SOCIAL CHANGE IN WESTERN EUROPE

THE PRIVATIZATION OF URBAN SERVICES
IN EUROPE

edited by
DOMINIQUE LORRAIN
and
GERRY STOKER

PINTER

PINTER
A Cassell Imprint
Wellington House, 125 Strand, London WC2R 0BB
PO Box 605, Herndon, VA 20172

First published in Great Britain in 1997

British Library Cataloguing in Publication Data
A catalogue record for this book is available from the British Library

ISBN 1 85567 364 9 (H/B)
    1 85567 365 7 (P/B)

Library of Congress Cataloging in Publication Data
Privatisation des services urbains en Europe. English
   The privatization of urban services in Europe/edited by
Dominique Lorrain and Gerry Stoker.
     p. cm.–(Social change in Western Europe)
   Includes bibliographical references (p.).
   ISBN 1-85567-364-9.–ISBN 1-85567-365-7 (pbk.)
   1. Municipal services–Europe, Western. 2. Privatization–
Europe, Western. I. Lorrain, Dominique. II. Stoker, Gerry. III. Series.
HD4644.A5P7513   1996
363′.094–dc20
                                        96-13
                                        CIP

Typeset by BookEns Ltd., Royston, Herts.
Printed and bound in Great Britain by Redwood Books, Trowbridge, Wiltshire

CONTENTS

DEDICATION

When we began this project in June 1993 we were nine colleagues and friends. As the British version comes out, one of us is missing. Kieron Walsh died suddenly in May 1995. His wife and children should know that for us, members of an international academic community, he was a good colleague. He was intelligent, very qualified in his field and full of human qualities. We shall miss him.

LIST OF CONTRIBUTORS

Henri Coing teaches at the Institut d'urbanisme in Paris. His publications include *La ville marché d'emploi* (Grenoble, Presses Universitaires, 1982). Over recent years his work has focused on changes in the management of urban services in the Third World and, particularly, in Latin America.

Nicolas Curien is Professor of Economics and Telecommunications Policies at the Conservatoire national des arts et métiers in Paris and heads the Department of Economics at the École Polytechnique. He has published a number of articles and studies on the economy of telecommunications and networks.

Tamás Fleischer is Senior Research Fellow at the Institute for World Economics of the Hungarian Academy of Sciences in Budapest. His studies are concerned with infrastructures and networks in economic development and the environment.

Carmen García Fernández holds a research appointment at the School of Civil Engineering in Madrid.

Dominique Lorrain holds a CNRS research appointment at the Centre d'études des mouvements sociaux in Paris. He is the author of a number of articles on urban government in *Sociologie du Travail*, among other publications.

Michael Reidenbach is Professor of Urban Economics at the Deutsches Institut für Urbanistik in Berlin. He is co-author (with G. Kuhn) of *Die Erhaltung der städtischen Infrastruktur* (Berlin, 1988) and has collaborated on other publications.

Gerry Stoker is Professor of Political Science at the University of Strathclyde; he also directs the research programme on local governance at the Economic and Social Research Council. In addition to a number of articles and studies, he has published *The Politics of Local Government* (London, Macmillan, 1991, 2nd edn).

Pawel Swianiewicz teaches at the European Institute for Local and Regional Development at the University of Warsaw and is also a Warsaw municipal councillor. A number of his articles have appeared in English publications.

Kieron Walsh was Professor of Public Administration at the Institute for Local Government, University of Birmingham. His recent research was into the introduction of market mechanisms and contracts into public service management in Britain. He published *Marketing and Local Government* (Harlow, Longman, 1989), *Competitive Tendering for Local Government Services* (London, HMSO, 1991) and *Competition and Services* (HMSO, 1993).

INTRODUCTION: THE EXPANSION OF THE MARKET

The series of major privatizations over the past ten years or so has had a considerable impact on public opinion; governments have sold off state enterprises, all symbols of a certain economic policy, including airline companies, coal mines and electricity corporations (Wright, 1993, Stoffaës, 1994). But there is less mention of the privatization of urban services, because generally speaking the issue fails to crystallize passions; it belongs by definition to another, more modest, more technical, register, one seen as having less bearing on the major options that face society. In our democratic systems, city government remains a secondary form of politics, one situated on a plane below the 'higher' politics of central government, involving ministers and presidents. The result is that what goes on there passes for a lesser form of public endeavour.

The texts assembled in this book invite the reader to reconsider this interpretation. Beneath its composed and unassuming exterior, the urban services sector is presently undergoing profound changes. Entire areas are in the sphere of private enterprise and a few names are beginning to be generally recognized, names such as Générale des eaux and Lyonnaise des eaux-Dumez, Veba or RWE, Thames Water or Rentokil. These enterprises are beginning to acquire the same significance as La Poste or Deutsche Telekom. New forms of public action have been devised. The model for public management, a legacy of the inter-war period, combining municipal socialism with Keynesian interventionism has been displaced by market-driven policies; and flexible government has taken over from direct administration.

There is a reason why urban services are becoming a driving force in the reconstruction of the whole field of local political action. First, urban technical services bear directly on economic development, with the result that their inadequacy may produce bottlenecks, hence restraints on the economy, as seen for example in deficient electricity supplies in Asia or outdated infrastructure in eastern Germany. Records in this section are sometimes a matter of urgency. Second, such services constitute the point of encounter between public service and the real world. This property has implications. Those engaged in local action are for ever being obliged to resolve problems that combine political principles, technical solutions and financial questions. The proposition normally put forward is that, leaving the technical aspects aside, the urban services sector has a direct bearing on the regeneration of public action as a whole. That is why it is the catalyst of a new emergent paradigm for urban government.

In this introductory chapter, we shall start by taking a panoramic look at various European countries and then proceed to a discussion of the factors behind these changes and the consequences both for the public and the private realm.

The European panorama

The situation of European countries in the matter of urban services may be classified in terms of two major variables: the intensity of political ambition with regard to local public services and the degree of significance given to management by private actors. Thus there emerges a panorama constructed around four points of reference (Figure I.1). Three (namely the United Kingdom, France and Germany) represent stabilized forms, while the fourth corresponds to countries seeking new solutions following the misgivings attaching to previous arrangements (Eastern European countries and to a lesser extent southern Europe).

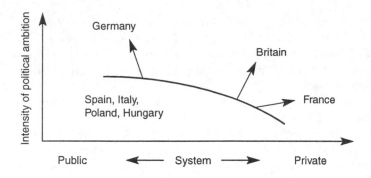

Figure I.1 *Trends towards privatization in various European countries*

Political resolve and pragmatism

The interplay of these two criteria enables us initially to position the United Kingdom and France. The first represents the most advanced form of determination for political change, given direct impetus by central government. After it came to power in 1979, the Thatcher government profoundly transformed the organization of local government. There have been a considerable number of reforms in spite of there having been no *a priori* strategy, as both Gerry Stoker and Kieron Walsh[1] emphasize. One after another, changes took place in the taxation system and control of capital spending, then in the structure of institutions. Urban services have been at the centre of these changes, with the selling off of much council housing, the privatizing of a number of major utilities – telecommunications, gas and electricity, water and sewerage – and the introducing of competitive tendering whereby in-house services are invited to compete against private bidders. At the other extreme, the case of France is one of unplanned change. Whole areas of urban service management have become privatized, more because the logic of the system inclined towards this, with firms being highly structured, than because of any deliberate political programme. Despite this contrast between planned and unplanned reform, the surprising factor in the situation is that now, for all their divergence of approach to the question, the two countries find themselves in an appreciably similar position in regard both to the form government takes and the structure of privatized delivery.

In both cases, local government has been facing fundamental reappraisal and reorganization. Local councillors tend to prefer contracting out to privatized services rather than relying on their own. Market values are becoming increasingly significant in local public administration.

The term 'enabling government' is close to the term 'flexible government' used to typify the French case. Similarly, the development of 'non-elected local governments' instanced by Gerry Stoker corresponds to what I have termed the 'paramunicipal sector'. Added to this, in both countries the retraction of local government is counterbalanced by the robust development of private tendering, with large firms capable of moving into a range of submarkets and functions. This has been traditional in France, but the United Kingdom is undergoing a rapid reorganization of enterprises in urban services and civil engineering. The United Kingdom's major enterprises compete internationally in large-scale tendering, as for example urban services in Sydney, Buenos Aires, Mexico and Bangkok, or bridges (over the Tagus and the Severn) and toll motorways (around Birmingham).

This development has engendered considerable passion in the United Kingdom for three reasons. In the first place, the background is one of strong local government, which since the nineteenth century has made its presence felt extensively in daily life alongside that of central government, which has assumed a less active role (Sharpe, 1978). Second, to a considerable extent the development itself is the product of political and ideological confrontation between the government of Margaret Thatcher and Labour, the market confronting the welfare state. Conversely, in France the transformation has occurred peacefully, probably because it has taken place in the newly evolved context of decentralization. Powers have been conferred on local institutions, consequently their prestige has been enhanced and elected members have suffered no sense of loss in making over large segments of local public services. They would certainly have had a different attitude if the initiative had come from central government; they would have been incensed by such unacceptable amputation of their authority. Hence, relativity of context and attitude on opposite sides of the Channel. Third, the vigour of the debate points also to a characteristically British method of implementing reform. Traditionally, the United Kingdom accords importance to preliminary reports and studies, and appears to elevate political economy to a fine art (Jeunemaître and Dumez, 1991). The controversy thus brought into the open clearly has the negative effect of hardening positions and so imperilling implementation; at the same time, the fact that it exists obliges those concerned to be systematic and clear, and to produce carefully thought out lines of argument, all of which is helpful subsequently in propagating conclusions. And this perhaps explains the apparent contradiction of the short-lived nature of the British experience and the huge influence it has had both on international organizations and on developing countries, the Argentinian experience described by Henri Coing being a case in point; one might further cite the cases of Mexico, Malaysia and Thailand, as well as of Australia.

Gradualism

Other countries have adopted a more flexible approach. Germany is a good example, as are Denmark (Villadsen, forthcoming) and the Netherlands. These countries share a combination of having marked convictions in regard to local government, frequently developed in the latter half on the nineteenth century (Häussermann, 1992), and public administration of urban services. It is a policy that contains sufficient inner resources to adapt. This implies that the provision of urban services is largely in the hands of various types of public enterprise: municipal department, public corporation (*Eigenbetrieb*), or private company with public capital (*Eigengesellschaft*). Such adaptability of legal forms to the requirements of efficient management is evidence of the strength of pro-public conviction in the running of local affairs. When municipal services became stretched, the response in this group of countries was not to appeal to the private sector because of the shortcomings of the public one, as was the case in France; it was to modernize the public sector. Michael Reidenbach explains how German cities created new legal forms in order to free themselves from the pressures of strict public management yet still retain major control. French *sociétés d'économie mixte (SEM)* also belong to this tradition.

The strength of the public model does not signify indifference to the pressure for change in these sectors. So much is clear from the favourable attitude towards market-driven policies, the reaction of the tax-paying electorate to the fiscal burden imposed by the welfare state, and the strength of large corporations. Nor, with change occurring, is the 'local public' model impervious to change, as many instances bear out: greater accountability introduced into public administration; a larger role for private enterprise in urban development schemes (Heinz, 1994; Goldberg and Janssen, 1992); and privatization of specific services in sewerage and waste to the benefit of family businesses or giant electrical corporations, such as RWE and Veba.

Given these factors, one might have expected the reunification with the eastern *Länder* and the turmoil it has entailed to open the door to privatization. Certainly a number of technical arguments were forthcoming calling into question the initial public model: the sheer volume of capital required to rebuild the infrastructure, the range and variety of infrastructure concerned – telecommunications, electricity, urban services, road networks, all pointed to the need to call upon the resources of German and non-German private enterprise. Yet five years after the Wall came down, there are still only limited instances of privatization in urban services.

There is the instance of the concession of the Rostock water supply to Eurawasser, linking Lyonnaise des eaux-Dumez with the Thyssen group. To understand the degree of publicity this received in Germany one needs to have an idea of the objectives the two groups had in mind when they formed this association in 1990. Such a partnership – between a supplier of services and an industrial enterprise – had clearly set its sights on the huge market for concessions which was bound to open up. What actually happened fell well short of expectations. And the same goes for other – German – enterprises in Halle and Cottbus. The Rostock concession remains the exception that provides ammunition for the critics of the pro-public lobby in Germany in their campaign to partition urban services.[2]

In other words, there are no grounds for supposing that reunification is likely to make much impact on the already existing model – public and local – whose promoters have faced the challenge with resourcefulness. Cities in the East have taken legal action so as not to be divested of their role as electricity suppliers by the cartel of major producers: RWE, Veba and Byernwerk. Officials of the Deutsches Institut für Urbanistik in collaboration with their municipal colleagues have carried out a number of surveys in order to acquaint themselves with the private sector elsewhere and acquire the knowledge to adapt in a positive way. They provide their colleagues in the East with advice and help, and propagate their ideas. The public sector in Germany is showing itself capable of taking on board a degree of change and development without sacrificing its principles. It declines to give way on the essential point of being itself the provider of local public services.

But if the model in its essence is able to withstand the wave of privatization and contracting out of urban services, its periphery is undergoing change in line with changes to the larger public companies in Germany. Until now those that sought access to these markets were largely energy-based conglomerates, firms with environmental interests and large construction firms. Now such enterprises tend to be more diversified. For example, RWE, the energy leader, having effected a degree of vertical integration in electricity, has moved into engineering, public works, water treatment, refuse and communications; and Veba, the number two company, has similarly diversified into waste treatment, waste-to-energy, housing and mobile phones. Prior to running into major difficulties at the end of 1993, Metallgesellschaft, the leader in non-ferrous metals, had diversified on an impressive scale in the environment. In a massive restructuring operation such as that undertaken at Halle, the group moved into a number of services – water provision, sewerage, waste disposal – as both industrial supplier and engineer. The larger construction companies are quitting their 'passive productive role' (Goldberg and Janssen, 1992) and becoming directly involved in projects. Some of them have become providers of services or are applying the *Betreibermo-delle* concept in waste water treatment. And their involvement in foreign markets inclines them to set up joint ventures. For example, the stake owned by Hochtief, a subsidiary of RWE and number two in the sector, in the number one, Philipp Holzmann, has increased to 30 per cent. Some family enterprises in waste disposal have become merged with major service groups, Otto making over 50 per cent of its capital to the American number two, Browning Ferris Industries, and Edelhoff being taken over by an electrical firm, VEW. Such changes in the supply market will have consequences, with the firms concerned being in a position to propose integrated projects to local authorities, since (as in France or Britain) the services they provide have become all-embracing.

Where the prerequisites for action remain to be determined

The fourth point of reference corresponds to countries where a public model, organized around large state or municipal enterprises, closely linked to the political authority, has been in force, and where the economic environment has held back market forces. As a result their situation has become destabilized. In Poland and in Hungary, the collapse of the previous system has created a vacuum; in Spain and in Italy, the context of an emerging market, institutional reforms that favour independence on the part of local authorities and the tensions surrounding public budgets have created a mood of indecisiveness. In all four of these countries there is a self-questioning and the search for a new accommodation. For all, the starting point is a similar public premise that stems from thinking in the inter-war period and that has affected work methods as well as the institutional choices made. With such assumptions called into question, they are faced with having to provide a new framework while problems demand attention. Previous investment undertaken was inadequate; technology applied no longer corresponds with current norms. Systems such as those involving water or refuse treatment, the production of electricity or telecommunications, require urgent modernization.

Eastern European countries provide an extreme case in that they are quite undecided as to the lines of reform to adopt; and while wavering on the question of principle they call on the whole gamut of experience – German, French and British – and appeal to the World Bank. Thus they have become an arena for competing conceptions and enterprises. Poland, for instance, sought inspiration first from British experience. A number of teams of consultants put forward reform schemes in the electrical industry and housing, based on their own experience and without regard for the considerable difference in circumstances and environment.

Certainly the situation in Spain is less dramatic. Even so, the transition is taking place without the prerequisites being clearly established, and as a result a number of possibilities are being tried out. Since 1978 Spain has undergone a political transition characterized by a new demarcation between central and local government. This process is still not completed; as Carmen García Fernández emphasizes, equilibrium between the state and the autonomous regions continues to be subject to subtle fluctuations which nonetheless enable the country to deal with its regional question. In the matter of urban services, the process tends to conflict with the other major process of economic modernization. This sector inherited the Franco legacy of public monopolies providing the major services. They rapidly became market-oriented, a trend that accelerated in and after 1990 with the preparation of sites for the Barcelona Olympics and the Seville Expo, which acted as a spur on the Spanish urban economy and brought in the major private groups from abroad.

What direction is Spain likely to take? Private firms – Spanish (FCC, Dragados and SCAB) as well as foreign (Lyonnaise des eaux and Waste Management) – are already strongly represented in urban services; other are trying to gain a foothold. Assumptions in urban planning are changing but there is uncertainty in regard both to the extent to which foreign capital should be allowed into the urban services industry and to that of reform within the overall institutional framework. Spain today constitutes a strategic area in the trend towards privatization, being the means of access into the Latin American market, where the problems are again of a different order. Consortia that have tendered successfully in Argentian privatization are made up Spanish companies, sometimes associated with other European groups (Telefonica, Agbar and Lyonnaise des eaux, for example, in Buenos Aires).

Forms of privatization

Privatization is a generic term covering a series of gradations. Four major modes are distinguished:

1. Sales of assets, or the sale of public enterprises to private bidders. This is the most visible, the most symbolic form since it constitutes an irrevocable transfer which has implications for several actors: those employed by the company, the supervisory administration, the banking system responsible for launching the operation, the shareholders and the consumers. This is the solution that was adopted in Britain for water in 1989 and for electricity in 1990. It remains a minority solution, hence it would be more appropriate to speak of market expansion than of privatization.

2. The tendering of a public service constitutes the commonest system of recourse to private enterprise. It amounts to a form of

subcontracting of a public activity to a private actor. One can also speak here of contractualization. In effect the solutions adopted are variable in the extreme, going from short-term contracts involving only a part of the service provided – contracting out, operation and maintenance, *marché d'exploitation*, *régie intéressée* – to more ambitious contracts that apply to an entire service and for a longer term – leasing, *affermage*, BOT, concession. In such cases, the public authority continues to own the assets, which will be restored to it when the contract expires, hence exploitation is effected on its behalf with a degree of freedom established by the contract. It is a solution altogether different from privatization.

3. Market expansion may also manifest itself in the public sphere by transforming ministerial departments into joint-stock companies, which amounts to autonomizing ordinary administration and introducing objective-led management into the public arena. This is a formula which has been much applied in Germany and which has also been adopted in Eastern Europe as a first stage in the process of dismantling the major public concerns.

4. A fourth mechanism for change involves the introduction of mathematical calculation and cost measurement, and provides a means of introducing competition into the public sector. In order to be able to sustain comparison with their private competitors, nationalized enterprises forsake their purely administrative role and adopt the practices of business enterprise. Illustration of this is afforded by the evolution of French nationalized firms and their German counterparts. In Britain the reforms in tendering have not produced the expected benefits for the private sector; in the vast majority of cases the municipal services bids have been successful but, as Gerry Stoker remarks in Chapter 3, competition 'has forced productivity gains'.[3]

All in all, if the sale of assets pointed to one solution, it remained a minority one, involving as it does considerable upheaval. In many instances substantial changes were effected as it were imperceptibly by modifying the operation of the system itself.

Forces for change

A social observer cannot but be struck by the swing of the pendulum over the past fifty years. Governments are selling what they then acquired, and state planning is giving way to the market. What is the explanation for such a shift at the close of the 1980s?

The fiscal argument

The development of the welfare state was accompanied by a marked rise in public expenditure, accounting for up to 45 per cent of GNP, and taxation has been more and more called into question by those it burdens. Against this background, cities have made over areas of their activity to reduce their indebtedness and realize new revenue, or at least call a halt to the escalation of public expenditure. In economic terms we are witnessing a massive reduction in the budget, with taxation being transferred to charges. The final impact on household budgets will depend on the effectiveness of the new participants. It will be observed that the areas returning to the private sector generally speaking have an industrial or commercial character.

The productive argument

The public authority is ill-equipped to produce since it pursues diverse objectives that override one another and reduce its productive efficiency, frequently inducing distortions in the productive function of municipal concerns. Arguments in the name of social justice result in price levels being too low to realize investment and safeguard the future. Strictly political interests in controlling resources lead to overmanning in public administration and municipal concerns. In other words, since their social objective is a multiple one, public authorities are ill-suited to production. Conversely, industry's specialization in the matter of social objectives is to effect economies of scale and strive for increasing returns. This is an important factor. The movement in favour of the market is fed by the imperfections of public corporations and correspondingly enhanced by the performance of private companies.

Economic theory and the optimum

The argument over the best possible form of social organization continues to divide economic liberals and those who favour interventionism (Keynesians, institutionalists and planners), for all that the latter appeared to have won their case in the aftermath of World War II. Liberal economists have produced well-documented arguments to reformulate fundamental questions (Beaud and Dostaler, 1993). With their aim of permanently adjusting production to consumer demand, they see the market as providing a better instrument than does planning, the corollary being the need for competitive organizations that are flexible and capable of speedy response. When the public authority intervenes, it fails to assess the effects of the actors adjusting to the conditions they create. A number of studies have questioned the validity of public interventionism in showing the unexpected consequences of its effects;[4] these studies have had an influence on regulation policies by setting out a simple proposition: before regulating, the public authority should give free rein to the actors; it needs to appreciate the mechanisms of self-regulation (Garrison, and Kirzner, 1989; Williamson, 1985).

Business strategies

The term 'privatization' is still often equated with a sale of assets by the public authority in implementation of a political programme, hence with the emphasis on political factors. Corporate strategy, embracing the credo of growth and competition with the public sector, is not considered by way of explanation. The point of view is that of political science, tangential to business but blind to its real function. In fact, when one surveys urban services it is clear that the process of market expansion is also the result of business activity in its constant search for development. Illustration of this is today provided by the markets for the upkeep of parks and gardens or for the cleaning and maintenance of public buildings. This aspect of the question, the corporate strategy, is an important explanatory factor, and this is substantiated when one takes a close look at the way in which those in government draw up their public policies. Across a variety of mechanisms, working committees, professional associations, groups of experts representing political parties, they are in close touch with private-sector managers. And the flow of ideas between the two spheres is such that public policies in their conception inevitably draw in part upon business strategies. This little-regarded aspect of privatization is destined to acquire greater significance as gradual withdrawal by the public sector means that private corporations are coming more out into the open both as service operators and as problem-solvers. Such an appreciation has the effect of shifting the boundaries between disciplines, inclining political science to become more open to the industrial economy.

All these familiar and widely rehearsed arguments contain part of the answer. Yet the very strength of the movement in favour of the market inclines one to search for cultural causes and to ask oneself what the deeper mechanisms are that drive human societies to innovate.

The frontier argument

An analogy can be drawn between systems for corporate action and the life of industrial products. They traverse several phases: birth, development, maturity, ageing. No social system can survive for long unless it submits to change; the collapse of the Soviet system provides a ready illustration. Every now and then, social positions need reordering, new opportunities have to be provided, new prospects put on line as proof that society has not reached an impasse. It is no coincidence that the metaphor of the frontier regularly makes its appearance in politics, with its proposition to alter the rules of the game, set out a new deal – thus, in other terms, giving new overall expression to a fundamental principle of resilience and adaptability, failure to adapt being tantamount to atrophy and inevitable disappearance.

A culture of autonomy

The trend towards contractualization in urban management should be seen in the context of a fundamental trend towards reordering collective action in industry as well as in administration. The organizational forms of industry are changing. Over a period of twenty years, hierarchical, pyramidal structures have lost ground to decentralized, cellular and matrix-like structures. The tendency is a deep-seated one and is confirmed by a number of economic and sociological studies.[5] There are two major reasons for this.

The first is that values are changing. People are becoming increasingly intolerant of hard-and-fast forms as a means to achievement and self-realization. They want space, a measure of independence; hence the development of work modes involving participation and flexibility where once strict functional specialization was dominant. In the public sphere, the criticism of big government is not merely that it is unwieldy and inefficient; it is too remote, too arrogant even: 'I know what's right for you, hence you should be grateful and let me get on with it.'

The second reason is that markets are changing. By way of response to higher risks and greater variation in customer demand (a tendency to prefer the custom-made to the mass product), industry seeks to become highly tuned in its receptiveness, more flexible in its organization. Here ties based on partnership or on subcontracting are as valid as financial links. So a cellular, decentralized pattern of organization, affording as it does greater elasticity and resilience, is found to be appropriate to industry. The growing partnership nexus provides practical illustration of this. Local authorities, too, with the uncertainties they face, have adopted similar solutions.

Thus hierarchical systems have given way to more flexible ones. What has occurred bears witness at some level to a profound cultural change accompanying the shift of a conception appropriate to wartime to one reflecting a time marked by recession. The period of hostilities imposed hierarchical organization in the name of efficiency (Rioux, 1980). Action categories are based on order and prediction; in outline, analysis, decision-making and execution are three distinct functions. The formula is to be found in the conception of action once adopted by the *secrétaires généraux de mairies* in France: 'Our function is to carry out the decisions made by those elected.' The climate of recession is marked at once by the assertion of the subject and by uncertainty. War acted as a vector to decision-making, imposing its own necessity. One characteristic of a recessionary period will be this uncertainty. And the words that have significance are 'flexibility', 'interaction', 'retroactive effect', 'just-in-time'. We are witnessing a decline in hypothetical and deductive models, with more attention being focused on uncertainty, fuzzy logic and limited equilibrium.

The disruptive impact of shock

From the case so far presented the transformation undergone in the public sphere would appear self-evident, but what factors account for commitment to the course taken becoming more and more pressing at a given juncture? This is where the role of crises and the disruptive effects of shock need to be stressed; forces that challenge routine and established interests have to be taken account of. In each of the countries examined a change of direction took place at a given moment and carried the actors with it.

In Spain, the death of Franco in 1975, followed by the promulgation of a new constitution in 1978 and the move into Europe, represented a total change. In the United Kingdom, one needs to go back to 1976 when a Labour government, faced with an unemployment figure – 1,269,000 – double that for 1974 – 600,000 – declared 'the party' to be 'over' (Pickvance, 1985) and was obliged to have recourse to a loan from the International Monetary Fund. Clearly, the trauma occasioned may well have made the Opposition all the more determined to attack the welfare state and every form of rigidity responsible for bringing such humiliation upon the country. In the East, the end of the order based on Moscow clearly represents a moment at which a new order seeks to emerge.

And in France everything passed off smoothly; there was no confrontation, no major debate. Even so, there too the acceleration of the trend is the result of the – threefold – impact of events. First, the advent of the left traumatized the right into feeling dispossessed of institutions it claimed as its own; thereupon it sought to strengthen its support in local government as a means of providing a foretaste of its national policy against an eventual return to power. Second, the scenario was hastened by a reversal of economic policy that put a stop to collective expectations of expansion. Local government spending became tighter, and recourse to private capital provided a margin for initiative. Decentralization, which made official the power of locally elected representatives when times were difficult, constituted the third impact. Mayors, seeking partners on whom they could rely and faced with the withdrawal of central government, turned naturally to the major providers of urban services.

Setting up markets

If so many shocks were needed to bring about reform, the implementation of those reforms has shown varying degrees of success. Examples provided for Poland by Pawel Swianiewicz (Chapter 8) and for Hungary by Tamás Fleischer (Chapter 9) show the slowness of progress. In the case of Hungary we are told how 'new difficulties constantly crop up and delay a programme that was seemingly well conceived'. At the start everyone thought all that was required was to sell off utilities and the market process would get under way again. However, reforms have hung fire. What has occurred in Eastern Europe is a reminder that the market is not a natural state; it is a social construct which presupposes that certain conditions are met in order to function properly. In order to be able to privatize, property rights need to be established. It needs to be known who can be a shareholder, and whether the government should invariably retain a majority of shares. Agreement also needs to be reached on the value of the assets, hence on the method of evaluation. There needs to be a capital market.

Suppose now that one wishes merely to call on a foreign associate to operate an urban service that has been contracted out; the role of each participant will need to be defined. How will the price-setting mechanism, until then the perquisite of the state, be determined, bearing in mind that a degree of freedom represents a necessary condition in order to attract investors? Mechanisms will also be needed by which to resolve conflicting interests, and it is of paramount importance that the overall structure affords reasonable stability.

All this points to a concern for learning processes (Mintzberg, 1993) and the existence of phases of crisis in the framing of rules for collective action, even in its most discredited manifestations such as the return of interpersonal relationships or the spread of corruption. If the main scenario involves contraction of the public realm and extension of the market, then money takes on a new role. While a new system of rules is being formulated, excesses will occur. They can be interpreted in moral terms; or they can be seen as linked to a shift in a society, in which new collective rules are being devised. In cases where this process is delayed, limited forms of stabilization offer a solution. Former state enterprises in a monopoly situation can ensure this function; they incorporate several degrees of activity and help to give an organized form to the ambient instability. A small group of actors who share the same values can compensate for the inadequacies of a system undergoing change. Thus the shared values of company directors in post-Soviet Russia (Kharkhordin, 1993) or of electrical-company directors in Hungary served to ensure economic transactions based on barter and trust and so avoid total collapse. 'Comecon exists no longer but some of the links between directors survive; industry lives on their credibility' (Bonaïti, 1992).

These remarks serve to illuminate the several mechanisms of transition to the market. To the question, who constructs the market? replies will vary with the type of society and its stage of development; the state, major firms, the nexus of actors that form society can all play a part. In the absence of a formal set of rules, or before their elaboration, collective action is sustainable only by interpersonal codes; small groupings (some would call them mafias) come into their own.

Classification of the source of the code that operates – a formal, legal body of rules, interpersonal code – as of the level of market development is of assistance in accounting for some of the problems encountered in Eastern Europe. Initially, a planned economy operated, outside the market but with a framework of formal rules. This system, established by law, was called into question. Consultants representing the World Bank, Goldman Sachs and various organizations came with their schemes for unadulterated privatization, identical to those applied in Venezuela between 1989 and 1993 (Coing, 1994), in Argentina, in the United Kingdom, in Australia and in New Zealand in the spheres of energy and telecommunications. And the system began to seize up, which is scarcely surprising since two problems required solving at one and the same time: that of shifting from one legal framework to another set of rules, and that of substituting a market economy for one outside the market. In the event the acts negotiated the changes by making a detour (curve 2 in Figure I.2). The initial stage in constructing a market economy saw a greater role emerging for interpersonal relationships, first across the major enterprises, thereby initially serving to maintain a degree of order in the economy, and subsequently across family-run firms as small-scale trades and industry got under way. Indeed, development in China has not proceeded in any other way (Li You Mei and Pavé, 1995).

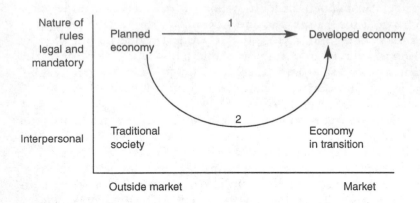

1 = Direct transition to developed market economy
2 = Negotiation rebuilding economic system on basis of interpersonal relations

Figure I.2   *Transition to the market*

Towards a new paradigm for collective action

Local authorities are disengaging from direct productive activity. Increasingly they have recourse to contractualization, introducing market mechanisms at all levels. This new state of affairs obliges them to set out their aims and their definition of a public service. Those in government are obliged to confront issues they tended to mask when they intervened directly through 'their' public enterprises. They have joined an economic debate on the issue of global control.

This debate over whether to apply global control or regulation is at once theoretical and highly concrete, and touches on considerations of economics, constitutional law and political science. Clearly, what is at issue has to do with more than is strictly contained in the notion of regulation, which concerns the definition of norms and price levels. Global control specifies the organization applying to the whole sphere of collective action (Simon, 1991; Vickers and Yarrow, 1988), the important point being that, once they turn to the private sector in the need to resolve a purely technical problem, local authorities end up having to reorganize their whole method of approach:

- extent of monopoly: total or partial?
- duration: short- or long-term contracts? (These points reflect current economic debate, as Chapter 2 shows.)
- selection procedure: *'intuitu personae'*,[6] competitive bidding, prior shortlisting?
- nature of controlling body: specialized agency, ministry, municipal service?
- definition of organizing authority: *commune* (district council), *agglomération* (urban district), county, region?

Furthermore, there are questions regarding the manner in which public action is conceived that call for a reply – questions as to whether the exercise of control should be comprehensive or specific, or how far the powers of the controlling body should extend, or again, whether the controlling body should involve itself in management decisions or merely ensure that competition is preserved in a market environment that may take on an oligopolistic character, as economists of the second Chicago school (Beaud, 1994) and the German 'global regulators' think (Dumez and Jeunemaître, 1991). Global regulation thus does not imply simply a mechanism for monitoring price and profit levels; it has a function in reconstructing collective action. Administering global regulation amounts to shaping socio-economic systems and defining principles of action; 'privatizations' are retroactive in regard to political systems.

The sphere of action or questions of institutional design

A survey of different countries serves to bring out the contrast in choices made, choices which have effects in the medium term upon the way urban government is organized, on political practices and on industrial systems. It very much has to do with the response given to specific questions whose technical character to a degree precludes all their implications being foreseen.

A first question arises when urban services face reorganization: Who is organizing and who is responsible? Is it the municipality, or is it a special authority relating to a larger urban community, a region or a body at national level? The choice is of considerable importance since it affects the sphere of competence of local

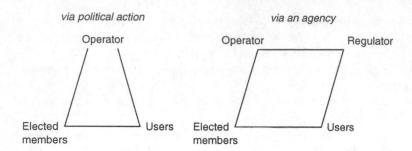

Fig. I.3   *Patterns of global regulation: left, via political action; right, via an agency*

elected representatives, hence the outcome of further questions. It may be decided to entrust the organization of a sector to a wide-ranging institution, in which case the authority at a local level is deprived of a potential area of competence. This is the pattern adopted in Anglo-Saxon countries across agencies, appointed bodies (quangos) and special districts. Conversely, if the responsibility for urban services resides with the locality in question, elected representatives come to have greater technical, hence political, legitimacy; and since they oversee those who operate the system a controlling third party is unnecessary. Moreover, such a structure creates its own dynamic for apprenticeship. Those elected are not confined to social or narrowly political functions; they have to tackle problems of a technical nature that presuppose negotiating with industrial firms. Such choices place Britain on one side of a divide, France and Germany on the other (Figure I.3)

A further strategic question concerns the form of operation to be adopted: modernized public enterprises as in Germany or private firms as in France. Primarily this has an effect on the political system. If there is municipal enterprise, the local authority enhances its productive capacity and controls a considerable economic sector which can act as a prop by which to realize other objectives, such as using charges as a mechanism for social adjustment or adopting exemplary policies for labour. A wide sphere of activity is of course a guarantee of influence.

If elected representatives opt for private enterprise, as in France or the United Kingdom, it is up to municipal government to elaborate functions for exercising overall control, which is an altogether different question. This issue merits discussion by examining the extent of contractualization in respect of services in any given city. The local authority will be working with an increasing number of business partners, which in itself poses a problem of coordination; and increasing complexity in the system contains a real risk of fragmentation (Lorrain, 1989).

It is all a question of balance. With a view to mitigating the consequences of too much confusion between the political authority as organizer and the monopoly position of the operator, a principle of separation between organizer and operator has been laid down. This has the advantage of defining responsibilities and of enabling economies of scale and scope to be realized. But it presents the risk of weakening the local authority insofar as it is unable to assimilate these different specialists. So the drive for productive efficiency is at the cost of territorial integration, which constitutes a third formula for efficiency, one unquestionably adopted by Germany with its *Stadtwerke*.

Further, these choices have effects on industrial structures provided the time factor is introduced. When an operation is kept within the public sphere, the private sector appears only in an industrial capacity, which accounts in fairly broad terms for the profile of German firms. Conversely, the fact that in France the institutional set-up by definition allowed for the operation of urban technical services by private companies explains the presence there of some uniquely gigantic ones.

Principles for action

The introduction of market principles into the public sphere from which they were previously excluded is of major significance. In public organizations it finds expression in the setting up of new information systems (Chapter 1) and mechanisms for performance as in the case of nationalized enterprises in France.

The generalization of performance is a substantial factor characterizing the society that is emerging. Rural societies allowed for an imponderable element: nature, rainfall and sunshine. The inability to exert control over natural phenomena along with lack of knowledge in regard to certain social mechanisms led to a degree of unconcern, allowed a margin of free play. Technological progress conduces to measuring time and movement and to calculating cost (Etner, 1987). We are moving into a society that is more precise, more tightly organized, one where performance and reckoning are implicit. In the public sphere this entails reviewing policies of cross-subsidizing. Hence social relationships are redefined, becoming initially tougher, as is clear from the move to a true pricing policy for public services in Hungary, Poland and Latin America.

By definition, a contract implies at the very least the existence of two partners. The previous direct management model allowed for only one actor – a ministry or a town hall – and no distinction was made between the town hall in its 'responsibility' for the administrative side and in its capacity as 'operator' of its monopoly enterprise. The transformation now taking place calls for a clear distinction to be drawn between the operator, be it public or private, and the organizing authority. In Britain local authorities are required to tender for services, thus placing their own departments in competition with the private sector. The generalization of a mechanism of this kind is occasioning a shake-up in the way that public services are organized.

The effects on supply

As Nicolas Curien explains in Chapter 2, when public departments are transformed into joint-stock companies there is a concomitant change in the attitude of directors. They must be mindful of their shareholders, mindful too that their companies are not under-capitalized, otherwise they run the risk of being a prey to takeover bids. They are obliged to embark on policies for growth and ones that offer prospects to their shareholders. There is indeed no common ground between a municipal department and an independent firm, even if it retains public shareholding.

Moreover, the transition affects the structure of supply itself. Since the beginning, the sector of urban services was organized on national bases as regards both firms and regulation; it was specialized in terms of infrastructure. The process of market expansion entails changes; the firms involved are taking on international and global dimensions; they are initiating a variety of policies so as to position themselves in growing markets, incorporating sectors above and below them, diversifying into other areas, concentrating on their chief activity by absorbing other firms; and they are setting off to conquer foreign markets. The recent history of two major French groups – Générale des eaux and Lyonnaise des eaux-Dumez – puts them in the vanguard here; but there are others close behind: German energy-based corporations, British, German and Italian engineering and construction firms, British water companies, and some Spanish firms.

These movements take on various forms. Privatizations in Britain have been instrumental in reordering the sectors of water, gas and electricity, and now the enterprises concerned – British Gas, PowerGen, Thames Water, Severn Trent, North West Water, etc. – are represented in every foreign market. Yet the outcome is not guaranteed; it is by no means certain that the wave of privatization in Argentina serves to strengthen local enterprises; all too often they are in partnership with the world leaders in each privatization sector, and are thus forced to play the role of intermediary or sleeping partner.

The important point remains that major multi-sector groups are being formed in all industrialized countries; they are set on being present everywhere, bringing their solutions, methods, standards and principles. They are backed up in this role by a number of securities firms, engineering companies and international organizations preparing major reforms in these sectors, and this represents a significant change. Hitherto the initiative was with the public sector, and firms would intervene according to a prearranged scenario. This has all changed. The public and the private arena now balance each other out. Large-scale enterprises are directly involved in the agenda because they have very considerable resources at their disposal. It is far from certain whether these changes, with all their implications, are fully appreciated by the parties involved. Authorities continue to see themselves as solely legitimate, though their legitimacy is now shared. Private industry continues to see its initiatives in terms of necessary strategies for growth, while it is bound to take on further responsibilities within the public sphere. So a point has been reached where the process of market expansion calls for a clarification of roles, a task which is at various stages of accomplishment according to the country concerned.

Redefining categories of public service

How far can the public sector be reduced? Reforms undertaken represent an alternative to bureaucracy with its strata and organization. If the aim is to improve the product yet with fewer resources, 'excess' weight is shed with the consequent risk of job losses and the widespread occurrence of insecure or low-qualified jobs in the various services. If the public realm is leaner, will it thereby be made more fragile? A host of new problems has arisen as a result of doctrinaire policies. For instance:

- The level of competence within the public sector has fallen because top civil servants have left, and this in turn is compounded by a loss of legitimacy. It is clear in the case of politicians that their legitimacy derives mainly from what they achieve, consequently the shrinking area of municipal action renders them less effective. The British case in particular illustrates this, whereas the perceived success of the German government is primarily due to its having a larger perimeter for action. Government commands respect insofar as its impact is direct. The result of this may well be that the role of the public sector is again called into question. Where formerly it was seen as unwieldy and invasive, it may come to have to answer the charge of being uninformed and unmindful of problems.

- The sale of assets is akin to a sector-recapitalizing operation. Governments sell off to reduce their debts, as do local authorities; and even when they merely relinquish their operating rights, the change cannot be reviewed before the contract terminates. Thus these policies are by nature limited.

- What is taking place is introducing duality of principle between actors: a pole of efficiency, applying market principles and flexible 'new public' management, cost measurement and marginal cost price-setting; and a social pole to which it falls alone to repair the damage wrought by application of the former principles. A case in point is provided by urban policy in France or Britain which, having largely been forced to abdicate as regards the provision of housing, is reduced to the provision of welfare for the resulting fall-out. In the last resort and so as to show themselves up-to-date and efficient, local authorities have developed an 'economic service' to further the introduction of market principles, while in its wake their 'damage-limitation service' takes care of the casualties. It may be considered that this inherent conflict between two poles is not the best way to organize society.

Thus the panorama set out above at some point produces an impasse owing to the contradictions between the world of enterprise with its logic of growth – go on or go under – and that of local public administration. But maybe it is no more than the effect of a reading which applies earlier categories of public service and public initiative to modern urban society. In France at the end of the nineteenth century the concept of *industrial and commercial public service* was forged between traditional administration and private industry (Lorrain, 1993a). In the United Kingdom there exists the notion of *public utilities*, in Germany that of *offentlicher Dienst* (Commissariat Général du Plan, 1994). The notion I should like to stress here by way of conclusion is that the formidable expansion of private initiative in urban management prefigures a new frontier between the realm proper to public service and activities applicable to the market.

In regard to the distinction between what is relevant to public service and what to private activity, French jurisprudence has always been pragmatic. In the course of time the frontier between the two areas has shifted considerably. At the end of the nineteenth century, the supply of bread, milk and hygiene represented strategic sectors. Bakeries were municipalized, milk was distributed at school, municipal baths and wash-houses were provided. Today such provision is made within the private sphere and the debate has lost much of its force.

Three arguments give grounds for thinking that a new concept of public service within urban services is emerging at the close of this century. There is the example from the past of a mobile frontier; the fact that continuing expansion of the private sector in a context where public and private realms are unchanged will lead to an impasse; and finally, that the urban environment represents a growing market. The context is changing and now the time is ripe for a new category – globally regulated private services – alongside public administration and commercial and industrial public services.

Notes

1. Other references on this period: King (1987), Rhodes (1988), Pickvance (1985).
2. See the debates in the *Städtetag* or in '*Kommunal' Wissenschaft*.
3. See also Department of the Environment reports and those published in *Local Government Chronicle* (13 July 1990 and 26 April 1991).

4. See the chapters by James Buchanan: 'Constitutional economics' and by David Friedman: 'Law and economics' in Eatwell *et al.* (1989).
5. See *Sociologie du travail*, 1993, no. 1 (*Systèmes productifs: les modèles en question*) and 1994, no. 5, special issue on models of production.
6. Granting a concession without open bidding as a public procurement. The underlying reasoning is that the choice cannot be made on the basis of price alone.

1

MARKETS AND THE PUBLIC SERVICE

Kieron Walsh

Introduction

The move to market-based approaches to the management of public service presents a challenge to traditional understandings of the role of the public services in a modern state. Market mechanisms can be of great value in ensuring that producers are not dominant, that the consumer's interests are represented, and in ensuring efficiency. The state, with its emphasis upon planning, is subject to problems of bureaucracy and unresponsiveness, and the market, with its unplanned mode of coordination, has much to offer.

At the same time, one cannot replace the state with the market. The process of government is not one of exchange, but of authoritative decision based in legitimacy, which is necessarily a political process. The issue that has been raised by the move to the new public service management is how market and government can be brought together. The basis of the argument for the new public service management lies in theories of political economy that have emerged in the past thirty or so years, notably public choice theory, principal–agent theory and property rights theory. The developing critique of the organization of the state that is based upon economic arguments must be supplemented by political and philosophical arguments which recognize the variations in the legal traditions and political cultures and structures of different countries. This chapter will draw particularly on change in the United Kingdom, which has undergone a wide-ranging process of public service management reform.

The nature of change

A range of market-based mechanisms have been introduced to change public service management, notably:

- contracts
- competitive tendering
- purchaser–provider splits
- vouchers
- user choice
- charges
- internal markets
- the establishment of companies
- devolved budgets
- the creation of internal agencies
- opting out
- the establishment of special-purpose bodies.

In most cases public services are being changed by a combination of these approaches. For example, in the British National Health Service, internal markets, opting out, contracts and devolved budgets are being used. In the United States of America Osborne and Gaebler (1992) cite many examples of the use of these mechanisms, and European countries have made use of various combinations of them.

Contracts are at the base of the reform of the public sector, and are required in a number of forms. In some cases there is straightforward contracting out of services to the private sector, either by the buying in of services from external providers, or by 'externalizing' service provision, for example through management buy-outs or buy-ins. It is common in many countries to contract with voluntary or private organizations for the provision of social care.

Where services are provided within the organization itself there may be a requirement to operate a purchaser–provider split, for example in health services in the United Kingdom, Sweden, Germany and the Netherlands. The separation of purchaser and provider is necessary if an internal market is to be established within public service organizations.

On the face of it, the most straightforward way of introducing the market into public services would be to give people the money or resources, perhaps in the form of vouchers, that would allow them to exercise choice. Vouchers have been widely used in the public services in the United States and, less commonly, in other countries. Some processes of direct subsidy of services, such as housing benefits in Britain, can be viewed as vouchers. Experiments with vouchers in education are commonly regarded as having failed, though proponents argue against this (Seldon, 1986), saying that there is a riddle as to why vouchers have not been more widely used. The underdevelopment of the use of vouchers is significant in that it is indicative of the general lack of the development of the role of the individual as customer exercising choice.

Changes have developed extensively *within* the public service as internal markets have been developed. The internal market can be seen as a combination of the purchaser–provider split, charging, contracts and purchaser choice. As internal markets develop, the public-sector organization become a complex structure of interacting internal contracts.

The company form is being widely used within the public service, for example in the United Kingdom, Canada and the United States of America. Municipal companies, in a variety of forms, are common in Europe.

The devolution of budgets within public service organizations has been central to the international movement for the reform of the public service, particularly in civil services. The most important example of the devolution of finance is giving schools control of their own funding. The central issue is the freedom granted to cost centre managers. There is always a tension between the assertion of central control and uniformity, on the one hand, and, at the same time, allowing the necessary freedom to manage at the local level.

Internal agencies, operating with a relatively high degree of independence, are the natural development of devolved finance, particularly in central government, and have developed rapidly since the late 1980s, for example in New Zealand, the Netherlands and the United Kingdom. Agencies operate within framework agreements or contracts made with ministers, which define missions and broad performance requirements. The freedom of agencies tends to be greater the less central the work they do is to the policy concerns of the departments within which they operate.

Opting out of direct control has been developed in the United Kingdom in education, health and housing. Schools, hospitals and housing associations are able to manage independently, with control of their own staff, capital and spending.

Finally, there is the use of special-purpose agencies, again most developed in the United Kingdom, such as urban Development Corporations, Training and Enterprise Councils and Housing Action Trusts, appointed directly by central government ministers to deliver specific services. The development of agencies raises the issue of whether public services should be delivered by elected or appointed bodies, and whether government should be service or territorially focused.

The programme of change in public service management is at a relatively early stage but the pace of change is rapid. The traditional bureaucratic approach to government is increasingly to be superseded by market-based approaches.

The contract metaphor

In some cases there has been explicit use of legally enforceable contracts within the public service, notably where services have been contracted out to private-sector organizations. In most cases, though, the contract has a more metaphorical character. Mather has been the most explicit proponent of the contract model. He argues, for example, that local government in future

> should be seen in this sense of a series of contracts: with central government responsible for the 'purchase' of particular grant-supported services; with contractor for the operation of execution of functions and services; with residents through more closely defined charging mechanisms ... and with partners, including the voluntary sector and the business community.

> (Mather, 1989, p. 233)

The public service is coming to be seen as a nexus of contracts, or, perhaps better, as a nexus of treaties (Aoki et al., 1990). Integrated hierarchies are being broken up into independent agencies, with varying degrees of property rights over the resources that they use, which must relate to each other through contracts or quasi-contracts. Exchange relationships replace authoritative orders as the means of coordination and control. Contracts may be seen as being of varying forms. There is the political contract, for example the agreement for the management of a civil service agency, which political principals have with managerial agents. These political contracts, by establishing clear measures of performance, allow politicians to hold managers accountable for performance without the politicians' direct involvement, at least in theory. Performance contracting generally can be seen as allowing such control at a distance. Managers and service delivery agencies may be seen, in turn, as having contracts with the public, which may be made explicit in service charters or service contracts.

The rights of the public as users, have, in practice, been increased only to a limited degree by the extension of contracting within the public service (Harden, 1992), and it has proved difficult to develop the involvement of the public in defining services and setting standards, though improved methods for doing so are beginning to emerge (Audit Commission, 1993; Ham, 1992, Ham and Spurgeon, 1992).

Quasi-contracts operate extensively within public organizations between internal purchasers and providers. Such internal contracting relationships may be multi-layered, with one part of the organization acting as provider to another, and purchasing other services from a third.

The public service as a whole can be seen as a complex of contracts, turning back upon and interacting with each other. Central government ministers, ultimately responsible for the definition of policy, have contracts on the one hand with the public and, on the other, with delivery agencies, either directly or as part of the grant process. Delivery agencies then can be seen as having contracts with their clients. Internal relations operate on a contractual basis. Individual staff relate to the organizations that employ them through contracts.

The contract metaphor has much value. It helps to clarify responsibilities and purposes. The effectiveness of contracts will depend upon the extent to which services can be defined before they are delivered, and the effectiveness with which delivery can be monitored. In complex services, such as those providing health and social care, there are significant information issues, with professionals having information advantages. The contracts metaphor raises organizational and legal issues, and concerns about the overall nature of the state as it moves towards the markets. These issues will be considered in turn.

Organizational implications

The move from hierarchy to contracts and markets as the means of managing the public service has fundamental implications for the way in which public services are organized. The size and structure of public service agencies are changing. New processes are being developed, and different organizational cultures emerging. The pattern of industrial relations in the public service is having to change in order to adapt to market principles. These changes are at an early stage of development, but some patterns are clear. The public service is becoming a network of interacting agencies, in which organizational boundaries are blurred. The network of agencies replaces the integrated governmental organization as a unit of analysis.

Public administration has been characterized by an emphasis on organizational size, which was seen as necessary in order to gain economies of scale, and to make coherent planning possible. The argument for size went along with that for self-sufficiency; that is, that organizations should normally employ directly those who delivered services. The result was extended hierarchical lines of control, with detailed rule systems to enable the centre to control what happened at the periphery of the organization. The development of markets has largely made arguments based upon size redundant. Separate agencies can, at least in theory, be brought together by contract and market exchange, so that integrated management is not necessary. Equally, large size does not necessarily mean integrated organization; the internal contract can serve to separate parts of the organization from one another. Hierarchy is not necessary and the contract replaces bureaucratic rule systems.

The development of purchaser–provider splits is intended to lead to greater differentiation within the organization, to allow the small to exist within the large. The argument is that there will be greater efficiency and quality of service if there is a strict division between those who define services and those who deliver them. The public choice phenomenon of producer dominance will be overcome. The degree of differentiation in public organizations depends upon the extent to which financial control is devolved to lower-level managers. In some cases the differenentiation between purchaser and provider takes place at a highly centralized level, with a single purchaser and provider, or a small number of

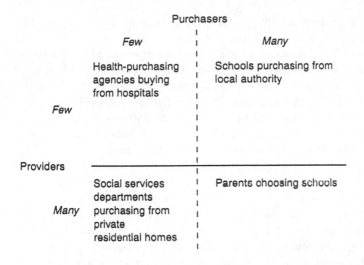

Figure 1.1 *Different types of organization in relation to the numbers of purchasers and providers*

purchasers and providers. In effect there is a situation of bilateral monopoly. In other cases there are highly dispersed patterns of organization, with many providers and many purchasers, as may happen in school systems. The possible patterns may be summarized by distinguishing whether there are few or many providers, and few or many purchasers, as in Figure 1.1, using examples drawn from the United Kingdom. The extent to which there are multiple purchasers and providers is important for the control of the use of monopoly power, by which either purchaser or provider may be tyrannized. Where there is monopoly there will need to be some process of regulation of the market in order to ensure that power is exercised responsibly.

The greater the level of differentiation of purchasing and provision, the more they must be integrated. To some degree the market will act as an integrating mechanism, as it does in the private sector, but there are differences between the public sector and the market. The quasi-market for public services is often highly regulated for political rather than efficiency reasons. No government, however market oriented, can choose to leave health provision as a purely private matter, as the continuing debate in the United States of America has shown. The issues of market failure, even if they are less constraining than has traditionally been thought to be the case, must also be addressed.

Organizational processes have become more complex as a result of the development of contracts and market process. Information systems need to be developed to cope with trading, for example the ability to operate management accounting systems. Purchasers need to be able to determine how much services will cost, and providers to set unit prices. Traditional organizational accounting systems, organized for public reporting, are poorly adapted to the development of public service markets. Public bodies have had to make major investments in information technology to cope with the development of trading and markets. Contract forms are becoming more complex, as managers try to relate the work done to price, and to calculate more accurately the quantity of work done. In effect, public organizations must now have two information systems, one for management accounting and one for public reporting. Research has shown that the introduction of markets and competition has led to significant information problems (Appleby *et al.*, 1992; Walsh and Davis, 1993).

Purchaser–provider relationships are tending to be increasingly formal in character. Formal systems for checking work and agreeing changes in the nature of services are becoming established.

The introduction of various forms of market mechanism within the public service leads to substantial change in the nature of financial management in government organizations. In traditional systems there is little concern about issues of cash flow, or balancing income and expenditure. Public-sector accounting has been to do with the ability to be able to report overall patterns of expenditure, and to control expenditure within budgets. Many public service managers are now responsible for their own budgets on a cost centre basis, and are increasingly being required to operate trading accounts, which means that they must be responsible for income as well as expenditure.

At the present, relatively early, stage there is little evidence of how the introduction of contracts and markets will influence the pattern of public service organization. It is, though, more or less inevitable that there will be failures of various sorts in the future. The purpose of the market is, precisely, that the inefficient shall fail, and the efficient expand. It is not at all clear that governments will be willing to let this process of creative destruction operate unhindered, especially where it might leave local people without particular services.

The development of purchaser and provider divisions, and trading relations based on contracts or quasi-contracts, is changing the culture and power structures of public organizations. Monopolies tend to be developed, though government can also have great influence as a large purchaser. The development of market-based approaches has also tended to lead to a focus on management as against professionalism, for example in health and education, and the number of managers has grown rapidly as market mechanisms have been extended. In large part, the purpose of the change in public service management has been to control professional producers, such as teachers and doctors. The difficulty is that their cooperation is necessary to the effective implementation of the new market policies.

The most fundamental change is to the culture of the public service, with a move from a service orientation to a more business-oriented approach. Citizens are increasingly defined as customers or consumers of services, for example in the United Kingdom's Citizen's Charter. There is a concern for quality and quality assurance, and the development of third-party certification for the quality assurance system. Service units within public-sector organizations are being defined as business units, concerned with business planning. There is, certainly, some clash between traditional public service values of professionalism and service commitment, and the demands of commercialism, for example where hospitals and schools try to avoid providing for difficult cases. Such developments raise clear issues about equity in the public service, which, whether it was effective or not, was the purpose of bureaucracy.

The development of market approaches has been effected in many cases without any great change in the nature of relationships within organizations. Conflict may result from the separation between purchaser and provider, and arbitration systems have had to be devised to overcome differences. Conflict is more likely at the lower levels of organization, where day-to-day problems must be dealt with, for example over inspection of service. Managers generally argue the value of trust in maintaining effective operation in market-based systems, as has, typically, been the case for contracts in private-sector organizations (Vincent-Jones, 1989). Without trust, the costs of monitoring and checking, or, as

Williamson (1985) argues, the costs of transactions, are likely to be high.

The development of market approaches has had a major impact upon the relationship between public organizations and their employees. The public service has traditionally been seen as offering security of employment, and public-sector organizations have been committed to being 'in the front rank of good employers'. A result of the move towards the market has been a worsening of the position of employees. Competitive tendering makes it more or less impossible to preserve jobs if contracts are lost to the private sector. The public employees may be taken on by private companies which win contracts, but pay and conditions will often be worse. Private employers generally operate less advantageous sick-pay, holiday and pension schemes. Many public-sector organizations have been changing their pay and conditions in order to enhance their competitiveness; part-time work and temporary contracts have become more common. In part, what is emerging is organizations that are made up of a relatively advantaged managerial and professional core, and a periphery that is less firmly attached to the organization. The tradition of integrated hierarchies of employees is being eroded.

Performance pay is an important component of the new public service. Senior managers, in particular, are likely to be paid on a performance-related basis. They are also likely to be on short-term contracts. The result has generally been higher pay for senior managers and a widening of differentials between staff at the top of the organization and those lower down.

Industrial relations are having to change to recognize the diversification and decentralization of the public services. Traditionally, public-sector industrial relations have been highly centralized, with the emphasis on uniformity of approach. It is no longer possible to sustain this pattern of industrial relations, and industrial relations and personnel issues are increasingly being delegated to cost centre managers. Trade unions are finding it difficult to cope with these changes, which challenge their traditional centralism. The main group who have suffered have been staff who have seen their working conditions becoming more demanding and whose pay and conditions have worsened.

Public service organizations are changing from being large, hierarchically organized, professionally based bodies to being diversified networks, emphasizing management responsibilities.

There is no longer a clear distinction between public and private organizations, with private-sector organizations providing public services and public organizations operating according to private-sector principles. The organizational world of the public service is becoming complex as the number of organizations proliferates.

Markets and law

The development of market-based approaches to the management of the public service raises specific legal issues in the United Kingdom, with its tradition of applying private law in the public sector. There is no specific body of law that governs the nature of contracts in the public service. Where a public organization makes a contract with a private organization, or with another public body, the contract is treated as having been made between two independent legal persons. Lawyers have argued (Harden, 1992) that there is a need for recognition of the special character of contracts in the public sector, and the creation of a 'public law' contract that recognizes the particular issues involved.

The forms of contract that have developed in public services have often involved large quantities of work being purchased by public organizations on behalf of individual users. Members of the public, for example as individual patients or residents, are not party to the contract. Nor does the contract give them any legal rights that they did not have before. To some degree individuals may have less influence, through having to fit into preconceived contracts. The involvement of the public in the specification of contracts has been limited. In effect they are able to complain, after the event, that the service was not effectively delivered.

Where contracts are with the private sector, voluntary agencies, or other public bodies they are legally enforceable, and aggrieved parties may have recourse to the courts. Almost all contracts with the private sector have an arbitration clause specifying how differences are to be resolved. In practice most difficulties are resolved informally.

Just as the contract does not give the individual citizen many more rights, so it does little to increase redress. In some cases it makes it either more complex or more distant. The separation of purchaser and provider can create uncertainty over who should deal with complaints.

A further legal issue concerns the way that different aspects of the law governing public services relate to each other, and the impact of European Union (EU) law. Countries where local government has a power of general competence find it easier to develop market based mechanisms in the public service, compared to the United Kingdom where the powers of local government bodies are strictly defined.

EU law has an impact upon the market-based approach to the management of the public service, and is making the position increasingly unclear. Public bodies must follow EU rules about how tendering should operate for the public service. In some cases these do not fit with the law in particular countries about how public tendering is to operate. There is increasing confusion in the United Kingdom over how employees are to be treated following contracting out, as a result of conflict between EU and British law. European law, through the Transfer of Undertakings (Protection of Employment) Regulations, provides for continuity of employment and preservation of rights in cases of workers transferring from one employer to another. In the United Kingdom, contracting out has led to worsening pay and conditions. If the regulations were to be applied it would be less easy for the private sector to compete. The debate over the applicability of the regulations is likely to be long-drawn-out.

The introduction of market principles into the public services raises issues of the relationship between the public and the private realms. The nature of this division, and the rights of the consumers of public services, will vary in the legal systems of different countries. Harden, in his discussion of the changing nature of public law, argues that

> In the Anglo-American legal tradition, contract has come to be thought of as quintessentially private law, separate and distinct from the law governing the relations between the individual and the state. However, the conceptual divide between 'public' and 'private' has now ceased to correspond to the way the world actually works. Legal structures and ways of thought need to be re-adapted accordingly.
>
> (Harden, 1992, p. 4)

The development of new approaches to the management of the public service involves the erosion of barriers between the public and the private, and, in consequence, the need for a legal system that recognizes the uncertain nature of that boundary. The particular models and approach that emerge will vary from one country to another.

The changing state

The move to the mingling of the public and private has major implications for the role of the state, and the link between state and citizen. The state's role is to ensure that provision of service is made, not necessarily to provide. The concept of citizen that is involved is the individual as a consumer of a set of services, so that citizenship has no overarching integrating function in defining a relation between individual, community and state. The approach is most clearly expressed in the notion of the 'enabling state' (Ridley, 1988) which works to ensure provision rather than provide. In theory, at least, the state need not employ anybody, contracting out all its functions, perhaps even defence and the maintenance of law and order.

The 'enabling' state, in the minimalist version, argues that the role of the state is to define standards, check on performance and ensure redress. Where standards are clear, citizens will be able to make clear choices about what level of service they want.

The development of the 'evaluative state' (Henkel, 1991), focusing on the performances achieved by public bodies, follows naturally from standard-setting. There has been a considerable extension of inspection within the public services. Inspectors play a strong role in the introduction of new, market-based approaches, as the Social Services Inspectorate has done for community care in the United Kingdom. The issue that then arises is whether one can define effective and clear standards. This is relatively easy for simple services, such as street cleaning; its is much more difficult to devise effective measures for education, health or social care. The debate over the introduction of market principles has been accompanied by a debate on quality of service.

The effectiveness of the operation of market principles for the management of the public service depends on the ability of users to choose. In education and social care, for example, there is generally a strong emphasis on the role of choice for the individual. There have been extensions of choice of school for parents, for example in the United States of America, New Zealand and the United Kingdom. In health, choice has been extended, for example in

Sweden. Choice is central to the operation of the new public-sector markets, and is meant to put pressure on providers. If there is poor provision, then people can go elsewhere. It can be argued that the ability to choose is, at best, a limited check on the power of providers. Either individual citizens have only limited information upon which to make choices, or the choice itself is actually limited by the level of supply. If the public service is to operate as a market, then there will need to be development of institutions that allow more choice, such as advocacy, and more ability to vary supply in response to demand.

The separation of purchaser and provider can have the effect of blurring accountability. It is not easy to distinguish failure that results from inadequate analysis and definition of service by purchasers, and poor service delivery by providers. In the United States of America operation through contracts has given rise to issues of accountability. Saloman has argued that such developments

> continually place federal officials in the uncomfortable position of being responsible for programmes they do not really control. ... Instead of a hierarchical relationship between the federal government and its agents, therefore, what exists in practice is a far more complex bargaining relationship in which the federal government has the weaker hand.
>
> (Saloman, 1981, p. 260)

The more complex the service, the greater the danger that the separation between purchasers and provider will lead to difficulties of accountability and producer dominance, as was apparent in the early stages of change in the National Health Service in the United Kingdom. Where purchasers are dominant they may act without considering the needs of providers.

The separation of purchaser and provider also has implications for learning and redress. In the case of complex services there can be difficulties in gaining adequate knowledge and understanding of the service when an organization is no longer involved in provision. Economists have argued the importance of information in the development of effective markets and contractual relationships. Where information is differentially available to the provider there will be difficulties in policy-making and strategy development. Redress may also be difficult if there is not adequate access to providers. Complaints systems may need to be reconsidered to ensure that they have the necessary access. Commercial secrecy may also act as a brake on effective accountability. Increasingly, private contractors and internal trading providers are wishing to keep information secret to protect their competitive positions.

The operation of the market within the state does not simply involve the introduction of a new mechanism for the production and delivery of public services. It raises crucial issues about the nature of the public realm and of public law. Standards of conduct and probity are necessarily different in the public sector because of its public nature. The state has the role of exercising force and control over civil society, which, in a democratic system, is accepted in the basis of legitimacy. The question of whether it can delegate those functions is difficult. If we accept private prisons would we accept private courts? The more those involved in providing a service are expected to exercise discretion, the less plausible exernalization would seem.

Conclusion

The introduction of market principles to the operation of the public service cannot be assessed simply on the grounds of efficiency. Economic arguments that the state is necessary to compensate for market failure, or that it should be replaced by the market because of government failure, do not exhaust the universe of discussion. The state is justified, or not justified, on the basis of its own political purposes, which need to be reflected in its organizational and institutional framework. Walzer (1983) has argued that different spheres will operate according to different criteria, and different modes of distribution will operate: 'Every social good or set of goods constitutes, as it were, a distributive sphere within which only certain criteria and arrangements are appropriate' (p. 10). One does not have to go all the way with Walzer to accept that there are limits to the operation of the market as an effective mechanism for ensuring the production and delivery of public services. Consider, for example, the case of social care. The greater proportion of social care is provided on a voluntary basis. There is an obvious danger that an excessive emphasis on market principles could lead to the erosion of voluntary commitment.

The market clearly has a role to play in the production and distribution of public services, but, by its very nature, the governmental sector demands its own institutional framework. As

Saltman and von Otter argue, any market system needs to be coordinated

> in the adaptation of market mechanisms to publicly operated health systems, key economic questions become directly subordinated to the political or normative objectives of the political decision-makers who construct planned markets, and who will be held publicly accountable for their performance.
>
> (Saltman and von Otter, 1992)

Economic efficiency is neither the only nor the dominating value for those who would design public organizations.

2

THE ECONOMICS OF NETWORKS[1]

Nicolas Curien

Deregulation: a single word, a threefold process

Over recent years, a profound transformation has been taking place in the technical, economic and regulatory conditions governing public utilities linked to a network infrastructure. This development, given the generic name 'deregulation', started in the United States during the 1970s, first in air transportation then in telecommunications. Subsequently, it spread to the United Kingdom where, on the initiative of the governments led by Margaret Thatcher, most of the utilities were privatized and opened to competition. Now the movement is proliferating within the European Union as the Brussels Commission issues directives setting out the terms for increased competition in the sectors of electricity, transport and telecommunications.

The trend towards deregulation does not conform to a single pattern. Sector by sector and country by country, three processes are variously combined: the transfer of rights of ownership from the public to the private sector, i.e. *privatization*; the opening to competition of markets that had previously been monopolistic or narrowly oligopolistic, i.e. *liberalization*; and the change in the regulatory mechanisms implemented to supervise these markets, *deregulation*, properly speaking, which it would be nearer the mark to term *trans*regulation so as to signify that it is not a case of *de*posing but of *trans*posing a regulatory practice and device. These three processes are frequently fused in discourse on deregulation, even though they cover quite distinct intentions in terms of economic efficiency; although not entirely independent of each other, they gain by being disassociated, at least when first examined.

The first process relates to changes in the *form of the company* operating the network which, from being a government department, becomes a public and later a private enterprise. This process is likely to further economic efficiency in the sense that it does away with the functional confusion between the state as shareholder and the state as entrepreneur, that it raises the incentive of the firm's directors to manage the firm efficiently and that, by way of the share price on the stock-market, it provides investors with an indicator of the firm's value.

Nevertheless, it would appear that privatization is not in itself a sufficient condition – any more indeed than it is a necessary condition – for improved economic performance. It does no more than modify the geometry of the system by which the market is ordered, and its potentially beneficial effects manifest themselves only if the structure of the market is adapted in other respects.

The second process concerns the *size and structure of the industry*, according to whether a single firm or a small or large number of firms are present in the sector under survey, and according to the way in which such firms are linked, whether 'vertically' or 'horizontally'. The criterion for efficiency relevant here relates to the cost structure and the degree of economies of scale. The entry of operators competing with the dominant firm is in effect efficient only if it occurs within an area of activity where there are no significant economies of scale and if it is accompanied by lower costs, hence lower prices. When these conditions are fulfilled, a fragmented market structure further enables an improved adjustment of the supply of services to the needs of diversified, flexible demand to take place.

The opening of the market disturbs and complicates the aims of regulation. Instead of providing an incentive to a monopoly, whether public or private, to administer itself efficiently, it is a case of preventing an ex-monopoly from abusing its still dominant position, and also of stopping cross-subsidies from going from activity that remains monopolistic towards activity exposed to competition. In network activities, it is the supply of services rather than the exploitation of infrastructures that lends itself most naturally to competition, and this requires three specific tasks of the regulator: to bring into play quasi-competitive mechanisms in order to simulate the virtues of genuine competition, itself difficult to achieve in the realm of infrastructures; to guarantee equal conditions of access to the various service providers jointly using a network infrastructure; and to ensure that competition does not transform the network into a Tower of Babel, where services are mutually incompatible or undermine the customers' security. Further, major networks are also public utilities and the obligations that correspond to them should not be impaired by the introduction of competition; organizing the supply and financing of public service obligations in a competitive system is an aspect of regulation that must be given priority.

The third process has to do with the nature of the *regulating process*. It alters the position of the regulator and the extent of his or her authority in such a way as to correct anomalies in control, which experience tends to show may prove to be insufficiently independent, too selective, pertinacious or implausible. 'Deregulation' further affects the way in which the regulating authority intervenes, so affording a transition from rigid administrative procedures that impose unnecessary and demanding requirements for information supply to ones that foster incentive, offer more flexibility and are more genuinely informative.

Regulation systems and privatization

Regulation, taken in the strict sense of a body laying down rules and seeing that they are applied, is only one element in the overall system of market control. Such a system may be defined as the ordering of relations between all the agents whose interaction determines how the market functions: public authority, regulatory body, firms active in the market, shareholders in the dominant company, creditors of the same company, and so on.

The process of privatization may thus be analysed as a mutation in the system of control. Where public property is concerned, the chain of control functions in the following way:

- At the top of the chain, electors are presumed to be motivated by social welfare in that they desire to have the benefit of high-quality services at moderate prices. Yet their means of attaining this objective are limited: it is costly for them to be reliably informed as to the real effectiveness of the public sector; moreover, their vote is largely influenced by factors other than the performance of the various public utilities. Hence with their expectations in this area being at best uncertain, as voters they are little influenced by the issue.

- The government elected has as its declared objective economic efficiency and social well-being. Nevertheless, its primary objective is to win votes, which does not necessarily amount to the same thing. For example, it may seem appropriate to limit productivity gains in order to reduce the costs of unemployment compensation thus engendered; or conversely it may be tempting artificially to lower the price of a public service and finance the operation through a covert fiscal measure.

- The regulating authority theoretically has the objective of assisting the government in seeking the general interest and to this effect exercising effective control of the market. Nevertheless, its overseeing role is naturally matched by a desire to increase its influence as well as its budget, and this entails a specific cost and provides no guarantee of efficiency. In addition to this, one has to reckon with an element of inefficiency inherent in bureaucratic procedures.

- The directors of the public enterprise dominant in the market are certainly well-disposed and not indifferent to the cause of social welfare. On the other hand, they are frequently less intent on cost reduction and, in their capacity as heads of a major industrial and commercial company, they are generally motivated to increase their share of the market, which is not necessarily synonymous with efficiency. Also, they are not prepared to go all out in the exercise of management, in the absence of an appropriate system of remuneration.

The chain of actors here described is governed by a cascade of relations which economists qualify by the term 'principal–agent'. At each link in the chain, the actor in the role of principal sets the rules of the game, though not in possession of all the relevant information, whereas the actor in the agent's role abides by the rules, while controlling the margin of uncertainty conferred by the advantage he or she has in terms of information. Thus the elector has the role of principal *vis-à-vis* the agent represented as the government, the government *vis-à-vis* the regulator, the regulator *vis-à-vis* the managers.

The imperfections of the regime stem from a chronic information gap that is not susceptible to remedy by means of feasible contracts between principal and agent. The result is that each actor, as agent, is able to pursue an objective that deviates appreciably from the objective set by his principal, and, as principal, finds himself with only limited power to induce the agent under his control to perform efficiently. Seen in this light, the defects in the system of public control can be summarized in four points, corresponding to the different degrees of the principal–agent relationship: the substitution of political objectives for social objectives; the tendency for the political factor to be brought to bear directly on the public sector of the economy instead of exerting its influence via the instruments of regulation; the weaknesses of the regulating bureaucracy, the extension of whose authority does not always coincide with the general interest; and the amount of discretion left to the heads of public enterprises, whose incentive to lower the cost of supplying services is insufficient.

The defects of the public regime of control particularly affect what economists refer to by the term *productive efficiency*:

- The state as shareholder is insufficiently concerned with profitability and production costs are too high; public service obligations apart, a number of activities – in particular, diversification – are sometimes structurally in deficit and financed with the help of cross-subsidies.
- There is an element of waste in the allocation and utilization of factors of production, and this is encouraged by the ready access public enterprises have to the capital market, in the form of raising loans at preferential rates or acquiring exceptional grants, as well as to the labour market, in the form of aid to boost employment and regrading.
- The adoption of improved technologies is not always optimized; sometimes new technologies are introduced before there is sufficient demand for them to justify their cost.

On the other hand, public management presents the advantage of giving consideration, however imperfectly, to social welfare. Economists speak of its being satisfactory from the viewpoint of *allocative efficiency*: services are provided in appropriate quantity and variety; consumer prices are in general not excessive; and public service benefits are available on affordable terms to users who are either socially or geographically disadvantaged.

The transition from public to private management can, as a first approximation, be understood as an intent to give preference to the direct pursuit of productive efficiency, resulting from the managers' concern to increase profits – so as to increase their own incomes – subject to the control exercised by shareholders and creditors. As for allocative efficiency, it is in part brought about through productive efficiency – lower costs in particular bringing about lower prices, in part guaranteed by intervention of the regulator.

More precisely, in the case of private management, the chain of control is given greater strength with three new principals, so to speak duplicating the control exercised over the managers by the regulatory body. These are shareholders in the company itself, shareholders in other companies, acting across the stock market, and creditors with whom the company negotiates its long-term indebtedness. In each of the three cases the characteristics and imperfections inherent in principal–agent relations are to be found:

- Private shareholders in the company endeavour to raise their dividend expectations, hence company profits. But the fact that shareholders are dispersed reduces the effectiveness of their control. Moreover, control involves a cost, and each shareholder tends to adopt the attitude of a 'free rider', hoping to reap benefit from the control exercised by other shareholders.

- Shareholders in other companies are likely to mount a takeover operation if the private firm exploiting the network is unsuitably managed; in which case the raiders' gain is equal to the difference between the *ex post* and *ex ante* share value, less the cost of the transaction. This certainly represents an incentive towards productive efficiency, but one limited by two factors at least: in the first instance, a takeover bid may be motivated not by profit-seeking but by the desire for market power, or again for fiscal reasons; hence the possibility of a takeover constitutes just as much of a threat to a well-run company; in the second place, a large company is in practice seldom under threat from a takeover bid.

- A private firm's creditors have a lever of control that manifests itself to the managers in terms of the risk of bankruptcy, a risk that is virtually non-existent for a public enterprise. Yet the greater the long-term debt the higher the risk is; and the ratio of debt to capital stock is generally under the direct control of the managers. Moreover, a sizeable debt makes for decisions that favour the short term, which is in fact detrimental to productive efficiency. In effect, the threat of bankruptcy is plausible, hence an incentive, only when demand is depressed or when the company is exposed to severe competition.

Thus, despite many limitations, shareholding, along with stock and financial markets, does tend to encourage productive efficiency where private management is concerned. The presence of these actors, who are absent from the system of public control, offers another advantage in that the regulatory body is no longer sole intermediary between government and company, which reduces the risk of collusion of interest between regulator and company, described as 'capture' by economists. Even so, the risk of capture of the regulator by government remains, under private as under public management.

Thus, except to those who take a doctrinaire position on private capitalism, privatization is not a panacea nor is it an end in itself. Rather it should be looked upon as one possible form of aid, in the pursuit of other objectives such as facilitating the introduction of competition, clearly separating regulation from operation, creating a more dynamic professional environment, and giving the management of the company greater motivation and momentum – or further, reducing the influence of trade unions. But privatization is not the only means of attaining these objectives. Similar effects can be obtained in other ways, for example by transforming an administration into a company with a public majority holding, by changing the way in which senior executives are nominated, by breaking up the enterprise and creating subsidiaries, or by removing the legal character of its monopoly.

In the United Kingdom, where public ownership was widespread, where public-sector performance was mediocre and where the Conservative government made a credo of private ownership, the path to privatization was taken. In other European countries, such as Germany, the Netherlands and probably France, it would seem that the course chosen has been to restructure companies without radically altering property rights.

Opening up to competition and regulatory issues

In the supply of network services one invariably finds a structure comprising two components: the infrastructure itself and the services it enables to be delivered. The services themselves are of two types: *intermediate* services, whose – internal – function is to maximize efficiency in managing the flow of traffic across the infrastructure; and the *final* services, whose – external – function is to satisfy demand on the part of network users. In most networks, and in telecommunications especially, greater weight is at present being given to the 'services' component. Intermediate services have become more sophisticated and are ensured through data processing; final services are diversifying and equipment associated with them is interconnected with the network's basic infrastructure, which has thus become multi-service, or 'service-integrated' in telecommunications language.

Generally speaking, the infrastructure gives rise to a significant outlay on investment which is planned, carried through and then recouped over a long period; it is 'sunk' in the sense that it is not subject to sell-off in the case of an exit from the market, nor readily to dismantling and reprogramming towards goals other than those originally set. Together these features pinpoint what is known among economists as a 'natural monopoly'; that is, an area of activity where several firms are less efficient than a single one. Hence in operating an infrastructure a monopoly is able to benefit from economies of scale – that is, to amortize costs that are sunk and fixed by a high level of activity – whereas a fragmented industry structure is likely to lead to at least partial duplication of such costs.

That argument, however, has limits. For example, in the United States, three firms compete in providing three long-distance telecom networks, and as far as one can see active competition is taking place in the operation of local networks; losses in economies of scale are probably being compensated for by economies in marketing, benefiting for instance a cable operator making use of the same commercial network to sell both cable TV and telephone calls; and 'static' inefficiency, arising from a degree of infrastructural duplication, is probably counterbalanced by 'dynamic' efficiency induced by the interplay of competition itself. Normally, however, infrastructural management requires a concentrated if not monopolistic industry structure.

On the other hand, in the sphere of services, whether intermediate or final, natural monopoly is not present. Investment, in software more than hardware, is much less substantial than in the sphere of infrastructure and is generally capable of being reversed and redirected. Indeed, it needs to have this capability, now and then in real time– in respect of intermediate services, so as the better to manage fluctuations in traffic across the infrastructure and, as regards final services, so as to respond to a clientele, business customers in particular, where demand is increasing rapidly.

Here it is flexibility of supply and short-term adaptability which are dominant to a point where an extended market, with several providers of services competing with one other, would appear to afford the most suitable structure. Clearly, however, the services market cannot be left totally uncontrolled on account of the presence of marked external factors. These relate, on the one hand, to the safety of infrastructures, especially in regard to transport, and, on the other, to compatibility between the services on offer from different suppliers on the same infrastructure. One of the roles of regulation is to set up a form of competition which takes these various effects into account, hence having overall welfare at heart.

What of the empirical evidence? The trend observed recently or likely in the short run in the energy, transport or telecommunications networks would seem to give confirmation to the theory, even though competition occasionally spreads beyond service provision into infrastructures. What is now becoming quite clear is that the era of integrated monopolies operating infrastructure and providing the totality of services is over. The 'industrial structure' of future networks is a complex one, where a dominant firm, the former monopoly, maintains its monopoly over some segments of the market, is subject to competition in others, and does not intervene at all in segments where there are other providers.

Competing operators, or those proposing services which are not provided by the dominant operator, are found only on particular sections of the vertical chain which allows a service to be rendered to the final customer from start to finish. Hence they must gain access to other sections and buy interconnection to 'essential resources' – typically infrastructures – from the dominating operator who is in a monopoly position to exploit these. An 'open' industrial structure of this type provides regulation with six essential objectives, covering (1) the control of abuse of the dominant position; (2) stopping cross-subsidies from monopoly activity towards competitive activity; (3) arranging equal and efficient conditions of access to essential resources; (4) urging the operators of essential resources to efficient management; (5) bearing in mind external factors such as security and compatibility; and (6) maintaining public service obligations:

1. When a large company coexists with smaller companies in the same market, this dominant position is likely to result in abuses and distort competition. It may be a matter of agreements, if not mergers, with the major company absorbing one or more of the smaller. If the major company is present both in a market providing equipment and in one providing services, it may be tempted to prescribe its own equipment to its service customers or its services to those buying its equipment. Or it may try to do its competitors down, if it offers a wider range of services than they do, by proposing linked sales or multi-service contracts to its customers. Or, if it operates infrastructures as well as providing services, it may try to win over a captive clientele in the services sphere and bind them by long-term contracts, even though such contracts are only truly justified in the sphere of infrastructures.

2. In order to display artificially low prices – i.e. lower than cost price – in markets where it faces competition, the dominant firm may practise cross-subsidizing, in other words set prices higher than costs in sections of the market where it is still in a monopoly position. If the firm in question remains integrated when the market is opened to competition, this practice is made simpler by the absence of accounting transparency, as well as by the – always arbitrary – procedures of cost allocation and transfer of expenses, which enable the prices of competing services to be reduced and those of monopolistic services raised. The task of the regulator is not made any easier by the fact that the cross-subsidies are often disguised or non-material: for example, the same personnel or the same equipment can be employed primarily to provide for the main occupation, as well as, in a secondary capacity, to help supply competing services; or the public service image, acquired in the main occupation, may be abused in order to achieve customer loyalty in areas of diversification. The subsidiarization of competitive activity is one means of remedying these problems, by imposing clarification in accounting, separating the measures applied to the two types of activity and allowing for customers to be less exposed to confusing images.

3. The company which, as a monopoly, exploits infrastructures that are of necessity used by those providing services so as to reach their final customers is obliged to practise no discrimination in access either in price or of a technical nature. In the latter

case, normalization requires interfaces for access to infrastructures to be defined and the different suppliers to be guaranteed equal conditions for being interconnected. The question is more complex in regard to price. If the dominant company remains integrated, it first needs to be established that the internal transfer price whereby it invoices itself for the essential resource is not at variance with the market price at which it makes it available to its competitors; in that case, too, subsidiarization guarantees a degree of transparency. Further to this, the method adopted for calculating the price of access to infrastructures needs to be defined.

4. Monopolies operating essential resources must be induced to carry out efficient management. Since effective competition is not practicable in segments where there is a 'natural monopoly', the regulator must try to replace it with mechanisms that reproduce competition's virtues yet at the same time maintain monopoly – *quasi-competitive* mechanisms. Several types can be distinguished.

Potential competition consists in not protecting the monopoly, either by law or through regulation, and in authorizing the entry of potential competitors. If the market is 'contestable' – that is to say, if the entry investments are not sunk, i.e. irrecoverable in the eventuality of exiting from the market – entry is plausible and the threat it represents acts as an invitation to the monopoly to become disciplined.

Fringe competition results from the institution of a highly dissymmetrical duopoly, as instanced in the United Kingdom by British Telecom and Mercury. The smaller company, enjoying favourable conditions of entry laid down by the regulator, acts as a spur to the larger one. When this has produced its effect and if competition is viable, it can be adjusted to become more symmetrical, with it being possible even to authorize entry by new competitors.

Prior competition is that which prevails *ex ante*, when the monopoly concession is accorded at the conclusion of bidding. The company that wins the bid is the one which undertakes to conform to the remit at the best price. The concession is granted for a limited duration, with the result that the company chosen, anticipating future competition, is not in a position to benefit from a rent.

'Yardstick' competition is what the regulator instils when

comparing the performance of the managing company with that of other comparable ones, operating either a similar infrastructure in a different geographic area, or a different infrastructure in the same zone. As an example, the price imposed by the regulating authority is the lowest price observed.

5. Cohabitation of a number of services on the same infrastructure constitutes a real advantage for customers only if the increase in variety is not paid for by a deterioration in quality or a threat to safety. Thus competition between services cannot be entirely left to itself. Or, more specifically, competition between final services must be accompanied by cooperation between intermediate services, those destined to provide optimum use of the infrastructure. Here the role of the regulator is not to lay down the specifications for such systems, but to guarantee norms of quality, compatibility and safety, by setting definition and verification procedures for these norms, which link the management of the infrastructure, providers of services and the final customers.

6. When a public utility is exploited from a monopoly position, whether public or private, the regulating authority requires the monopoly to take on a certain number of obligations, more particularly the supply of non-profitable services such as universal access to infrastructures, so as not to penalize excessively categories of customer who are geographically isolated or economically deprived. If it is opened up to competition, the maintenance and financing of these public service obligations is at stake, the former monopoly being unable to take entire responsibility for them, without compensation at least. There are several options open to the regulating authority, some which require effective provision of such obligations by the dominant company alone, others treating all operators in the same way.

'Deregulation': selectiveness and incentives

The purpose of regulation is to mitigate the failure of the market, to remedy, that is, the inefficiencies – productive or allocative – which the free play of economic agents may lead to. Hence regulation has meaning only insofar as it does not bring about inefficiencies of a higher degree than those it sets out to correct. The term 'deregulation' may be so interpreted: it does not signify termination of regulation but its being reordered in the interests of greater efficiency. Two aspects of this, one relating to the sphere and powers of regulation, the other to regulatory contracts, are outlined below.

- Effective regulation does not imply total regulation. The field of regulation should be selective and restricted to areas where market forces on their own are clearly imperfect: the allocation of rare resources, such as the Hertzian spectrum in telecommunications; giving attention to external effects such as transport safety; non-discrimination in access to essential resources, viz. network infrastructures; supervision of dominant firms; and so on. Whenever direct interaction between economic agents is not the evident source of inefficiency, the best form of regulation is not to intervene or, in the last resort, have recourse to arbitration.

  On the other hand, once the scope of regulation is determined, it is important that the body charged with the task is given sufficient powers to have thorough credibility. To this end, it needs both to be seen to be independent of political and market influence and to dispose of suitably swift means of intervening at the three stages: imposing regulations, controlling their application and penalizing abuse. So deregulating implies enabling the regulating process to function more smoothly, by preserving it from the illusion of omnicompetence, role confusion and the built-in resistance of bureaucracy.

- Deregulation also means moving as effectively as possible from a prescribing to an incentive-creating function. It means seeking out contractual procedures which induce economic agents to move spontaneously in the desired direction, without their being directly constrained to do so. Prescribing is demanding in terms of the amount of information demanded, hence lacking in efficiency and credibility if the data are missing whereby the rules can be laid down and enforced, whereas fostering incentives generally involves disclosure of information via the response of the agent to the incentive offered (though it may prove to be financially costly to obtain the desired level of effort). Yet it is better to spend money in enlisting the agent's cooperation than mobilize methods that are inquisitorial and unproductive.

One example of incentive-providing regulation is to apply control over an operator through 'price capping' rather than by limiting profit levels. By imposing a cap on price movements, the regulator actuates a lowering of costs, whereas setting profit limits guarantees that costs, however high, are reimbursed. In the United States, there has been a move away from cost plus- to price cap-type regulatory contracts, and these are the types of contract now used in Europe to control public utilities. Yet one should not have unlimited confidence in the virtues of such contracts. In the first place, they truly serve as an incentive only if they have credibility; that is, if the firm is really certain to benefit from the productivity gains achieved while the contract lasts. Secondly, they do not exempt the regulator altogether from becoming informed about costs, this being an initial requirement in order for the contract to be calibrated and subsequently renegotiated. Thirdly, price control has to be matched by quality control, so that the firm does not lower its costs to the detriment of the service it provides to its customers.

Conclusion

Over and above its primary legal dimension, regulation comprises an economic dimension that is by no means negligible; and it is desirable for this to be borne in mind at every stage of the regulatory function.

In the same way that companies apply economic calculation to the process of decision-making, it would be sensible practice for regulators to estimate *ex ante* the costs and benefits of measures they contemplate and rules they lay down. Costs include the direct cost of regulating, the cost of acquiring the information necessary for drawing up rules, and the cost of seeing to their application. Its usefulness lies in the increase in social surplus attributable to regulation. Costs and benefit are certainly hard to quantify with precision, but a rough calculation frequently allows an ill-chosen decision to be avoided. Besides, the mere fact of scrutinizing the effort employed and the results expected invites reflection and directs regulation where it can be most beneficial. Finally, once a regulatory decision is taken, it is desirable than an *ex post* follow-up should assess the short- and long-term consequences.

It follows that regulation can be effective only as a result of lawyers and economists combining their efforts. This is already so in the North American tradition of regulation. In Europe such combining of skills is only just beginning. It needs to be encouraged. In the coming years European networks will without question represent a choice terrain for action and for regulatory 'inventiveness'.

Notes

1. As a supplement to this article the reader may wish to consult three books which the present author has drawn upon: Vickers and Yarrow (1988); Curien and Gensollen (1992); and Simon (1991).

3

THE PRIVATIZATION OF URBAN SERVICES IN THE UNITED KINGDOM

Gerry Stoker

Introduction

The British experience of privatization stems from 1979 when the Conservatives won political control of Parliament and began a long period of domination in national politics. Privatization became one of the distinctive policy approaches of the Conservatives and has attracted considerable attention both within the United Kingdom and beyond. The British privatization programme is often promoted as a major economic and political success. In addition, the scale of the programme has been greater than elsewhere and the British experience is often presented as an exemplar to other countries (see, for example, Marsh, 1991). The British experience provides an illustration of a politically driven privatization programme.

One issue that needs to be addressed immediately is what the British mean when they refer to privatization. There is no denying a degree of ambiguity and uncertainty surrounding the term. At times politicians have wanted to reserve the word 'privatization' to describe only the sale of nationalized industries and other state-owned companies back to the private sector. In particular, in the debate about the National Health Service (NHS) the Conservatives have been sensitive to accusations of privatization, claiming that state provision and funding are not under threat and that therefore the claim that they are privatizing the NHS is unfounded. Yet central to Conservative thinking beyond the sale of public assets has been the introduction of various elements of commercialization, competitive tendering and quasi-market mechanisms in the provision of public services including the operations of the NHS.

In this context many academics have deemed it appropriate to use the term 'privatization' to describe a broad range of programmes 'which aim to limit the role of the public sector, and increase the role of the private sector, while improving the performance of the remaining public sector' (Young, 1986, p. 236). This may seem a vague formula, perhaps confirming people's prejudices about the imprecision of academic debate. Yet the kernel of truth contained within this approach should not be lost. Privatization is best understood as a broad package of programmes aimed at restructuring the role of the state and the nature of public provision.

In this sense, it is clear that in the United Kingdom there has been a radical shift towards privatized provision. To put this change in context requires a brief review of the development of urban services in the United Kingdom. The dominance of provision through elected local government, the National Health Service and various quasi-governmental agencies (all organized on a large scale by European standards) emerges as the core characteristic of the pre-1979 system. As modern industrial capitalism evolved so the role of the state expanded.

The next three sections examine in some detail major elements of the Conservatives' privatization programme post-1979. The focus, in turn, is on council house sales, the privatization of key public utilities and the development of compulsory competitive tendering for a range of local authority services. A further section seeks to capture how the mechanisms of privatization have also had an impact across almost all urban services, from social security to health care provision. Almost all areas of urban service provision in Britain have felt the pressure of privatization.

The development of urban services

Each country has its own unique history in terms of the development of its system of local government. In Britain the modern system of local government is closely associated with the rise of industrial capitalism.

In the nineteenth and early twentieth centuries, local authorities pioneered key urban services such as highways, gas, sewage treatment, water supply and public transport that were central to the infrastructure for industrial production. Police and fire services and poor relief provided a response to the tensions and grinding poverty associated with the rapid growth in towns and cities in this period. Later, health care, housing and education were also services pioneered by local authorities, among other institutions. Other activities that were undertaken by local councils included the provision of a racecourse (Doncaster), a municipal bank (Birmingham), river ferries (Birkenhead), a telephone system (Hull), a civic theatre (Manchester) and numerous crematoria, slaughterhouses and dock undertakings.

In this process of 'municipalization' local authorities became the owners and managers of many buildings and much machinery and land. From the late nineteenth century to the mid-1930s local government is seen by many commentators as having enjoyed a golden age of expansion (Robson, 1966). Between 1900 and 1938 total local authority expenditure increased nearly fourfold in real terms. The services provided by local authorities remained patchy and underdeveloped, and ran alongside the efforts of others, but few could dispute the authorities' domination in the provision of urban infrastructure and welfare support systems to industrialization. At the start of 1939 local authorities provided most of the water supply, two-thirds of the nation's electricity, and one-third of the nation's gas consumption, controlled over half the hospitals in the country and ran many other elements of a growing welfare state.

The post-war settlement marked a shift in emphasis in the role of local authorities. Functions were removed from their control and placed in the hands of various nationally organized quasi-government agencies.

Gas and electricity facilities were nationalized in 1947–48. Local authority hospitals were absorbed into the National Health Service in 1946. The National Assistance Board, established in 1948, completed the removal of responsibility for public assistance and social security from local government (a process begun in 1929 with the abolition of the Boards of Guardians). Local authorities passed their responsibility for water supply to joint water boards, and eventually, in 1973, responsibility for water and sewerage in England and Wales was passed to regional water authorities. As new functions arose they too became the responsibility of various *ad hoc* agencies. From 1946, New Town Development Corporations were established to oversee the expansion of purpose-built new cities and towns to overcome the problems of overcrowding and provide new sites for industrial expansion. The truck and motorway building programmes were taken as a direct responsibility by central government.

Yet alongside the loss of functions, funding was provided to expand the welfare state functions of local authorities. Between 1955 and 1975 local authority current expenditure increased threefold in real terms and local authority capital spending more than doubled. Slum clearance and the provision of new council housing improved the standards enjoyed by many households and led to a dramatic increase in the proportion of households renting from a local authority from roughly 10 per cent in 1938 to nearly 30 per cent in 1975. Local authorities were active in building new schools, better local roads, community centres and various welfare facilities. The numbers employed by local authorities also leaped; between 1952 and 1972 there was a 50 per cent increase in the number of full-time employees and an over 200 per cent increase in the number of part-time local authority workers.

Despite their loss of functions, local authorities by the mid-1970s were 'big business'. In tune with the concerns of modernization they had been reorganized into 514 principal authorities serving on average a population of over 120,000 in England, over 90,000 in Scotland and over 75,000 in Wales. Local authorities accounted for about a quarter of all public expenditure and over a tenth of the gross domestic product. They employed roughly three million full and part-time employees.

This brief review does not provide an adequate history of the development of urban services (for a further discussion see Byrne, 1986; Loughlin et al., 1985), but it does help provide the context for the programme of privatization launched from 1979 onwards (see Table 3.1). A final scene setting matter is provided by the economic 'crisis' of the early 1970s and the subsequent concern to rein back public spending. It was a Labour government that first expressed concern on this issue and told local authorities that the 'party' was 'over'. Cuts in capital spending and cash limits on current spending were introduced. The long-established trend of growth in spending gave way to standstill. For Thatcher and her ministers, Labour's measures were not sufficient. What was required was a more radical attempt to 'roll back the state'. The programmes of privatization emerged as a key element in the Conservatives'

Table 3.1 The changing organization of provision in key urban services 1880s–1990s

Service	Early development and municipal provision (1880s–1930s)	Dominant provider	
		Nationalization and expanding welfare state (1930s–1970s)	Privatization (1970s–1990s)
Water and sewerage	Local authorities	*Ad hoc* agencies	Private company
Electricity	Local authorities	Nationalized industry	Private company
Gas	Local authorities and others	Nationalized industry	Private company
Telecommunications	n/a	Nationalized industry	Private company
Education	Local authorities and others	Local authorities and others	Separately managed schools and colleges
Public rented housing	Local authorities	Local authorities	Local authorities and others
Social services	Local authorities and others	Local authorities	Local authorities and others
Social security	Local authorities	National administration	National agency and contractors
Ports	Local authorities and others	Mixed	Private companies
Regional airports	n/a	Local authorities	Private companies (by end of decade)
Rail transport	Private companies	Nationalized industry	Private companies (by end of decade)
Bus transport	Local authorities	Local authorities and other public bodies	Private companies
Refuse disposal	Local authorities	Local authorities	Local authorities and contractors
Police	Local authorities	Local authorities	Hybrid national administration
Fire	Local authorities	Local authorities	Local authorities
Health	Local authorities	National administration	Locally managed providers in national administration

response as they started a long period of control over national government in 1979.

Council house sales

Housing was one of the first areas to experience the challenge of privatization. The conservatives came to power with a clear manifesto commitment to increase home ownership and in particular to give council tenants the right to buy their own homes. The Housing Act 1980 gave most council tenants the 'right to buy' their dwellings.

The Act also established a discount rate for these tenants, varying from 33 to 50 per cent of the market value (depending mainly on the length of a tenant's tenure). It came into force in October 1980 and a surge of sales followed (see Table 3.2). When interest showed signs of drying up, the government decided to offer more incentives to prospective purchasers. In the 1984 and 1986 Housing Acts, discount rates were increased to 60 per cent for houses and 70 per cent for flats. Also, those two Acts extended the range of tenants and housing types that were eligible for purchase. Again a surge in sales followed, although this has again slowed down, not least because of the general impact of recession and unemployment on the housing market (see Table 3.2). In total, over 1.4 million homes have been sold and a new advertising campaign was launched in 1993 pushing the virtues of the 'Right to Buy'. With tight controls restricting new building by local authorities and other measures to increase the rents they charge for their existing stock, the context for the success of Right to Buy was set. Kemp (1992, p. 71) concludes: 'The Conservatives were successful in extending home ownership. It expanded from 55 per cent of all dwellings in Britain in 1979 to 67 per cent in 1989'. He goes on to note that Right to Buy accounted for two-fifths of the increase and that during the same period the proportion of council housing fell from 31 per cent to 23 per cent of the total stock.

Local authority resistance was overcome after a brief struggle in Norwich in which central government took over the administration of sales. Because of the perceived popularity of the policy neither the Labour Party nor public service unions representing housing officials were confident that they could mount viable broad-based anti-sales campaigns. The direct impact of the sales policy on voting

Table 3.2   Right to Buy housing sales

| Year | Sales completed to sitting tenants | | |
	Local authorities	New towns	Housing associations
1981	79,430	2,427	547
1982	196,430	3,963	2,003
1983	138,511	3,638	2,140
1984	100,149	2,655	1,965
1985	92,230	2,113	1,522
1986	89,250	1,656	2,876
1987	103,309	2,277	2,447
1988	160,568	3,275	3,766
1989	181,367	4,608	4,191
1990	126,210	2,539	3,701
1991	73,458	1,535	2,111
1992	67,000*	1,700*	3,000*

Source: Department of the Environment *Housing Statistics* (1992 and 1993).
* Estimate based on figures for three-quarters of the year.

patterns is a matter of dispute but the crucial point from our perspective is that among leading politicians of both the left and the right, the policy was perceived as irresistible because of its popular appeal.

The limits to the sales policy are set by economic rather than political considerations. Right to buy has contributed to the loss of much of the better stock and most of the higher-income tenants from the local authority sector. Nearly three-quarters of council tenants now rely on state welfare benefits as their main source of income. In the light of such considerations the Housing Act 1988 gave the remaining local authority tenants the right to opt out and choose another landlord. Yet relatively few tenants so far have exercised that right. Renting from a non-local authority landlord might involve a reduced security of tenure and a tougher attitude to rent arrears. The loss of political accountability was also a concern for many.

Kemp (1992) points out that one unplanned outcome of the conservatives' challenge to the local authorities' role in providing rented housing has been the emergence of wholesale voluntary stock transfer. These involve a local authority selling its entire stock to a new landlord, generally a housing association established specifically for the purpose. By the end of 1992 eighteen authorities had engaged in such transfers, although all involved relatively small amounts of stock and were mainly in Conservative-controlled districts.

The Leasehold Reform, Housing and Urban Development Act 1993 expresses the government's concern to continue its challenge to the role of local authorities in housing provision. It pushes the 'Right to Buy' still further by providing for the establishment of 'rent to mortgage' schemes. Tenants may have their rent payments treated as payments on a mortgage. The Act also paves the way for introducing competitive tendering into housing management (see later discussion).

The Conservatives' housing policies have succeeded in undermining the quasi-monopoly position of local authorities in providing rented housing and satisfied the aspirations of many individual tenants. Yet they have created a substantial gap in strategic capacity in many localities. Local authorities find themselves in many cases unable to provide housing to meet local needs, and no other agency has the responsibility or resources to fill the gap.

The sale of public utilities

Beyond the sale of council houses the Conservatives had in their 1979 manifesto pledged themselves to sell back to private ownership the recently nationalized aerospace and shipbuilding concerns, as well as sell shares in the National Freight Corporation. Out of these rather modest proposals there developed, in the course of the next few years, a major programme of privatization extending to seventeen major asset sales between 1979 and 1991 and providing net proceeds to the government of over £33,000 million (see Marsh, 1991, Table 1). Indeed, some writers have argued that the policy was adopted almost by accident, without any clear-cut objectives (Bishop and Kay, 1988). It would probably be more accurate to argue that the Conservatives lacked a clear and detailed plan when they came to office but that privatization was on their agenda, and it took until the second term for a full programme to emerge (Young, 1986; Dobek 1993). What is equally clear is that 'the privatisation policy had a number of aims, which at different stages and to different observers among both academics and Conservative politicians, received different emphasis' (Marsh, 1991, p. 463).

From the perspective of a concern with urban services the key asset sales are set out in Table 3.3. Telecommunications, gas,

Table 3.3 Sales of public utilities 1979–91

Company	Financial year of initial flotation	Golden share	Net proceeds to government (£ millions)	Number of times oversubscribed	Discount on share price (%)
British Telecom	1985/86	Yes	3,681	3.0	21
British Gas	1986/87	Yes	7,731	4.0	11
Ten water companies of England and Wales	1989/90	Yes	3,480	2.8	17
Electric companies	1990/91	Yes	5,200	10.7	21
Two electricity generating companies (Powergen and National Power)	1991/92	Yes	2,000	4.0	37

Source: Adapted from Marsh (1991, Table 1).

electricity and water supply (in England and Wales) are now in the hands of private companies. The sale of each of the utilities attracted a great deal of investment interest and all the share issues were handsomely over-subscribed.

Modest efforts to create the conditions for competition were developed, for example in the encouragement of Mercury to compete with British Telecom and in the splitting of the electricity generating industry into two companies. Overall, 'almost all observers are agreed that asset sales have very rarely led to increased competition' (Marsh, 1991, p. 466). Indeed, part of the attraction of the privatized companies to investors was that their monopoly position was largely unchallenged. The government, concerned to ensure a successful share launch and eager for quick action, recognized that it was to its benefit if the company retained much of its monopoly position (and the established managers of the companies were not likely to disagree from their perspective). In the case of privatization of public utilities there is also a sense in which the services they provide are natural monopolies, although changes in technology may begin to challenge this characteristic. Measures to increase competition are under consideration.

In some respects the privatized utilities are hybrid, mixed-economy undertakings similar to those in other European countries. The government has in some cases retained a 'golden share' which provides it with a variety of powers to block types of shareholding, share issues and asset disposals. The golden share may allow some scope for influencing the companies behaviour. In addition, a series of new state regulatory agencies have been established to oversee the work of the utilities (see Table 3.4 for details). Moreover, existing watchdogs have been given new powers. The Monopolies and Mergers Commission, for example, has been given powers not only on the costs and efficiency of the formerly nationalized industries but also a brief to promote the competitive aspects of those utilities now in the private sector. The new watchdogs have powers to control prices charged for some services; to ensure that the private companies conform to the terms of their licences; to monitor service quality and act as conduit for consumer complaints; and generally to promote competition within the industry.

The new regulatory provisions clearly do not provide governments with the direct control and influence that was available to them in previously nationalized sectors. The regulators in the judgement of many lack power: 'at best they have influence which

Table 3.4   New regulatory agencies for privatized utilities (as of 1990)

Agency	Budget (£ millions)	Staff	Date formed	Self-financing
Office of Telecommunications	4.5	120	1984	Yes
Office of Gas Supply	1.4	28	1986	Yes
Cable Authority	0.4	5	1984	Yes
National River Authority	30.0	6,500	1989	Yes
Office of Water Service	–	–	1989	Yes
Office of Electricity Regulation	–	–	1990	Yes

Source: Adapted from Veljanovski (1990, Table 13.2)

they can exercise through a process of negotiation and consultation with the privatised company' (Marsh, 1991, p. 470). Regulators often have limited budgets and staff. They may lack expertise and rely on the privatized company for their information. For others, especially those on the political Right, the fear is that the regulators are becoming too powerful (Adam Smith Institute, 1993). The regulators, they argue, have considerable discretion. They use their powers in an unaccountable and inappropriate way. Price controls that were supposed to be a stop-gap measure are becoming a permanent feature of the operation of the newly privatized utilities. The pressure to regulate in other areas of their activities may grow: 'It starts with regulating the most obvious monopoly abuses, squeezing the problems into progressively harder to regulate areas. Soon the regulator discovers that he is shadowing management, second-guessing them and virtually running the company' (Veljanovski, 1990, p. 304).

For the Conservatives, the utility privatizations are counted as a considerable success. Various aims have been achieved. Trade union power in former nationalized industries has been curbed to a degree. Privatized companies have been able to undertake major redundancies. Management salaries have risen substantially after privatization but that has not generally been the experience of workers. Yet the trade unions remain in place in most of the privatized industries and it is debatable whether the challenges they have faced in the newly privatized sector are greater than those faced elsewhere in the economy (Marsh, 1991). The spread of share ownership is undoubtedly a side-effect of privatization, increasing from 7 per cent in 1979 to 20 per cent in 1991 the proportion of shareholders in the population. Substantial sums of money were brought into the Treasury's coffers, helping the Conservatives to promote a policy of income tax cuts at the same time as maintaining much public spending. In addition, the burden of raising funds for capital spending was shifted out of the government's orbit. Above all, there has been a massive transfer from the public to the private sector. Between 1979 and 1991 650,000 workers changed sectors and the proportion of the UK output accounted for by the nationalized sector shrank from 9 per cent to less than 5 per cent (Marsh, 1991, p. 463).

In the light of the above it should not be a surprise to learn that in their fourth term of office, the Conservatives are continuing their programme of privatization of utilities. Yet what is also clear is that the political opposition to further privatizations is gaining in strength despite considerable opposition. British Rail remains the major privatization target, and measures to force local authorities to sell their regional airports are still under consideration. However, opposition has meant that the plans to deregulate and privatize London's buses have been delayed, and the proposal to privatize water and sewerage systems in Scotland has been dropped. Instead, this service is to be taken out of local authority hands and given to three centrally appointed water authorities to run. For many observers, the Conservatives' long-term interest in privatizing 'Scotland's water' remains.

What is important from the perspective of urban services is that the key pricing and investment decisions of the privatized utilities have shifted from the openly political sphere to a shadowy and unaccountable world in which the managers of the privatized companies and the regulators are the key actors. The sensitivity of these companies to the concerns of specific urban policy-makers is likely to be non-existent compared to the modest political and official influences of the past available through the national level for telecommunications, gas and electricity and at the local level for water supply.

Compulsory competitive tendering

Competitive tendering is widely used throughout the world to decide how public services shall be delivered. However, as Walsh

(1991, p. 7) comments: 'The British experience of competition is probably, now, the most systematic and comprehensive. Britain is also the only country in which competitive tendering for local authority services is compulsory.' Competitive tendering has been widely used in the 1980s in the National Health Service for catering, domestic and laundry services. Competitive tendering has also been extensively used in the civil service for similar functions. The discussion in this section will concentrate on the experience of local authorities.

The competitive tendering which is a focus of attention here involves services previously provided by in-house workers. British local authorities have been, according to some observers, 'peculiarly dominated by direct public service provision' (Batley, 1991, p. 217). The right-wing 'think tanks' that have emerged around the Conservatives in the past decade or so were quick to push the virtues of competitive tendering, claiming it would lead to savings in public spending and undermine the power of local authority trade unions. A number of pioneering Conservative local authorities aggressively pushed ahead with a tendering programme. Private contractors looking for new opportunities were also instrumental in promoting the spread of tendering.

The essence of competitive tendering is that the in-house workforce is asked to compete against interested private bidders. If it wins the work then the contract price becomes its budget (subject generally to yearly adjustment for inflation), and it operates at arm's length from the local authority for the specified years of the contract. If it loses then the service is contracted to the winning bidder in the private sector and the direct labour force is disbanded (although individual employees may be taken on by the private contractor). This form of competitive tendering has been made compulsory for an expanding range of services and has grown to become a central plank of the Conservatives' privatization programme.

At the national level the Local Government Planning and Land Act 1980 introduced the first requirement to subject services to competitive tender, covering a proportion of construction and maintenance works on buildings and highways. These activities have always in part been undertaken by private contractors but the proportion of work subject to tender was increased so that as of 1989 four-fifths of the total value of work was included. Regulations introduced in 1989, bringing in even more highways work, will increase the proportion further. As a result of competitive tendering the share of work (by value) undertaken by direct labour in construction and maintenance has declined between 1981–82 and 1988–89 from 44 per cent to 40 per cent. To retain such a substantial, if reduced, proportion of work, direct labour organizations have undertaken extensive managerial reforms and have shed several thousand direct employees. Productivity, measured in terms of turnover (at constant prices) per employee, increased by 22 per cent between 1981–82 and 1988–89 (Institute of Public Finance, 1992, p. 2).

The most comprehensive measure to extend competitive tendering came with the Local Government Act 1988. This Act requires competition for a number of 'defined activities' and gave the Secretary of State the power to add other services. The initial defined activities were refuse collection, buildings cleaning, other cleaning, catering, schools and welfare catering, grounds maintenance and vehicle maintenance. The management of sports and leisure facilities was added to the list by Parliamentary Order in November 1989 (Walsh, 1991, p. 10). With some minor exemptions all work performed by the staff of local authorities and other local governmental agencies in these areas was to be the subject of competitive tender.

Drawing on figures covering contracts awarded until November 1992, Table 3.5 indicates that in-house staff (direct service organizations, DSOs) have been successful in winning contracts across all areas of activities. DSOs have won on average 83.9 per cent of contracts by value although the proportion of DSO success drops to 69 per cent in terms of the number of contracts let (Local Authorities Association, 1992, p. 7). If the scent of victory is suggested by these results, the government has been able to counter with the claim that even though competitive tendering has not proved a bonanza for private contractors, it has forced efficiency gains. The financial effects of competition are not easy to assess, but careful and detailed research based on a panel of twenty-four authorities has concluded that on average the estimated annual cost for the relevant services was 5.7 per cent lower than the cost before competition (Walsh, 1991, p. 125).

The Major government has shown itself keen to extend the operation of competitive tendering. A consultation paper, *Competing for Quality in 1991* (Department of the Environment, 1991), outlined its proposals and the Local Government Act 1992 provides the mechanism for extending compulsory tendering to a whole

Table 3.5 Compulsory competitive tendering 1989–92

Activity	DSO success (% of contracts)	DSO success (% value won)	Average value of contract (£ p.a.)	Average length (years)
Building cleaning	54.1	83.3	350,155	3.7
Refuse collection	72.1	75.2	1,251,087	5.2
Other cleaning	71.1	80.6	445,493	4.4
Vehicle maintenance	78.6	88.5	509,609	4.6
Catering (education and welfare)	91.6	97.2	1,995,245	4.1
Other catering	76.1	82.3	178,838	4.2
Ground maintenance	67.3	81.5	299,327	3.8
Sports and leisure management	82.4	84.4	573,776	4.6
Average	69.0	83.9	*	n/a

Source: Adapted from Local Authorities Association (1992, pp. 7–8).
Note: The total value of current contracts reported in the survey is £1898 m p.a. at unadjusted prices.

range of white-collar and some additional blue-collar areas. The consultation paper suggested that compulsory tendering would be extended into four classes of service:

- *'Direct to the public' services*: the management of theatres and arts facilities; library support services; and parking services are to become new defined activities under the Local Government Act 1988;
- *manual services*: cleaning of police buildings and the maintenance of police vehicles; maintenance of fire vehicles; and provision of home-to-school transport will become defined activities under the 1988 Act; as will
- *construction-related services*: architecture; and engineering and property management; and
- *corporate services*: including legal, financial, personnel, computing and other administrative tasks.

The list is not exhaustive; other services can be added later. Further, as noted earlier, in 1993 legislation was passed paving the way for the tendering of housing management.

The extension of tendering looks set to bring into its orbit hundreds of thousands of local authority jobs. In November 1992 the government announced various changes designed to ease the extension of the process. Councils are to be given greater freedom to decide on the relative merits of different tenders and consulted about changes in accounting procedures in the setting up of internal trading accounts. Some local authorities seem keen to jump before they are pushed. Oxfordshire County Council in April 1993 contracted out the administration of its payroll, pension and revenue administration. Several other authorities in the Home Counties and London areas are also experimenting with competitive tendering in areas beyond even those identified in the government's consultation paper and legislation.

Several issues, however, have made the extension of the programme of competitive tendering problematic. Resistance from white-collar staff appears more vocal and better organized than that of the blue-collar employees affected by the first phases of tendering. The complication of local government reorganization running in parallel with the extension of tendering has created difficulties. If a new structure of local authorities is to be established, then the running of contracts by new authorities on terms set by abolished councils seems a recipe for chaos. Moreover, the administrative work associated with organizing a large-scale structural reform makes meeting deadlines for tendering problematic. These factors make the timetable for extending competitive tendering uncertain.

A further threat is posed by the legal confusion over the rules to be applied to competitive tendering. The unresolved issue is to what extent the 1981 Transfer of Undertakings Protection of Employment (TUPE) regulations apply. These regulations were created by the British government in response to a directive from the European Community. Where TUPE applies, a successful bidder must take over the workforce on existing terms and conditions. Such a provision plainly limits the scope for 'efficiency savings' and is seen as likely to deter private-sector competition for local authority work. Despite an effort by the government in September 1993 to resolve the issue, a great deal of uncertainty remains. Many local authorities, both Conservative and Labour, have adopted a procedure of stating that TUPE rules apply to their tendered contracts. However, in November 1993, European Union officials made statements suggesting that they never intended the rule to apply to public procurement contracts. At the time of writing the issue is unresolved and a cloud of uncertainty hangs over competitive tendering.

The spread of competitive tendering and other quasi-market forces across the range of local authority services is seen by many observers as threatening the strategic capacity of local government. Stewart (1989, p. 17a) comments:

> The danger is that the local authority will become a series of separate units each with its own defined task, and that there will be no capacity to look beyond the units or to consider the interrelationship between them. Local government will be lost between the fragments.

Efficiency gains in particular aspects of service delivery may be won at the expense of a capacity for coordinated and effective governmental action at the local level.

The spread of privatization

In the discussion so far, some of the main privatization initiatives have been examined and some further developments noted. In this section the analysis is extended to show that virtually every area of urban service provision has felt the pressure of privatization. Most service areas have experienced a mixture of the various elements of privatization: asset sales, commercialization, competitive tendering and the introduction of various quasi-market mechanisms.

Transport is a prime target for privatization. Mention has already been made of proposals in relation to British Rail and the regional airports. Already the national airline (British Airways), airports, ferries, road freight and bus companies have been sold. Plans to build more toll roads have been widely promoted by the government. A particular impact on urban areas was made by the deregulation of bus services. The Transport Act 1980 made it easier for new private-sector operators to gain licences to provide bus services. The Transport Act 1985 took further measures to break the monopoly position of public-sector operators. The local passenger transport executives and district councils that ran bus undertakings had to form their operations into companies. The system of licensing was abolished and replaced by a streamlined registration scheme. Subsidies provided by local authorities were allowed only to support unprofitable but socially desirable services and only after bids to operate the route had been subject to competitive tender. In most towns and cities the established former local authority providers remain as substantial players in the market but they operate in a competitive environment. In particular, the number of minibus services has increased. However, the quality of service at off-peak times and to outlying areas has in many cases declined.

Education has also seen an extensive process of privatization. First the number of children attending private, fee-paying schools increased during the 1980s, although the recession of the early 1990s caused a drop in demand. The Conservatives have introduced a number of tax breaks and other mechanisms to support the sending of children to private schools. The public sector has seen the introduction of market-like mechanism.

The Education Reform Act 1988 introduced open enrolment to schools in accordance with parental preference. All larger schools were to be freed from detailed control by local authorities, through the establishment of devolved budgets and local management via governing bodies. Parents were also to have the right to vote for their local school to opt out of the local authority sector and become a free-standing grant-maintained school, funded directly by central government. Competition was also to be provided by a network of city technology colleges (CTCs) based in various localities, which were to be funded jointly by central government and business interests. Later, sixth-form and further education colleges were removed from local authority control. The Education Act 1993 confirms this policy direction and it extends the process of competition, ensuring that failing schools can be phased out and downplaying further the role of local authorities. Paradoxically, in this process of encouraging school-based management and parental choice, it is central government that gains a range of extensive powers of intervention and direction.

The National Health Service, too, has seen some government encouragement to the growth of private health care through tax incentives and other mechanisms. At the same time the state-funded sector has been subject to market disciplines. On the demand side of the market for hospital care there are two types of purchaser: district health authorities (DHAs) and some general practitioners (GPs). They will 'purchase' health care on the part of their population and patients. On the provision side there are local managed hospitals with DHAs, self-governing opted-out hospital trusts and private-sector providers. Elements of quasi-market mechanisms and commercialization have also been introduced in primary health care.

The reach of privatization programmes and principles is extending throughout the public sector. Social security administration and benefit provision is to be market-tested with competitive tendering to undertake a proportion of the work. Social services provision for the elderly has an extensive role for private nursery and residential homes. Community care mechanisms are extending the net of competitive tender and contracts to voluntary organizations providing support to various disadvantaged and disabled groups in the community. Prisons and related services have seen private provision and tendering for escorting duties to and from courts. Public–private partnerships have blossomed in urban development, training and local economic initiatives. Batley comments:

> The British system which was peculiarly dominated by direct public service provision is being pushed into a wider web of relationships with other providers as is the case in most European countries. However, a new peculiarity has developed which is the emphasis on competition between providers and the imposition of competitive practices by central government.
>
> (Batley, 1991, p. 217)

Conclusions

The privatization programmes of the conservatives have a range of different aims and purposes. For Mrs Thatcher the overarching theme was, perhaps, captured by the slogan 'Market processes good, public intervention bad'. Various government ministers tried in the 1980s to provide a broader rationale for privatization. The pamphlet published by Nicholas Ridley (1988) when he was Secretary of State for the Environment is particularly relevant to the urban focus of this paper since it makes the case for the privatization strategy applied to local government. In the pamphlet Ridley lays out a vision of the enabling authority which no longer sees itself as the universal provider but tries to ensure that needs are met by working through other agencies and making greater use of private and voluntary resources.

In the 1990s and under the Major government, much of this rationale for privatization remains in place. It has been embellished by a management concern to ensure that the benefits of privatization are experienced by individual citizens. In July 1991 the Citizen's Charter initiative was launched, aimed at improving the performance of public services: to raise quality, increase choice, secure better value and extend accountability. Asset sales, competition and market-testing continue to be seen as central to improving public provision – a view confirmed in a pamphlet published in 1993 by government minister William Waldegrave (1993).

The British case, as stated at the beginning of the chapter, is of a politically driven privatization programme. Yet the development of privatization reflects a complex mixture of strategic planning and *ad hoc* reaction to events. The Conservatives have shown a consistent desire to challenge the post-war consensus about the role of the state and public provision but their more specific goals and instruments have varied and their lines of attack have reflected a pragmatism characteristic of much political decision-making.

A further, slightly paradoxical, lesson is that privatization in its various forms has involved a very active form of government. This point is reflected not only in the range and detailed nature of the legislation that has been passed but also by the active commitment to monitoring, overseeing and implementing their programmes shown by the Conservative governments since 1979. The Conservatives have given central government considerable new powers to control funding and guide policy development in localities. The implementation of the privatization programme has required the Conservatives to show a considerable display of tenacity and determination. There have been failures and problems, but, given the complexity of what has been attempted and the range of obstacles that had to be overcome, the Conservatives have achieved many of their objectives.

The greatest doubts that have been raised about the privatization programme concern its impact on the system of urban government. Accountability appears to be blurred in much of the reform programme. Privatization appears to create a certain ambiguity. Old-style political accountability through elected representatives has given way in many cases to institutions where the key levers of control rest with professionals, managers, regulators and appointed governors in the context of greater central control over funding and objectives. This process of centralization, combined with the creation of a range of unaccountable 'partners', has led to the rise of a substantial 'accountability gap' (Stewart, 1993).

A final issue is *capacity* to govern. Central government, in taking new powers to itself, runs the risk of overload. Elected local government has lost control of various functions and may lack the resources and coordinating capacity to bring together the dispersed public and private institutions and agencies of the new local governance. Have the privatization reforms created the conditions for non-government in urban areas?

4

THE PRIVATIZATION OF URBAN SERVICES IN GERMANY

Michael Reidenbach

The (re-)unification of the two German states in 1990 has had a profound effect on the political and economic situation in Germany. The conversion of the former East German socialist economy to a market-oriented economy demands the transfer of billions of Deutschmarks annually over a long time period. This transfer is putting such strain on the financial abilities of the western German public sector that privatization on all government levels is seen – at least by the federal government – as one remedy by which to stabilize or reduce the public deficit. Until now privatization has mainly comprised the selling of industrial and financial assets belonging to the federal government and the *Land* governments (Esser, 1993), but debate is now turning, with strong political momentum, to the privatization of urban services.

For analytical and practical reasons it is necessary to distinguish between the situation in western and in eastern German (the former GDR). Whereas the privatization discussion has been going on for a very long time in western Germany, the experience in eastern Germany is naturally very short. The situation in eastern Germany is still somewhat uncertain, but most of the new organizational structures have now emerged. Some solutions for privatization of urban services which have hitherto been rejected in western Germany are being tested in eastern Germany.

The present situation of urban services in Germany must be seen in the context of historical developments since the last century. The first provision of services, in a modern sense, was made at the beginning of the last century. While the state and local administration themselves were slowly becoming more and more service oriented, the construction and operation of new services were often given over to private companies. This was mainly accomplished by granting long-term concessions to private companies (also known as the French system!). The provision of gas for domestic and industrial purposes is a good example in this respect.

In the later decades of the last century, urban administrations gained a growing influence owing to much better management and the economic and financial importance of the larger cities. On the basis of the principle of comprehensive responsibility (*Allzuständigkeit*), administrations had to intervene more and more in the problems of the cities. In regard to the services run by private companies, very critical attitudes were voiced. The main arguments against these companies were ruthless exploitation of a monopolistic situation, excessive profits, reluctance to innovate along with a tendency to hinder technological progress, especially the introduction of electricity. Whether these arguments were valid or not seems to depend in large part on the situation. In the end the contracts for most private companies were not extended. The end of the concessions gave cities a welcome opportunity to take over the companies and to use the company profits for the financing of their own budgets. On the eve of World War I most urban services, with the exception of the public telephone system, were in the hands of the local public sector (joint company stake in parentheses): water 93 per cent; gas 78 per cent (3 per cent); electricity 40 per cent (5 per cent); tramways 50 per cent.

These activities of the cities were mainly opposed by liberal groups and by the newly created associations of industries and trades (*Industrie- und Handelskammern*). While the liberals would concede state involvement in economic activity only in exceptional circumstances (e.g. natural monopolies), the associations were more pragmatic since they were mostly interested in gaining contracts for their members.

Before and evenmore so after World War I, 'municipal socialism' (*Munizipalsozialismus*) was propagated by communist groups and many social democrats in respect of those parts of the economy passed over by central government. However, these attempts mostly failed, one reason being that the parties fostering socialism had different ideas as to whom the enterprises should serve: the customers, the employees or the general interest of the locality.

As a consequence there was no widespread further extension of municipal influence. On the contrary, in some fields, such as electricity production, the share of the local authorities fell (mainly for technical reasons).

In the wake of the world economic crisis and especially during the Third Reich the economic activities of local authorities were curtailed massively. Because they were seen as unfair competition to small and medium-sized industry, to use a modern term, their activities were restricted to those fields which were at that time not in competition with private commerce and industry. The rules of the game were set out in a new Local Authorities Ordinance (*Gemeindeordnung*) which described the legal framework in which local authorities could act.

After World War II the regulation of this ordinance was taken over by the *Länder* of the new republic which were now responsible, and hardly altered in the following decades. Only in the late 1970s and the 1980s did changes in the law occur. These changes consisted mainly in giving local authorities the option of 'spinning off' some of their activities from the budget and converting them into quasi-companies (see below).

The owners and operators of western German urban services

Germany is a federal republic in which the federal and state constitutions and a number of government acts grant specific responsibilities to the local level as the third tier of government. Among the tasks local authorities have to discharge is the provision of services for the public and for industry and commerce. It is therefore not surprising that the local authorities have organizational authority for most urban services. Exceptions to the rule are telecommunications and the national road system (motorways, etc.). Telekom, a subsidiary of the German Federal Post Office (DBP), directs telecommunications. The responsibility for the national road system lies in the hands of both the federal government and the state governments except for built-up areas within cities of more than 80,000 inhabitants, where the city itself is responsible. Table 4.1 gives the approximate share of the public sector and the local authorities in the field of urban services in West Germany in 1989.

Table 4.1 Estimation of the share of the western German public sector and the local authorities in the field of the urban services

Type of urban services	Measurement unit	Share of public sector	Share of local authorities only*
Road system	Road length	Nearly 100%	100% of local streets
Sewers	Connections	Nearly 100%	Nearly 100%
Waste water treatment plants	Cubic metres	95%	95%
Waste disposal			
Collection of waste of household waste	Tons	50%	50%
Waste disposal	Tons	95%	95%
Electricity generation	Kilowatt-hours	14% public, 85% mixed	11%
Electricity supply	Kilowatt-hours	n/a	29%
Gas supply			
regional distribution	Joules	12% public, 15% mixed	n/a
local distribution	Joules	70% public, 26% mixed	67%
Water supply	Cubic metres	85% public, 13% mixed	85%
District heating	Joule	n/a	50%
Mass transit	Persons	92%	64%
Telecommunications			
standard telephone	Connections	100%	0%
cellular digital telephones	Connections	40%	0%

*Cities, towns, villages, districts and their municipal corporation and joint authorities

About 8,500 cities, towns and villages and 237 administrative districts exist in western Germany. The average local authority is rather small and quite often lacks the professional skill necessary to plan and supervise public works. In the large and medium-sized towns the situation is different as their administrations are large enough to employ qualified professionals. Furthermore, in these cities the main operator is usually a municipal multi-purpose enterprise, the *Stadtwerke* (literally, city works). In the ideal case the *Stadtwerke* are the operator of electricity and gas supplies, district heating, water supplies and public transport (for legal and taxation reasons waste disposal is not yet included but these restrictions may soon change). The *Stadtwerke* are not covered by the city budget. They use commercial accounting systems and draw up balance sheets and profit and loss statements. They are run either in the special form of *Eigenbetrieb* or as a normal joint stock company of which all the shares belong to the city (*Eigengesellschaft*). In the case of the *Eigenbetriebe* a close link exists between the city administration and the managers of the company, whereas the *Eigengesellschaft* is more independent of city administration. For the supply of energy and water the company forms mentioned are obligatory if the size of the municipality exceeds 10,000 inhabitants.

Compared to the large public and private corporations which operate services in France and the UK (such as EdF, CGE, Lyonnaise des eaux-Dumez or British Gas), the typical western German municipal enterprise is rather small. Its activities are normally restricted to the city area but extend sometimes to the suburban areas too. However, the *Stadtwerke* of the larger West German cities have considerable financial power (with the backing of the cities) and are very often run by highly trained professionals who are often well-known experts in their respective fields. The largest such company, the Stadtwerke München, has a turnover of DM 3 billion and 10,000 employees.

The multi-purpose concept (*Querverbund*) gives management the possibility of coordinating different functions. According to a recent survey by the Stadtwerke Bochum, the – theoretical – separation of the management for different services would halve the profits made. The Stadtwerke Düsseldorf calculates that it can save nearly a quarter of the investment costs by laying gas and water pipes together. Possible diseconomies due to small scale are thus compensated by economics of scope, at least in part. Since the enterprises are largely independent of the pay structure of the civil service, they can attract better-qualified personnel. Proximity to the city administration gives management a chance to cooperate with other city planning activities, but also makes it dependent on political decisions by the city council.

Not all enterprises bearing the name *Stadtwerke* are wholly owned by the city. Sometimes the local saving banks own shares, in other cases large energy-generating companies provide assets (power supply systems) in return for a share in the *Stadtwerke* (e.g. in Leverkusen and Düsseldorf).

Where solutions at a local level are not economic (e.g. for large power plants) or where special districts were not set up, public enterprises on a regional or national level have been formed, very often with municipal shareholders (such as Rheinisch-Westfälische Elektrizitatswerke RWE AG or Vereinigte Elektrizitätswerke VEW AG). These enterprises once supplied only electricity or gas but today offer a wide range of products.

To form more efficient administrative units, western German local authorities quite often set up special single-purpose districts (*Zweckverbände* or *Wasserverbände*) by delegating the organizational authority from the town or village to such a district. Sometimes a special district or association is created by state act. About 450 special districts are responsible for waste water in their region; another 60 deal with solid waste. These districts cannot raise taxes, but receive their revenue from payments by the local authorities in relation to the benefits rendered. The large water management associations of the Ruhr area, which were founded before World War I, are widely known. Another example is the associations which serve the Stuttgart area with drinking water from the Bondensee (Lake Constance).

The privatization debate

The term 'privatization' is used to describe a vast array of activities in Germany:

- In its original meaning, 'privatization' describes the transfer to the private sector of activities previously carried out by the public sector without strings attached except for the payment of the value of the assets. Industry privatization is a case in point.

- Withdrawal or reduction of the activities of the public sector (such as the surveying or compulsory insurance of houses) in areas where private companies offer similar services. Here it is up to the private companies to fill the void left by the retreat of the public sector.
- The creation of mixed companies, where the state or local authorities hold a majority of the shares, quite often 51 per cent, and one or more private companies the remainder, is also called privatization. The hybrid structure still allows public authorities the final decision but private partners can provide capital and know-how. This variant is called the cooperation model.
- A lesser form of privatization is contracting out a service to a private entrepreneur. This form of privatization occurred quite often in the past for the cleaning of premises, the cultivation of green spaces, etc., and is still practised with sewer maintenance. These contracts are mostly concluded on a medium-term basis and do not involve the transfer of any assets or other rights.
- Finally, leasing or similar financial instruments are quite often regarded as privatization because some of the activities which a local authority performs are transferred to the public sector.

From these examples it is clear that the term 'privatization' is used to describe any transfer of activities from the public to the private sector in connection with the planning, plant construction, operation and financing of urban services.

In addition to these cases, the term 'privatization' is also used when an institution is 'spun off' the budget and transferred to a public enterprise in the form of a private company. This type of formal or organizational privatization, which leaves all the assets and property rights within the public sector, is very common at the moment. Though in most discussions these activities are left out, it is worth having a look at the motives for such a process since they tell us something about the problems of the public sector.

As was mentioned earlier, the Local Authorities Ordinance of the *Länder*, and other acts and ordinances, set the framework within which the local authorities can act. Some activities cannot be privatized at all. This is the case with the local road system. For other tasks a delegation to a third person is possible as long as the overall responsibility in the legal sense rests with the local authority. An example here is the collection of household waste. Finally, for those tasks which local authorities perform voluntarily within their mandate, they may choose whether to perform the tasks themselves or use a third party, which may be subsidized.

Furthermore, a distinction must be made between the choice of setting up a new activity and of privatizing an existing one. As a rule the privatization of existing facilities poses numerous tax and labour law problems. Since the staff concerned can be dismissed only under special circumstances the local authority must find ways of finding alternative employment for personnel who are not taken over by the privatized company.

Most of the arguments for the privatization of the urban services have not changed since the turn of the century:

- The assumption is made – explicitly or implicitly – that the production of services is done more efficiently and/or cheaply by the private sector than by the public sector.
- Because transfer to the private sector would save costs, a significant improvement in the budget deficit would follow.
- Labour productivity would rise because the public sector has few incentives to improve its performance; employees would be forced to work harder.
- Economies of scale could be reaped because machines and other tools could be better employed.
- Subsidies by local authorities could be concentrated on these really in need, while the other users should pay the real (market) price.

These arguments are in part explanations of why privatization ought to be better for the users of services. However, the empirical evidence for this hypothesis is not totally conclusive. It is possible to cite many cases for or against privatization, but it should be noted that in few cases cited in respect of Germany has a direct comparison been made between public and private performance, for example in a tender, and that there have been hardly any studies on the long-term effects of privatization except for a few historical studies from the last century.

An important question in every privatization debate is the treatment of wage differences between the public sector and activity that is privatized. In many of the cases mentioned above, such as the cleaning of windows or premises, such wage differences exist in Germany. In most cases the private employer pays minimum wages and uses every possibility for part-time work, which may be seen as a modern form of exploitation. The public sector cannot match its wages in the face of such business behaviour. But in most fields in the technical infrastructure skilled workers and engineers are employed. Here wage differences are more usually in the other direction, namely that the private sector pays better but sometimes also demands more.

One argument for privatization is that economies of scale can be made in the operation of urban services. This argument inclines one to make a distinction between small villages and towns on the one hand and large cities on the other. The good standing of the *Stadtwerke* comes in large part from the big cities where the personnel are highly professional.

Economic arguments against privatization revolve largely around the monopoly situation of the networks involved. Even if a natural monopoly is privatized there remains the problem of control since the risk of monopoly exploitation always exists. As a consequence, controlling institutions must be set up, the costs of which have to be subtracted from privatization gains. A similar problem is the appearance of large enterprises, either directly or via their subsidiaries on the service market. Since we know that large companies sometimes try to bully small local authorities, restricting possible local action if it is contrary to the aims of the company, some safeguards must be installed that will control such companies (the fast-growing market power of German waste management firms is a problem in this respect).

Privatization in the German water industry: the 'operator scheme'

The German water industry provides an instructive instance of the difficulties encountered on the way to privatization. The western German municipalities normally construct and operate public sewerage systems. This case study describes and evaluates a scheme to plan, construct, finance and operate sewerage works by private firms. The scheme was developed in the state of Niedersachsen (Lower Saxony), where it had already been tried out in several municipalities.

The general waste water management plan drawn up by the state authorities of Niedersachsen in 1984 estimated that about DM 5 billion was needed to finance necessary construction until 1998. Even with substantial support from the state government, local authorities would have difficulties in financing such capital expenditure since many municipalities have reached the limits of borrowing. The question was how to resolve the tension between urgent action for greater environmental protection and lack of funds in the public budgets. A possible answer was the privatization of government activities. The then state government in Niedersachsen, a coalition of Christian Democrats (CDU) and Liberals (FDP), was strongly in favour of such privatization, because it assumed that private firms are faster and more efficient than public administrations. The scheme of operation described below was seen as a chance to show that privatization can work even for a genuinely public task such as the collection and treatment of waste water. The Ministry of Economic Affairs engaged considerable manpower to prepare the legal contracts and help the first municipalities which intended to use the scheme, and to overcome any difficulties encountered. In the initial phase of the development of the scheme the Ministry paid up to 50 per cent of the costs for the necessary technical and economic examination of the projects.

According to the relevant government acts, municipalities are responsible for the collection and treatment of any waste water originating on their territory. In Niedersachsen the municipalities can transfer these functions to a third party (i.e. a private firm), but they cannot relinquish their ultimate responsibility.

The state has a twofold responsibility. First, it has to supervise the water quality of rivers and lakes. It sets and controls levels of permitted pollution for every form of discharge. Second, it has to provide the local authorities with enough funds to ensure the desired functions. Though the 'polluter-pays' principle is accepted policy for sewerage treatment, the ensuing costs to the individual citizens are quite often considered to be too expensive. This is especially true for politically important rural areas where specific costs are much higher than in densely populated areas. Grants by the state, normally of 30 per cent of construction costs for new plant – in extreme cases up to 80 per cent – diminish the individual burden.

Within this scheme, sewage treatment plant and sometimes sewers too are planned, financed, built and run by a private firm for a defined period. At the end of that period the plant reverts to the municipality. The scheme is named an 'operator scheme' (*Betreibermodell*). The expression, though rather unfortunate since it puts too little emphasis on the vital planning stage, will be employed below.

Privatization of waste water collection in the form of delegated management has been practised in other countries too. It can take the form of concession contracts, farm leases or management contracts. The innovative approach in Niedersachsen is a blend of several elements from these forms. Its value should be judged in relation to the German situation and the painstaking elaboration of the legal, financial and economic framework.

Traditionally, German waste water treatment is run by a department of municipal administration. Receipts and expenditure are part of the municipal budget. All major decisions are taken by the municipal council. The planning of construction is carried out partly by the administration but mostly by external engineering firms. All construction and equipment have to be tendered following strict rules. Capital expenditure is normally financed by contributions from residents, subsidies from the state and the federal government and loans from banks. The total amount of borrowing, which can include other items such as roads or school buildings, is subject to the consent of the state at the time of approval of the annual budget. Costs for operation and maintenance plus depreceiation and interest on capital employed are in principle recovered through consumer charges, though there is considerable room for varying the amount charged (e.g. by changing the interest rate or the valuation method).

This traditional procedure has been criticized for a variety of reasons:

- During the preparation, planning and actual building of the plant the planners seem to apply too little engineering experience. Since external engineers are paid their fees according to the volume of construction, little incentive exists to implement cost-saving solutions.
- State funds which are essential for the financing of the projects are given in instalments only. This forces the municipal administration to stretch the project over a longer time period than is technically necessary.
- The usual method of inviting tenders first for construction, then the machinery and finally the electrical engineering can prejudice optimal design of the whole project.

The 'operator scheme' was developed to overcome some of the weakness of this traditional procedure. Its main features are:

- The private operator not only builds the sewerage works, but also operates it over an extended period (twenty to thirty years) on his own responsibility.
- The private operator is required to finance investment sums which are not covered by state subsidies or contributions in such a way that the municipality incurs no further debts. The municipality pays a fixed price (e.g. per population equivalent (PE)), which has to cover all the expenses of the firm. The price can be revised only if a rise in the consumer price index exceeds a certain level or if substantial changes in the quantity or composition of the sewage occur or if the state demands improved treatment of sewage.
- Cost analysis has to show that private construction and operation is cheaper than the traditional system.
- The municipality still has the ultimate responsibility for sewage collection and treatment. It must supervise the private operator in order to intervene if norms are not respected. It continues to levy consumer charges. No legal ties exist between the individual consumer and the operating firm.
- The municipality has to make sure that any insolvency on the part of the private operator gives it the immediate right to run the plant on its own. It can attain this goal by granting a leasehold on the plant site with a fall-back clause. In that case, or when the contract reverts, the compensation for the remaining value of the plant is determined on a decreasing scale.

Evaluation of the 'operator scheme' must concentrate primarily on measuring financial benefits and costs. Cost savings in comparison to the original calculations have been considerable for some projects, ranging from 13.6 to 30 per cent of the original calculation sum. However, for five other projects the financial advantage has not been large enough for the tender to be granted. Perhaps the original plans drawn up by the municipalities left no room for substantial cost reductions.

What is the explanation for such cost saving? An analysis of construction planned shows that firms that work with the 'operator scheme' can be much more innovative and flexible than in the rather strict framework of conventional planning concepts. As an example, in municipality A, a simple treatment plant with low-cost earth basins was installed instead of an expensive 'normal' treatment plant. To take another case, in municipality E, two basins, each of 3,000 m^3, were bought on the 'spot market'. Thus cheaper and more efficient equipment and concepts were chosen. Traditional tendering is sometimes a piecemeal process. First the construction parts are tendered, then the mechanical equipment. This fact supports the thesis that the traditional separation of the engineering part and the construction part may lead to suboptimal solutions. Since the costs of capital (depreciation and interest) constitute the major part of consumer charges, low capital expenditure will be reflected in lower charges. It is interesting to note that the projects concentrate on the construction of treatment plant, omitting the construction of new sewers (except in one case).

Capital costs are further influenced by the costs of loans and the size of any grant given by the state government. Local authorities can normally obtain loans from the banking system at very favourable conditions since these loans bear no risk of default and are not included in the calculation for special deposits at the Deutsche Bundesbank. A private firm can never match these conditions. However, if the municipality agrees to give a collateral to the bank, the private firm may be granted loan conditions similar to those obtainable by the municipality.

With state grants of 30 per cent and more of construction volume, the conditions under which grants are distributed by state governments have a great influence on the possible organizational solutions. In denying such subsidies to private firms, as was the rule in some German states, a bias towards public ownership is introduced. Private firms cannot compensate a subsidy of such a dimension from their cost savings.

Concerning the costs of operation and maintenance (excluding capital cost), it is difficult to gain a clear picture of to what extent, if any, private firms are more effective than the municipality:

- Comprehensive planning gives a private firm the possibility of optimizing life-cycle costs and decreasing costs by closing down unnecessary plant.
- Wage advantages for a private firm may be more doubtful since quite often it has to employ the former staff of the municipality. Furthermore, experienced plant operators are hard to hire, so wage advantages obtained by employing unskilled workers – a factor that very often explains the financial advantages of other privatization projects – are hardly likely.

- Private firms may enjoy economies of scale at management level if they operate many sewerage systems. From the data available it does not seem that the successful firms in the seven municipalities under consideration are large enough to enjoy such benefits.

A special problem arises with the VAT tax code. Sewerage is not a taxable item as long as it is run by the municipality. A private firm has to levy VAT (currently 15 per cent), but it can get a tax credit on all purchases made in the course of business. Therefore it receives a tax credit on construction costs, which reduces its need to take up a loan. On the other hand, this advantage is gradually reduced because all services billed to the municipality must include VAT whereas such services performed by the municipality are tax free. Therefore, to whose advantage the system works depends on a number of factors.

The risk of failures and damage to the plant construction and equipment, which is normally covered for between six months and two years by a warranty on the part of the construction firms, is extended over the lifetime of the contract. For old sewers the operating risk is difficult to evaluate, since thorough inspection of sewers is difficult and costly. It is no surprise that the municipality of Wedemark still has to maintain its network of old sewers.

From an environmental standpoint, any speeding up of the construction or replacement of inefficient plant must be seen as a valuable benefit. Private firms do seem to enjoy some advantage in that respect. Whether this is true in the 'operator scheme' can be questioned. First, the whole procedure looks quite complicated. This may be due to initial difficulties. Second, the projects depend on state subsidies. Any speeding up can be attained only if the private firm pre-finances grant instalments.

The overall success of the scheme is quite modest when we consider only the quantitative effects. So far municipalities have made use of the scheme in relatively few of the waste water projects implemented. The initial impetus of the scheme has slowed down considerably. On the other hand, the scheme has certainly stimulated debate over privatization in the sewerage sector. It has attracted considerable approval and opposition. This is especially manifest in several series of articles in professional journals in which many detailed questions are examined. Apart from the Liberals, the main proponent of the scheme is the building industry, which hopes for faster orders when private enterprise takes over. Several banks have taken up the idea and are trying to promote the scheme even for the construction and operating of waste incineration plant.

Opposition to the scheme comes not only from the traditional foes of privatization – the trade unions and sometimes the Social Democrats – but also from the state administration in other German states. The city of Schorndorf (Baden-Württemberg), for example, tried to implement the scheme for the rehabilitation of its treatment plant (estimated costs DM 22 million). But the proposal was turned down by the state government because it was not prepared to alter the grant regulations.

Several general conclusions can be drawn from this case-study:

- Discussion and critical analysis of the 'operator scheme' presented has drawn attention to the weakness of the traditional system of constructing and operating sewerage works. Even if privatization is in the end not carried out, some changes should be made to the traditional way of constructing and operating sewerage plant.
- Since the public demands strong safeguards when it comes to the collection and treatment of sewerage, complete privatization of sewerage is quite difficult at present. This constitutes a marked difference as compared with the privatization of industries and the like that has been carried through in Germany during recent years.
- On several levels other restrictions to privatization are visible. The grant system as well as the tax code can play a major role in the decision as to whether and how to privatize. Decisions based on such restrictions do not reflect true cost savings.
- The debate on privatization should include all stages of the construction and operating process. Only comprehensive planning seems to guarantee minimal costs in the long run.

Further privatization activities in western German urban services

While theoretical discussion of the merits and shortcomings of privatization has reached no final conclusion, developments have been fairly rapid, on the side of the public authorities as well as on that of the supplier of private services.

The most important privatization of urban services has been taking place in the field of telecommunications, which is very important for urban areas but not managed by local authorities. Telekom will be privatized over the coming years in view of the liberalization of the telecommunication systems in the European Union beginning in 1998. For the fast-growing market of cellular telephones two systems have been introduced in order to foster competition and to start privatization. The first system, called D1, is run by Telekom. The second, D2, was tendered to a consortium of companies led by Mannesmann Mobilfunk GmbH (51 per cent of the shares), a subsidiary of Mannesmann AG. Further members of the consortium are a German bank (10 per cent), the central associations of German craftsmen and electricians (5.5 per cent), Pacific Telesis (21 per cent), Cable and Wireless (5 per cent) and Lyonnaise des eaux (5.5 per cent). The planned investment for the D2 system amounts to DM 5.7 billion. The D2 system has gained a market share of 60 per cent at present. The follow-up system, E1, will also be run by a private consortium.

Another important field for privatization is waste management. In 1973 the collection and disposal of solid waste from household became mandatory for all cities and administrative districts in West Germany. While the cities already had their organizations, most districts were not very familiar with waste management. Many preferred to delegate management to a private firm. Today collection is almost equally divided between local authorities and private companies which work in the name of the local authorities. The latter companies are active mainly in rural areas. Local authorities operate the disposal of the solid waste on sanitary landfills mainly by themselves. Because of the legal problems involved, and decreasing willingness by the populace to accept landfills, only local authorities can in practice open new landfills or expand existing ones. Sites for new landfills are very scarce. By increasing the amount of solid waste that is recycled, the capacities of landfills can be stretched considerably. Private companies in some cases offer to install and operate the necessary equipment for recycling. Where no landfills are available, more costly disposal processes are employed, such as burning or composting. Incineration plants and to a lesser degree composting plants generate considerable heat when domestic refuse is disposed of. Municipal enterprises – sometimes also as operators for special districts – have taken up the opportunity to construct and operate such plant to generate electricity and sometimes district heating too. Another example of the strong connections between city administration and the *Stadtwerke* at a local level should be mentioned in this context. Like sludge from treatment plants, landfills emit large quantities of methane gas. Close cooperation between municipal institutions means that more and more cities are collecting this gas and generating electricity from it. It is either used on the spot (i.e. for the aeration of waste water) or supplied to the public power grid. However, the waste management business is becoming so complex in comparison to the situation twenty years ago that cooperation with the private sector is almost inevitable. Private firms, especially the larger ones, are better able to sell recycling products. This trend towards larger private companies is further enhanced by the introduction of the dual system (*Das Duale System*, also known as *Der grüne Punkt*), which tries to recycle wrapping material, bottles, etc. and is paid for by the producers of the goods (and probably shifted on to consumers), thereby taking away some of the business of local authorities in the collection and disposal of waste.

Apart from waste management a recent survey among towns and villages in the state of Nordrhein-Westfalen indicates quite clearly that most of the privatization carried out in recent years falls under the category of 'contracting out' (Steinheuer, 1991). Typically the municipalities contract out the cleaning of premises and windows, washing of hospital laundry, inspection and maintenance of sewers or maintenance of parks and cemeteries. It is also worth mentioning that in the important field of public investment the use of private firms is the rule, and in some cities only minor maintenance work is carried out by municipal staff.

The Deutscher Städtetag (Association of German Cities), which has always been very cautious on privatization, concedes in its guidelines for privatization (*Leitlinien der Privatisierung*, 1993) that some tasks performed by cities may well be privatized. But it also states quite clearly that economic reasons should not be the only motive for privatization, and it fears the loss of control over such activities. The retention of this controlling competence is also an essential prerequisite to privatization for the Association of Social Democratic Local Politicians (Sozialdemokratische Gemeinschaft für Kommunalpolitik in der Bundesrepublik Deutschland eV), a body which, owing to its close links with the trade unions, has until now not been very favourable to the idea of privatization. But now total opposition to privatization has been replaced by a willingness to examine the individual situation. Discussion on the effectiveness of local government which is going on at the moment in Germany has aroused further interest in the issue of privatization. Keywords in this discussion are 'lean administration', 'the entrepreneurial city' or 'decentralized responsibility for resources'. One solution implied by these concepts is to break down the administration into flexible separate entities. In the long run these entities will be able to buy the resources needed not only from other departments or offices but also from the private market if they are cheaper.

In contrast to this caution in regard to privatization, the reigning liberal–conservative coalition is far more outspoken. An interministerial working group was set up which gave detailed recommendations on possible privatization in the public sector (*Bericht der Arbeitsgruppe der Bundesregierung*, 1991). The federal government has even tried to introduce a new ruling into its finance bill which would allow it to set up a new public enterprise or activity only when a financial advantage over private firms could be proved.

The private enterprises first entered the market by constructing and sometimes co-financing new installations in cooperation with local authorities. An example of this kind of cooperation is the construction of a waste-to-energy plant where the local authorities burn their household refuse and the private enterprise feeds the energy into its grids. Those firms which already had close ties with the authorities (for example, those partly owned by the local authorities) were at an advantage here. As the market for environmental protection installation grew, electricity companies, but also firms specialized in plant engineering, expanded considerably.

- RWE AG, by far the biggest German generator of power, has established a subsidiary which deals mainly with the problem of waste disposal (RWE Entsorgung AG). It has a turnover of DM 1.4 billion and is already running a large incinerator plant in Essen-Karnap. Furthermore, RWE has bought shares in seventy private waste disposal companies, among them 49 per cent of Trienekens, the second largest private company specializing in the collection of household and industrial waste with a turnover of DM 350 million and 1,000 employees.
- VEW AG, the second largest electricity company, changed its company statue in 1988 to work in this field too and has

acquired the majority of Edelhoff AG, one of the large middle-sized companies working in waste disposal. In 1992, together with the city of Dortmund, it set up Entsorgung Dortmund GmbH, which is responsible for waste disposal in the city (the city holds 51 per cent of the capital and a further 12 per cent via its *Stadtwerke*).

- Veba AG, another conglomerate with important interests in the electricity sector, is also active in the waste disposal business. Its subsidiary, Veba Kraftwerke Ruhr AG, has, together with Générale des Eaux, founded OEWA Wasser and Abwasser GmbH. OEWA plans to take over the water provision and the waste water disposal in eight towns with about 300,000 inhabitants.

On the one hand, this development is the consequence of a diversification policy on the part of power generation firms which possess a very good cash flow owing to depreciation on their power plant. On the other hand, it is an attempt to transfer some of the company know-how in the construction and operation of power plant into comparable engineering fields.

As a consequence, private firms are starting to look for privatization of already existing municipal activities, mostly in the form of cooperation models. In a typical case, like the collection of water and waste water in the city of Schwerte (50,000 inhabitants), the city management sets up a new company (*Besitzgesellschaft*) which owns the assets of the plant, etc. and in which the city holds the majority of shares. The private firm creates a subsidiary, which holds the rest of the shares, to operate this plant (*Betriebsgesellschaft*).

In these privatization initiatives the banking business is becoming more and more active, which is a sure sign of its future potential. The Deutsche Bank, which is by far the largest German bank, has founded DB-Kommunal, for instance, to finance such partnerships between industry and the local authorities. Its main operational field is at the moment in eastern Germany.

Developments in eastern Germany

With 7,800 local authorities, including 189 districts (*Landkreise*), eastern Germany has nearly the same number of local authorities as western Germany but only a quarter of its population. But in all the new *Länder* the number of districts was to be reduced drastically in 1993–94. Small villages have to join administrative units (Ämter) which will perform most of the daily administration. The new local government Act (*Kommunalverfassung*) gives the towns, villages and districts a large number of tasks, larger than those performed by local authorities in western Germany.

Before and shortly after World War II the same organizational structure of urban services existed in eastern Germany as in western Germany. But in the early 1950s the *Stadtwerke* were dissolved and their employees and assets transferred to branch-oriented *Kombinate*, which worked at the national or district level. The municipalities remained responsible only for local streets, garbage collection and disposal, and domestic heating.

After unification the aim of the federal government was the privatization of industry inherited from socialism. A federal agency, the Treuhandgesellschaft, was created to oversee this privatization scheme, which was probably the largest to be carried out in any Western economy. All the state-owned companies (*volkseigene Betriebe*) were transformed into limited-liability companies or public limited companies. Among these companies were the water industry, the energy industry and public transport. This, then, could have been a great opportunity to sell part of the urban services to western German or foreign companies, as was attempted with some success for companies in the manufacturing and service sector. But the outcome is quite different.

Water

Until 1990 the water industry in the former GDR consisted of only fifteen organizations (VEB Wasserversorgung und Abwasser Betriebe WAB) responsible for water supply and waste water treatment at administrative district level. According to the Act on the restitution of assets, the pipes, sewers and plant became in principle the property of local authorities. Before the spring of 1993 all fifteen organizations were transformed by the Treuhand into a limited-liability company belonging to all the towns and villages in the district. The next step, which is now well under way, consists of breaking up the assets of the company by transferring them either to the municipalities or to associations of municipalities. Structures similar to those in western Germany are appearing now. Some experts have regretted that such large companies were split up, but they were not very efficient and furthermore organized not on the basis of river basins but according to district boundaries.

The local authorities which were then responsible for the water industry faced two problems: lack of knowledge and of money. Both could be provided by private companies operating in Western markets. More especially, in the utility and water service fields many French, British and US companies tried to get a foot in a market from which they were largely excluded in western Germany. Since unification, several 'operator schemes' have been set up, mainly in small communities. The federal government and some of the *Land* governments supported the efforts towards more privatization because this move would help to create efficient installations more quickly and at lower cost.

At the beginning of 1993 about forty projects were registered in the waste water sector with private firms engaged. Among them was the Rostock region project, a new type of privatization which was well publicized. The Thyssen Handelsunion AG, a 100 per cent subsidiary of the steel company Thyssen AG and Lyonnaise des Eaux-Dumez, founded Eurawasser GmbH, the former holding 51 per cent of the shares. The group made several offers to towns to take over the water and waste water service on a concession basis. Most of these were turned down but in Rostock it managed to win a contract. The offer was to run the water and waste water system of the city of Rostock and its suburban and rural hinterland for twenty-five years. While the 'operator model' is in most cases limited to the construction and operation of the sewerage treatment plant, the Eurawasser model comprises the whole water service of a region.

From the very start the contract was the subject of fierce debate, both in the city administration and in the city council. In a last-minute effort to stop the acceptance of the Eurawasser offer, the newly founded *Stadtwerke* submitted a counter-offer but one which was obviously no match. The final vote in the city council saw a majority from the Social Democrats and the Bündnis 90 in favour of the contract and opposition from the Conservatives, who favoured the *Stadtwerke* solution. Since the agreement was seen by many as the long-intended breakthrough for privatization of urban services political pressure was correspondingly large. Even the German Minister for Economics, Möllemann, intervened in favour of Eurawasser. Yet the description of the privatization process makes it clear that success or failure depends on a number of imponderables. Therefore, it is not surprising that other cities developed other solutions. The city of Cottbus, for example, sold a 25 per cent share in its water supply to Metallgesellschaft AG, which has considerable knowledge in the field through its subsidiary Lurgi AG.

Electricity and gas

Electricity, gas and, in part, district heating were provided in East Germany by two state companies responsible for the national grid and fifteen state utilities (*Energiekombinate*) at district level. In June 1990 three West German *Verbundgesellschaften* (RWE Energie AG, PreussenElektra AG and Bayernwerke AG) concluded an energy contract with the GDR government by which they would take over the East German companies, but without the high-risk nuclear plants. The GDR government intended by this move to modernize the electricity industry thoroughly and guarantee the purchase of its huge lignite production with its thousands of work sites.

The contract gave the three utilities mentioned a 60 to 75 per cent maximum stake in the Vereinigte Energiewerke AG VEAG which, through the Treuhand, took over the national electricity grid and the large power plants from the state utilities. The remaining shares are divided between the remaining *Verbundgesellschaften*. Furthermore, the three companies took a 51 per cent share in eleven of the fifteen utilities at district level, while the remaining four districts fell to the smaller *Verbundgesellschaften*. The states, cities and towns were only allowed to have a combined share of 49 per cent in the regional companies, effectively depriving them of any major influence in the management of the companies.

This move met with stiff resistance from East German cities, which feared that they could not re-establish their *Stadtwerke* without the prosperous business of supplying electricity and the possibility of developing a local energy concept founded on the co-generation of electricity and heat. The 49 per cent stake meant that no room for manoeuvre existed for founding the *Stadtwerke* since the grid and other assets could not be separated. Since the treaty of unification included the transfer of administrative assets to the authority responsible for the field according to the Constitution, and, furthermore, upheld restitution claims on assets formerly owned, more than 150 cities sued before the Federal Constitutional Court to protect their rights. Their resistance was supported by the Association of German Cities (Deutscher Städtetag) as well by the Association of Municipal Works (Verband kommunaler Unternehmen).

The court, while allowing their complaint, shied away from pronouncing on the matter. It suggested, quite unusually, a compromise which was worked out in detail by the different parties involved. All the towns which were able to operate *Stadtwerke* and had the authorization of the government to do so would receive the grids and production facilities on their territory in kind without payment; the towns themselves would transfer their 49 per cent shareholding in the regional suppliers to the three electricity enterprises. As a rule, their own electricity production should not exceed 30 per cent of local demand so as to minimize consumption of lignite. Additionally, the *Stadtwerke* could supply gas and district heating. In August 1993 all municipalities suing before the court agreed to the compromise, though some smaller towns only after a lot of arm-twisting. The VKU (Association of Municipal Enterprises) estimates that about 135 cities will create or revive their own *Stadtwerke*, which will employ about 35,000 people.

The total privatization of the electricity sector was successfully prevented. At the moment it is very difficult to pronounce on this development. Has recommunalization prevented an efficient system of electricity supply? What will be the costs of establishing separate electricity circuits? But we have to recognize the fact that old structures are difficult to alter and that non-economic values can play an important part in debate.

In contrast to the infighting for the electricity domain in eastern Germany it seems that national gas distribution will be transferred to the cities and districts via their respective *Stadtwerke*. The reason for the smooth transfer is the lack of a general contract (like the *Stromvertrag* in the electricity sector), the willingness of the western German gas companies to accept minority participation in the *Stadtwerke* or regional supply companies and the realization by local authorities that they needed competence and financial support to construct new gas grids. The national pipeline system belongs to a new company called Verbundnetz AG (VNG), 35 per cent of whose shares are linked to Ruhrgas AG and 10 per cent to BEB Erdöl und Erdgas GmbH. It is quite possible that local authorities will take a 20 per cent stake in the company, which will be pre-financed by Ruhrgas AG.

Waste management

In eastern Germany, solid waste management has always been in the hands of the cities and villages. With fees for waste disposal being very low and not connected to the quantity collected, local authorities have usually had no means of installing proper sanitary landfills. As a result a large number of waste dumps exist which must be closed as soon as possible. In 1990 many local authorities contracted out waste management to private firms, which quite often took over the existing city works. Meanwhile, many forms of cooperation between the city works and private firms were established where the private firms holds a considerable share of the newly founded city works company.

Public transport

Public transport in eastern Germany is a task for local authorities, according to the Constitution. Until 1990, however, a large part of transport capacity was provided by the buses of industrial firms and state cooperatives especially in rural areas. Since these services were stopped or diminished, public transport companies have had to take over the service without the proper financial means. Large subsidies by the federal government but also by the *Länder* and the local authorities ensured survival, though the transport facilities offered had to be curtailed, sometimes quite drastically.

Like water services, public transport companies were first administered by the Treuhand, which had to transfer these companies back to the local authorities, though it would have preferred to privatize at least some of them. In mid-1993 the assets of nearly all public transport companies were transferred to the districts (*Landkreise*). Already all tramways are back in the possession of local authorities. Privatization of the public transport system is difficult to carry out. Since the price for a fare is a political issue in Germany and often less than half the costs are covered by receipts, any private enterprise would have to receive large subsidies to realize an adequate service. Nevertheless, in about 20 per cent of districts bus lines have been contracted out to private bus services with some success. In nine of these the public transport companies were taken over by private firms since the counties refused to take over the companies from the Treuhand.

Conclusion

Privatization of urban services seems to be much more difficult than privatizing public industries or banks because urban services are an essential part of the quality of life in the cities. It is therefore necessary that the city administration regulate and control these activities. Outright privatization combined with loss of the controlling facility is not acceptable to most city administrations.

Both debate about privatization and actual events are concentrating mainly on those services which are already cost-covering or where high profits are expected in the future. From the standpoint of industry or commerce, the privatization of urban services will be interesting only if, at least in the long run, profits can be made (taking subsidies into account) which are equal to profit margins in alternative investment opportunities. This principle will restrict the services available for privatization to those which already make a profit, such as electricity or gas provision, or to those in which through synergy with other activities new financially rewarding investment fields are opened. The great interest shown by private firms in waste management is a certain indicator that exceptional profits are made or are expected in the medium and long run. The privatization of loss-making services such as public transport will be much more difficult and will demand other provisions unless the aim of the privatization is to bring prices more into line with their real costs. The running of bus lines does not attract large firms.

In the German debate on the privatization of public services it is also remarkable that in most cases the transfer to an existing private enterprise is implied. The selling of *Stadtwerke* shares to the local public, for example, has not been considered. This hesitation may possibly be due to the smallness of the firms but may also reflect a lack of creative imagination on the part of the public sector.

If privatization policies in eastern Germany are successful, even stronger pressure will be put on local authorities in western Germany to privatize. But we have to remember the very different point of departure – the lack of qualified personnel and financial funds and the enormous time pressure to build new urban services to provide a basis for economic recovery. Technological changes as they occur in waste management will foster the trend towards privatization of urban services as well as the demand for leaner administrations. The new forms of cooperation between the private and the public sector will spread if they achieve what they promise.

5

FRANCE: SILENT CHANGE

Dominique Lorrain

Compared with the course of events in the United Kingdom and in certain other countries, the privatization of urban services has aroused little debate in France. Is this to say that nothing has occurred? Observation based on past experience has taught us to accord importance to silent changes. Again, the scant attention given to these questions belies the situation, since ten years after the decentralization measures there is a significant modification to record. Private management has continued to gain ground in different sectors and assuming multiple forms. In traditional public services, whether industrial or commercial, where from the outset an early form of privatization was applied, the utilities – water, sewerage, refuse, heating and transport – have been privatized; the private sector has come to play a leading role in new areas – planning development, promotion, construction, mobile phones, street-lighting, parking site management, cleaning, cable networks and urban cartography; and it has found its way into administrative services such as health provision, canteen services and leisure amenities.[1]

There is an explanation for what may appear as a paradox. France is a country provided with a pre-existing, formalized, highly developed model, one that is not disputed by elected local representatives and that in principle legitimizes private management within urban services. This is the contractual model. A handful of municipal engineers show signs of bitterness, a degree of resentment; but in an uncoordinated way, and they have never managed to develop a doctrine by which to buttress their preferences. It is now a number of years since passions ran high and not since the early 1970s has the choice of management type, that between public or private, direct public control or concession, been regarded as a choice that society has to make (Lorrain, 1987).

If the United Kingdom epitomizes political determination underpinned by economic argument, France finds itself at the other end of the spectrum, in that in the absence of debate or apparent political intention the private sector appears to have acted on its own. The grounds of such action are there, however inchoate, and little by little major private enterprises are making their mark on the sector as a whole. The picture is one that affords a clear understanding of how market forces take shape within a system that is set and long-standing, and what the consequences are when they come to occupy most of the ground; hence it has its usefulness for any country embarking on a policy of privatization.

The situation in France

The phrase 'privatization of urban services' denotes three features. The first is the running of local services by private contractors, municipal control being replaced by the subsidiaries of a few major groups. The same groups then peripherally extend their hold into the field of maintenance and conception. Subsequently, the principles informing privatized management are adopted by nationalized enterprises.

The fact of local authorities being empowered to call upon private firms to manage urban services is long-established, going back to the middle of the nineteenth century. Firms set up to supply water gradually established themselves in all areas of municipal provision and then diversified into other services. Paradoxically, the effect of the decentralization measures in 1982 was to accentuate the process.

The situation in France reveals a high degree of integration between the different urban services since the same firms have a role in this or that field, either as organizing authority or as operator. Responsibility for this lies initially with *communes*, which can come together to form larger groups, as either *syndicats intercommunaux à vocation unique*, *syndicats à vocation multiple*, *districts* or *communautés urbaines*. However, given the fact that the grouping of *communes* is not obligatory, as is the case in other European countries, initiative remains with *communes* themselves. Hence the overall picture is a highly varied one. A survey of urbanized France[2] has shown that coordination between *communes* is relatively slight as regards water and sewerage. Conversely, virtually all transport services come under an inter-communal authority. In waste disposal, the situation is different for collection and for treatment, *communes* acting individually in the first instance and, because of the outlay required, in combination in the second.

A second major factor of integration is that of operating services, with the notable exception that gas and electricity are in the hands of two major nationalized enterprises, Electricité de France (EDF) and Gaz de France (GDF). If, in law, municipalities are able to choose between direct public control and contracting out, observation over a considerable period reveals an unvarying tendency for the former to yield to the latter. The factors that have led to this will not be systematically examined here; nevertheless, the significant feature is that these private firms belong almost exclusively to the same major groups.

Water is now 75 per cent privatized. In 1983, when the figure was 60 per cent, the market was divided up as follows: Compagnie générale des eaux (CGE), 18 million users; Lyonnaise des eaux-Dumez, 8; Saur, 4.5; the remaining 3 million were divided between SOGEA, linked to the Saint-Gobain group, and SDEI. Générale des eaux, Lyonnaise des eaux and Saur also have a lesser role as operators of other public services in sewerage, waste disposal and heating systems via specialized subsidiaries. Furthermore, they are strongly represented in cable networks along with a third major operator, the Caisse des dépôts et consignations (CDC) group; in addition, Lyonnaise holds a 25 per cent stake in M6, as does the Générale in Canal Plus. The Bouygues group, a majority shareholder in the first national channel, with an audience of 40 per cent, has not managed to establish itself in the new local cable network market. In addition, the three groups are represented in mobile phones: CGE + Nokia in France, the SLE + Mannesman in Germany, and Bouygues, which won the bidding for a private network in 1994.

Until recently, the transport sector appeared out of phase with this pattern of integration. Three groups between them managed three-quarters of the 150 urban networks: one (Scet-transports) connected with the CDC group, another (Via-Transexel) with the

Compagnie de navigation mixte, the third (CGFTE) with the merchant bank Rivaud. In 1987 a transport subsidiary of Générale des eaux became majority shareholder of CGFTE. Early in 1990, CGFTE and Transexel signed an agreement to cooperate in the sector of urban transport and to extend their activity outside France, notably to Spain.

As a result of this process of concentration, the public authorities that chiefly ran urban services after World War II find themselves increasingly in a minority position. The main problem they encounter is their want of 'critical mass'. City engineers and technical specialists in France may well be numerous but it is evident that as a group they are fragmented. For any one city or for any specific problem, the resources that the authority - even the Lyon *communauté urbaine* - can mobilize are significantly fewer than those available within the major groups. Nor do the *communes* have available a central pool of resources by which to turn their experience to account and offset this inevitable fragmentation. Yet they all function with reasonably effective information networks that depend on the goodwill of those who constitute them rather than on internal organizational procedures. A second major problem springs from the fact that the authorities remain rooted in their particular locality. They have never succeeded in winning the political right to export their know-how - perhaps they have never considered asking - and this is the one condition that, by enabling the cost to be met, would justify them in developing technically advanced solutions.

The integration of the sector is reinforced by the presence of subsidiaries of the same groups in the other functions making up the full operation of a service, viz. engineering, public works, and supply of equipment. In France engineering has reached a relatively high degree of integration. So it is that the Compagnie générale des eaux and Lyonnaise des eaux-Dumez play a major role in water sewerage technology; Degrémont, owned by Lyonnaise, has acquired a world reputation. They are also involved in the design of urban heating plant, with Compagnie générale de chauffe and Elyo, and in plant for processing refuse, with Tiru and Sita. In urban transport, an engineering technology has developed round hi-tech products such as metro, automatic metro (*Val*) and tramway systems; but here subsidiaries of Matra and Alsthom engineering or, in the case of the RATP, Sofretu are more likely than local operators to have a role in transport engineering.

In regard to public works the situation is somewhat different. The sector is now highly concentrated, five groups playing the major role: Bouygues, Dumez-GTM-Entrepose, SGE, Spie-Batignolles and Eiffage. With an extremely dense network of subsidiary companies they function throughout France in every sphere of activity. This trend is a widespread one and common to a number of other economic sectors; more relevant to the present study is the fact of increasing integration between the public works and urban services sectors.

Throughout the 1970s and 1980s, Générale des eaux diversified into public works to become one of the leaders thanks to its many subsidiaries: Campenon-Bernard, Fougerolle, Compagnie générale de bâtiment, Société générale d'entreprise. Bouygues, which began in public works, where it gained a national reputation, has broadened its activities by diversifying into water services (Saur), television (TF1) and street-lighting (ETDE), among other directions. Over nearly ten years SLE followed a different pattern, having sold off its public works and construction subsidiaries so as to concentrate on engineering and operating urban services. Its merger with Dumez in 1990, resulting in a giant group with a turnover of FFr 93 billion and 110,000 employees, marks the end of this strategy.

With industrial equipment integration is much less developed. Générale des eaux in particular has carried out vertical integration in some sectors. In water, with Bonna, it supplies piping; in refuse one of its subsidiaries, SEMAT, manufactures trucks. In plant for refuse incineration, there are two firms, TNEE and SOCEA, that are subsidiaries of Saint-Gobain/CGE. In cable, CGE has recently acquired control of Tonna, which manufactures satellite dishes and provides cable installation; in heating systems it controls Montenay, which distributes fuel and electronic surveillance. Even so, it is unrepresented in certain areas of equipment, including fire apparatus. In the transport sector, Renault supplies a majority of municipal buses; Matra produces *Val* and Alsthom trams.

Generally speaking, the industrial side of these urban markets turns out to be much less highly organized in France than does the operational side, engineering and public works. No industrial group conducts a comprehensive strategy in urban equipment in the way that Saint-Gobain envisaged, with its aim of being represented everywhere in housing: glass production, insulating materials, piping, construction and urban services. Equipment is produced by different industrial groups or by the *Petites et moyennes enterprises* (PME). There is an organizational distinction here with Germany or Japan.

The 'privatization' of public enterprises

The privatization of urban services is also manifest in the growing influence exercised by market principles on the public sector, as effective in its results as privatization with the sale of capital assets in the conventional sense. One may pause for a moment to consider the cases of EDF, La Poste, and France Telecom, all three of which used to operate on public service principles. Today the groundswell has reached them so that their outlook has become entrepreneurial and they are reviewing their methods of pricing, their internal organization and even their role in regional development.

Over nearly fifty years, EDF has moved from an attitude of mind based on supply, as a monopoly within an economy characterized by shortages and the task of reconstruction, to one focused on demand, where the prevailing climate is one of abundance and the primacy of the market; it is this shift that has induced reform. What is now the priority for EDF is the sale of its product; the rationale of marketing has taken over and the enterprise for the time being is caught up in the process. On the ground, distribution centres have won independence, and their proximity in regard to elected officials and major clients has led them to adapt to demand:

> EDF no longer tries to press home its views on regional development; it can no longer claim to 'provide the resources for your welfare'. EDF is currently renewing its links with local authorities. ... It is revising its terms and conditions, setting up a mechanism for more open dialogue, diversifying its supply into cable network, waste incineration, carto-graphy and so on.[3]

One can follow the link between the methods of accounting and the ultimate consequences on regional development. Two methods of cost calculation can be formalized. One is the marginal cost method, which includes the cost of satisfying the last demand; the cost of the product is invoiced and this leads to different prices over distance and between customers. This method has not been adopted. Instead, a more evenly balanced one is applied. At present, operation is profitable in large and medium-sized towns and in suburban areas; it is not profitable in Paris or in rural areas. Yet the principle of equality between customers has not been called into question and the kilowatt-cost in consumer pricing remains the same all over France, and is even applied in the DOMs (overseas *départements*), where the selling price of electricity is barely higher than in France (FFr 0.68/KWh in the Caribbean as against FFr 0.57) in spite of the fact that production costs are far higher (by around FFr 3/KWh).

The principle of equality with cross-subsidizing is now facing challenge from different pressures: mayors with management preoccupations who are renegotiating prices, major industrial firms, and competition from other electrical undertakings, as introduced by Brussels rulings. Thus the principle of the equality of treatment of citizens as consumers by a public service which is recognized in pricing may give way to a concept of equality of satisfaction, implying a variation in the price and quality of the product in line with customers' wishes. In such a conception, three standards of public service expectation may be identified, and three corresponding supply responses. First, for basic consumer requirements, the objective would be to simplify problems insofar as possible, but provide a ready and efficient service, involving direct debit payment, and a maintenance back-up to minimize power failures, etc. Second, for special needs – mountain hut wardens, isolated farmsteads – it may be acceptable for the service to be interrupted at certain critical points in the year since a strict application of the equality principle would be too costly, in view of the high cost of virtually total security; this is where the notion of equality of satisfaction comes in. Third, for very heavy consumers – say, an aluminium plant or a local authority – each case is negotiated and the market price applied.

The Post Office in France is also moving towards a pricing policy based on costs. With 17,000 local branches, it certainly represents the largest neighbourhood network; and in rural areas it is perhaps the last public service remaining. The question of its continuing presence has now arisen because of the rationalization applied over the past ten years; analytic accounting makes clear the under-efficiency of rural as compared with urban areas. The debate is open, and the burden of argument is moving from a classical conception of public service, defined as one accessible to all at a uniform price, to a notion of comprehensive service, whereby in any given area the service is available to anyone at an acceptable price.

The obligation to provide a comprehensive service may be separated from its implementation, and this evidently has implications in rural areas. Two possibilities have been successively explored. One scheme was to put existing post offices to use as comprehensive service centres, combining them with other administrations and with travel and insurance agencies, etc. For the time being, the scenario of combining such services at one point has been abandoned. The government has not given extensive consideration to the problem of rural areas, and administrative coordination has been lacking. Another scheme being mooted starts from the premise that the Post Office is not required to use the time-honoured *bureau* for the service it provides. Its franchise can be conceded to others, to bakers or café proprietors or to service stations; one visualizes the *bistrot* as the ultimate comprehensive public service!

What is new and merits attention is that such calculations in terms of the market cost and price have become generalized. Most of the larger nationalized enterprises in France which are embracing business practice – EDF, GDF, La Poste, France Telecom – are currently reviewing their estimates and their pricing policy. The French railway company, SNCF, prices on the basis of distance and has introduced a timetabling adjustment through the reservations system. The Paris transport authority, RATP, prices according to zones, and France-Telecom according to distance and to time bracketing. La Poste combines the maintenance of basic rates with a range of new services that allow higher returns, such as 'chrono-post'. The principle of one and the same service is no longer adhered to and a new conception of public service is coming into being.

In urban services which are administered by private operators, the new principles of pricing have been in operation for a considerable time. What is new is their extension to non-commercial sectors which in French law are known as public administrative services; this has been made possible by virtue of finding mechanisms allowing a combination of private initiative and partial solvency in a sector. Urban transport systems in the provinces were forerunners here. Plans were developed for a share-out between public authorities and operators as well as methods of computing that enabled the cost of the selling price, hence market profitability, to be set apart. Between 1971 and 1981 a doctrine was gradually devised, stating in effect that if an asset cannot be priced at cost of production for reasons which pertain to consumer solvency and if, despite this, the same asset is required to be provided, then the public authority must make up the difference. The formula is a significant one and indicative of a degree of political culture, since in all other industrialized countries the response has been to say 'this asset can only be exploited by a public operator'. Such a situation in many services is causing subsidization to proliferate, and partnerships and cross-financing to become generalized, none of which contributes to economic transparency.

These concomitant changes therefore raise questions to do with regional development and parity between customer categories; in short, with social justice. The generalization of 'measurement' in all public service puts paid to the ongoing concern to reduce disparities and territorial differences.[4] With demands made on them by all the major operators, public as well as private, local authorities will find themselves at the end of the line, caught between the needs of their electors and the demands of true-cost pricing, between a social and a market rationale; in which case, to what extent can costs and prices remain transparent? How is it possible to maintain public service and its principle of equal access and at the same time adapt to more diversified demand?

If those who deliver urban services no longer ensure a degree of social adjustment, the task of doing so will revert to central or local government. Without its being admitted, such a method of proceeding introduces dual accounting, and thereby a distinction in kind between social participants. On one side, there are likely to be those whose vocation is to undertake only action which is profitable in market terms and who stand aside from the remainder, and, on the other, the public authority whose function is to look after this 'remainder'. Quite apart from any observation as to the overall efficiency of such a division of social roles, the consequences for France of such a pattern are clear: within a few years the state will have renounced its modernizing role for that of providing a safety net.

Corporate strategies

The contribution of the 1980s to the history of corporate strategies is a very important one, testifying to the consolidation of an age-old system as well as to its spread to new sectors and to new countries. Elsewhere I have laid stress on the reasons for this by proposing contextual explanations – economic recession, the political balance and the end of cultural taboos in regard to profit and enterprise – and by developing the special importance of the political factor, which is too often evaded (Lorrain, 1993b). Here and now my aim is to analyse the situation, since the term 'privatization' is a loose concept that embraces several forms in relation both to enterprises and to elected officials.

In order to understand what has been set in motion through the action of private enterprise it has to be recognized – and this commentators have all too frequently neglected to do – that a firm quoted on the stock exchange has either to expand or disappear since it finds itself in competition with every other sector of activity in order to keep its shareholders. And this implies that its management must be attentive to such needs and to every possibility for growth. Thus they are driven to conjure up solutions, propose services, in fact create their own market.

However, to use the term 'strategy' here calls for reservations. We need to be aware that observing a firm at a given moment tends to make its situation at that moment appear 'natural' and its development logical, and to incline one to attribute this to the effect of a strategy. Yet one should be wary of taking a deterministic view. What today seems self-evident was not so yesterday. A number of ventures may have been tried, a number of avenues explored; not all have been fruitful. Unless one is mindful of this, today's image tends to obscure past experience. Major firms do not invariably prevail nor is their progression continuous. Monitoring over a medium period, on the contrary, reveals a fantastic respiratory movement with purchases and withdrawals evolving in line with short-term opportunities and longer-term strategies. Hence so as not to risk imposing finality on them in terms of their success, their development needs to be studied comprehensively in its different stages over the medium term.

How, in fact, do firms achieve expansion? There are several avenues of approach to private management, varying in accordance with the time and the situation. Close inspection is rewarding in that it reveals how richly various are the forms of privatization.

Growth through winning contracts and increasing the number of municipalities serviced

This involves examining the particular reasons that may incline local politicians to call on the private sector (see the point following), but if firms win contracts it is because they are in contact with their clients. Cities are approached by the firms in question, their needs are listened to and proposals are made to them backed by sound arguments. It is an old story. In 1938, Jacques Rueff, the economist, at the time adviser to Paul Reynaud, Minister of Finance, observed on the subject of the provision of water and electricity and the requests in this connection constantly formulated by mayors to central government:

> If the industrialists interested in projects of this kind left *communes* alone, these would let the matter rest. All in all, they are not unlike those old women who send their children into the street to beg, and wait for them round the corner.
>
> (Baudant, 1980, p. 249)

A harsh observation, quoted by Alain Baudant in his voluminous thesis on Pont-à-Mousson (Baudant, 1980), yet one which attests the central structural factor: firms have to develop; they do not remain passive, waiting for mayors to decide to call on their services.

Acquisition of companies, frequently family companies

Technically this is done by buying up stock-market shares or by buying shares directly from shareholders where they are not quoted. There are a variety of reasons involved: the founder's intention to sell at a good price, problems of succession or inheritance, or financial difficulties. Each year numerous instances occur to account for changes in firms and growing market concentration. Mention may be made of a few significant cases.

Following constant acquisitions on the part of the two major operators in the water industry, the sector at the start of the 1980s was organized round five firms covering two-thirds of water sales, the remainder being assured by municipal authorities. Of the five, three – Saur, Sogea and SDEI – were smaller in size. Saur was bought up by the Bouygues family in 1984. Sogea, in the Saint-Gobain group, passed into the control of Générale des eaux in the share-out that followed the privatization of Saint-Gobain in 1987. SDEI, the fifth and last water enterprise, controlled by Merlin, the consultancy, was purchased by Lyonnaise des eaux-Dumez in 1991. Now the purchase of a company represents the acquisition of a number of assets – land, equipment and contracts – important indeed in a sector where contracts are for a long term. In this instance, company purchase is a means to gaining a footing in cities. Saur's assets included being established in rural areas, a contract with Nîmes and an established position in Africa. SDEI brought along the Grenoble water supply, privatized in 1989.

Such specific operations are important providers for firms since they enable them to gain a foothold in new sectors.

• In 1969, a takeover bid for the Compagnie de l'ouest atlantique enabled the Exploitations électriques industrielles group to supply Rennes and Le Mans. In 1977 the purchase of the Chemins de fer économiques du Nord (a subsidiary of the Empain group) added five networks in the Nord region: Boulogne, Douai, Valenciennes and two in Lille, whereas until then the group had boasted only seven 'historic' networks. Two financial operations saw it doubling its urban portfolio.[5]

• A stock-exchange dealing involving the Pompes funèbres générales gave Lyonnaise access to the lucrative funeral services sector in August 1981. Ten years later this foothold led to a significant share of the market in France and in the United Kingdom as well.

• The purchase of Locapark in 1984 enabled Générale des eaux to move into the parking sector and, by acquiring management of 15,000 parking bays, to catch up with the Société d'économie mixte of the Caisse des dépôts group.

• Likewise, Dumez achieved a prime position in the French construction market through vigorous pursuit of external growth, involving the acquisition of various regional enterprises which gave it a regional base and, in particular, in 1987 *rapprochement* with GTM-Entrepose, following difficulties with Vallourec, the parent firm. One deal enabled Dumez to become a star player.

Partnership

A further method of development is partnership between the firms leading the field, which enables a compromise to be reached where there is outside competition and larger markets beckon. Thus it is that several networks are operated jointly by the two major companies: Société des eaux du Nord (1902), Société des eaux de Marseille, Mosellane des eaux (1976) and Eaux de Saint-Étienne (1992). Paris water services were privatized in 1985 in such a way as to separate the provision of drinking water from its distribution, this being further divided, with Générale taking the Right Bank and Lyonnaise the Left. Water services in Lyon were privatized in 1986 and restructured to cover Greater Lyon. There the attribution was somewhat different. Générale, which already provided for several *communes*, took over the municipality itself and picked up operating services that Lyonnaise had been running in a number of *communes*. Some years later Lyonnaise was awarded the refuse collection contract, so having its presence substantially confirmed.

Minority entry into a firm as a means to self-establishment

Minority entry is an approach to business which in relation to takeover is not unlike a 'sale-or-return' trial marriage. It represents a discreet but pragmatic approach with all options open – disengagement, the status quo or deeper commitment. It involves purchase of a minority holding, in general with the knowledge of the directors. Mention is seldom made of these practices, yet they count. Firms analyse, 'test the water' with little risk attached. In the course of ten years or so, results become apparent. The larger firms in the sector have had recourse to this method as a means of progression. Let us take two groups of examples, starting with Générale des eaux in the refuse and cleaning sector. Part of the group's policy in this sector was based on (initially) minority association with family firms: Grange (35 per cent in 1980, number two producer of refuse trucks; Montenay (42 per cent in 1984); and Genest (associates in Comatec). Integration took place subsequently, thereby giving a new profile to these firms. A further example might be the international strategy adopted by Lyonnaise des eaux. On more than one occasion, the pattern adopted was to acquire participation in a foreign firm so as to become accustomed to the country and the form, thereby acquiring assurance.[6] Thus Lyonnaise took a share of Anglian Water, Wessex Water and Severn Trent (all in England), in Corporación Agbar in Spain and in Dai Nippon in Japan. Such 'trial marriages' were not always successful. It would appear that the regional water authorities put obstacles in the way of Lyonnaise getting very far in the United Kingdom. Lyonnaise sold off its share in Severn Trent in December 1990 as well as that in Wessex, which in January 1991 signed a major agreement with Waste Management, the world number one in refuse. As against this, cooperation with Dai Nippon led on to deals achieved in Tokyo. In Spain, partnership with Agbar resulted in a more far-reaching agreement with the parent company, Caixa, at the close of 1992. They have assembled their shares in water distribution – Aguas de Barcelona – and the motorway concession – Acesa – within a new company.

Major industrial manoeuvres

This is the reverse process: entry at the top and agreement on a programme concluded at directorial level with the aim of making delivery from the subsidiaries more effective. Such manoeuvres are somewhat rare. In this case too the outcome of the partnership is not known in advance. It is a less common way of proceeding since it corresponds less to the attitude of pragmatism and discretion that characterizes to the sector. Even so, one example is the 1972 agreement between Générale des eaux and the Swiss group Continentale, which enabled Générale to make progress in two sectors – street-lighting and waste disposal – where it was poorly represented. The organization was embodied in two companies, CGEA and UEER, of which the two groups shared ownership. Ten years later, the withdrawal of Continentale from the urban services market in France enabled Générale to move deftly into the two sectors and make up the ground lost to Lyonnaise in waste disposal (the Sita group). Mention should also be made of similar dealings conducted by the Lyonnaise group only recently: with Rhône-Poulenc in the field of waste disposal, with Total in energy, and, in Germany, with Thyssen (which resulted in the Rostock concession won by Eurawasser, their joint subsidiary).

Local political decision-making

Let us now consider the question from the point of view of the politician who, since he or she is at the head of the organizing authority, has a central role to play. To the question as to why private management should be preferred to public, strictly economic arguments provide an inadequate answer (Vickers and Yarrow, 1988; Lorrain, 1987, 1991). In fact, one needs to go back to considerations of political philosophy.

Among local elected representatives there is no marked political ambition, and this contrasts with the many ideas on industrial policy put forward both on the left and on the right. In central government there is action but without there being a public policy[7] that informs the sector as a whole. There is no real debate on these matters in France because, unconsciously, everyone considers these urban assets to be industrial assets along with electricity, gas, telephones, television and railways. The leading role played by politicians in privatization has the effect of annulling any serious economic measures that set out to compare the effectiveness of different types of management.

Local civil servants have concentrated their energies over ten years upon negotiating regulations and the issue of gradings. Nor from the point of view of elected officials is there a political philosophy, but only a pragmatic stance or the management of immediate business under pressure. Local administration in France is seen indeed in a narrow focus and on a day-to-day basis. Intellectually the paradigm is that of operational research applied to industrial management: the management under constraint of the Von Neumann games theory – 'mini-max', maximizing the advantages and minimizing the disadvantages. Today the constraint facing elected officials is to prove their drive and, at the same time, limit fiscal pressure. In this situation, contracting out – by enabling public budgets, along with staffing levels, to be cut and an out-of-the-ordinary revenue to be produced – is an opportune solution.

The absence of debate on these matters in France is reinforced by the attitude of the private sector towards local politicians, an attitude that is at once discreet, modest, flexible and pragmatic. Those who operate services know how to adopt a low profile and merge into the local institutional set-up, as into the locality itself. Two anecdotes are particularly eloquent. In the course of a survey into the management methods applied to seven utilities in France, in reply to the question 'Who is the organizing authority', several towns gave the name of the operator. That is to say that for the local civil servant who dealt with our questionnaire the image of a particular public service had become so confused with its operator that the legal difference was no longer distinguishable. A similar superimposing of image can be seen to this day in the relationship between municipalities and Electricité de France. Another example concerns the registry office in Kremlin-Bicêtre in the Paris suburbs. The municipality contains a large hospital with a high-level accident and emergency department, whose presence means that a considerable number of deaths are registered there. The registry has four direct telephone lines, three providing a link with a public administration – hospital, police and fire and rescue service – and one with the Pompes funèbres générales, a private funeral service and subsidiary of the Lyonnaise des eaux-Dumez group. There too a private firm is perceived and treated as part of the public service.

Elsewhere (Lorrain, 1991) I have drawn attention to the general factors that induce local politicians, mayors especially, to turn to the private sector. These are the structural differences between public and private actors, the shortcomings of local authorities, the competence and experience of groups that provide urban services, and the time factor. But there are further specific factors which weigh on the decision. One can make a distinction between those which are more directly political, those which touch on productive organization and those which have to do with networks.

The objective of recovering control of municipal services and restricting union power

Several privatizations took place in the immediate wake of right-wing victories in communist strongholds – Nîmes in 1983, La Seyne 1987, Amiens 1989. At Castres in 1989, the election of a former mayor who had been driven from office by the left in 1977 was immediately followed by the dismissal of the secrétaire-général and reinstatement of his predecessor, and by the contracting out of water services. In this way newly elected mayors clearly mark out their territory and, at the same time, send a clear message to unions. The privatizing of several services in Lorient in 1990, where the socialists had held office since 1965, testifies in part to punitive action on the part of the mayor for grave incidents which had taken place during a visit by the President of the Republic. At Liverpool too a not dissimilar sequence of confrontation between unions and elected officials led to the refuse services being privatized (with the contract going to Onyx, a subsidiary of Générale des eaux).

Desire on the part of the mayor to impose his or her authority on the council and, in particular, on his 'adjoints'

Choice 'intuitu personae'[8] proves to be crucial to private-sector development. The decision to privatize is in most cases taken by the mayor and his or her principal collaborators, whereupon the services are informed, this circumspection being justified on grounds of efficiency. In Montpellier, the decision to contract out water and sewerage services to the Compagnie générale des eaux in 1989 was negotiated within two months by three representatives of the municipality: the mayor, his financial adviser and the director of the service, whose chief role was to provide information required as to the condition of the installations. Similarly, in Caen in 1992 the Director-General of Technical Services, who had an important role in the Association des ingénieurs des villes de France, was informed by his mayor that the proposal for privatization would be presented to the council within a fortnight and that he could make his views known on the programme for contracting out. In Grenoble, three months after the March 1989 elections, the populace were informed that it had been decided by the mayor that water services should be contracted out, even though the subject had not been mentioned during the campaign. Direct action such as this has the effect of reinforcing the individual power of a small number of elected officials. Along with growing professionalism of elected officials and corporate work methods, privatization had led to tighter decision-making on the part of a small number of elected notables.

Applying a political programme

Those elected on a laissez-faire ticket intend their local policies to stand as an example for national policy should they be returned to power, so providing an instance of the pedagogical role that local administration plays in politics. Exemplarity has the virtue of sanctioning display and visibility. After 1983 the right appropriated methods put to use since 1971 by the left. One calls to mind Sète (1984), Paris (1985) and Lyon (1986).

Applying modernization programmes without raising taxes

This leads us to considerations affecting the internal methods of urban management. For reasons which have to do with their interpretation of public accounting, municipalities do not allow for depreciation, which would enable them to prepare for future investment. Furthermore, elected officials frequently apply a moderate level of pricing as a political argument for good management. Investment in this sector is heavy and non-linear. When a mains-drainage system is saturated, its capacity is not increased by the extra 10 per cent required; a new system is created. In other words, matters of budgetary technique municipalities do not constitute financial reserves, and investments in this sector are discontinuous. Therefore, in order to finance their investment programmes, mayors are forced to borrow, which is not in principle a problem but has the disadvantage, at a time of low inflation and high credit, of requiring them to resort to taxation. Contracting services out enables them to pass the investment expenditure on to the private operator and it will be up to the mayor to lessen the impact by providing the initial investment and arranging the return on investment in the medium term. Paris and many other cities exemplify this, while similar circumstances have caused Bordeaux and Marseille to move towards leasing.

Releasing revenue in order to finance other projects

Water privatization involves sometimes very considerable payment on the part of private firms, which provides revenue for the municipality: Toulouse (FFr400 million), Montpellier (FFr 250 m), Grenoble (FFr120 m), Caen (FFr200 m), Saint-Etienne (FFr1,120 m). These figures incline one to ask what sums were negotiated in other cities at other times, and what economic significance payment of this order carries; and, further, to remark on internal working methods in the local public sector in France. Private enterprise succeeds in doing what municipalities cannot – releasing considerable sums of money in the short term and ensuring a return on investment over a long period – because its accounting methods are different. It has been able to set up a system of time management, covering duration of contracts and accounting techniques for providing reserves and for depreciation. This capability contrasts with the schedules of local officials, chopped up into numerous commitments and broken down into different items.

Arguments based on safety and superior technology

Frequently, private groups come into the picture when municipalities are forced to invest in plant that is technologically complex – for water or refuse treatment, for instance, since they have the know-how and their presence provides local politicians with a guarantee of success. When in 1977 the Montpellier municipality decided to change its water supply by drawing on a subterranean reservoir, there was a fine set-to by experts in the matter. Geologists and academics confronted one another; *no one knew for certain that the plan would work*. Many feared that too intensive pumping from a source whose underground galleries had not been explored might drain it or deprive surrounding villages of their own sources. The city therefore issued a tender for an appropriate pumping station to be designed and constructed, the contract being won by Générale des eaux. The company undertook to provide a volume of production at a selling price of 14 centimes/cm 3, and, further, to finance construction of the station at a cost of FFr30 million (1989 value) and ensure its operation and that of the basin in question. As was remarked at the time about this decision: 'The fewer risks that face the municipality the better.' Today certain privatizations are justified by the need to bring infrastructure up to date and conform to directives from Brussels.

Enterprise and technological expertise as arguments in establishing a network rationale

Current developments in the water sector with a view to ensuring supply involve integration within an area of urbanization, so bringing in networks that were previously independent in terms of supply or operation. This results in morphological as well as an operational change with a network operator emerging. When one looks at factors in the breakthrough achieved by private companies in various urban areas, it appears that they established themselves in satellite *communes* while the city itself was still supplied by the public authority. This policy of encroaching occupation puts the enterprise in a position of strength when it comes to providing a network structure for the city, enabling it either to become the operator of the entire system or to obtain compensation in another sector. A converse pattern is observed. Establishment in the city itself is a means to being offered services in peripheral *communes*; there is the instance of Mosellane des eaux (CGE), whose objective is suburban *communes*. In the United Kingdom today the same tendency towards technological harmonization is at work in networks, with the water authorities buying up the smaller statutory water companies in their areas; in February 1993, for instance, Severn Trent bought Biwater's share in East Worcester Water.

Risk-covering in complex operations

Partnership represents one simple way in which a public authority can call upon outside minority partners for an operation deemed to be on too large a scale. In the course of time a change in the share balance can increase the private elements in the scheme or enable it to pull out. The functioning of the *société d'economie mixte* (*SEM*) shows how flexible this approach can be. Early in the 1960's, the *SEM* formula remained the prerogative of the Caisse des dépôts et consignation or of Paribas subsidiaries. Network operators preferred to intervene only across private companies. From the start of the 1980's, with the realization that what mattered was to establish a relationship with municipalities, the Via-Transexel group was ready to set up *SEM*s so as to run transport networks. Ten years later the two major service groups in their turn had a share in *SEM* capital, as was revealed in a Fédération nationale des SEM survey, in spite of its not being their usual practice.

Market dynamics and construction

To have observed the private sector over ten years and more is to be aware of its constant expansion without its being subject to any

Table 5.1 Share out of SEM capital (excluding local authorities)

Caisse des dépôts	12%	SLE/CGE	3%
Various financial bodies	18%	Social housing firms	2%
Companies	7%	Other SEM	1.5%
Public partners	3.7%		

Source: Fédération nationale des SEM, *Le Moniteur*, 13 November 1992.
SEM = société d'economie mixte.

Table 5.2 Examples of contracting out water services since 1983 (privatized share 60 per cent in 1983; list not exhaustive)

Sète	1984	*Amiens*	1989
Colombes		*Grenoble*	
Paris	1985	Castres	1990
Lille		*Montpellier*	
Avignon		Lorient	
Villeurbanne		*Toulouse*	
Saint-Malo		*Toulon*	
Lyon	1986	*Dijon*	1991
Angoulême		Châteauroux	
Qimper		Laon	
Saint-Lô		*Saint-Étienne*	1992
Lunéville		*Caen*	
Orléans	1987	*Mulhouse*	
Brest		Dunkerque	
Issoudun	1988	*Romans*	1993
		Colombes	

Sources: reports to shareholders, press and interviews
Note: Towns of more than 100,000 are in italics

coherent overall political programme. What does this teach us? A first interpretation supports the view that enterprises go hand in hand with markets. They adapt to needs as needs emerge. Water services link with sewerage, refuse collection with disposal then with cleaning services, operating services involve engineering and public works, constructing and operating car-parks are interlinked. This is what occurred between the 1950s and 1970s, when growth was self-generating. Today in a similar way the growth of urban environment markets produces a ripple effect which will benefit enterprises. Such an interpretation, which provides a clear explanation for what is occurring, sees this development as 'natural', the outcome of the encounter between market opportunity, corporate strategy and political decisions taken at a local level. With this first interpretation, which distinguishes three factors, the market is outside the firm; one remains within the classic figures of the subject and structures, actor and system, *Homo economicus* and 'invisible hand', in short within the concept of exteriority between actors and market.

Observation of these sectors suggests a different interpretation. These firms also form an integral part of the market, not wholly but to a substantial degree. They function by being alternatively inside and outside according to whether they command their environment or whether it eludes them. I should like to offer a second explanation in showing that their development involves a social edifice in which they actively relate to the market. Here one can speak of corporate strategy and co-production of markets, thus abandoning a notion of exteriority between actor and market and asserting that in certain circumstances certain actors may initiate action to create the conditions of their development.

What elements, then, are required for a market to function? The equation is a simple one: for a given product it requires there to be an instrument to measure consumption, a technique for pricing, a clientele that is solvent and rules of play that are stable. This notion of market construct takes on validity the more we study urban public activity. These sectors are not market sectors like the others, even if the market constantly feeds them. They do not see an automatic adjustment of demand to supply. Rules need to be framed for this to occur since the sectors are placed between domestic and collective spheres. They represent public goods which call on much effort and attention to be turned to account, since unquestionably all human activities call for prior agreement on terms of reference, even language and grammar. This requirement is especially the case with urban services. The market is not an automatic condition; its particularity is that it needs constructing.

This is what occurred for water at the end of the 1930s when the practice of delegated management – that is, of maintaining private operation despite a structural deficit – became generalized. Today this constructional process is to be seen in new fields where the rules of play are not set and where decisions taken by the authorities can have significant consequences on the forms these markets adopt. Similar situations are found in countries where privatization is taking place, whether in Europe or the developing world. Where an institutional environment needs to be constructed, major enterprises are induced to play an active role. Here are two examples.

At the moment cable represents a new market in France in which both technical and institutional solutions are sought. The example makes it clear that a market is in no position to develop unless a pricing policy or legal framework has been established. Ten years after being proclaimed, in about 1983, as a great adventure in technology and communications, disillusionment set in. The number of subscribers fell far short of that anticipated and the sector was gravely in deficit. The problem has to be appreciated at three levels: the overall population in the districts served by the network, the inhabitants of dwellings connected up and inhabitants of such dwellings who are subscribers; in other words, across the rate of connection and the rate of subscription.

For the time being, cable network operators face heavy initial investment – on networks and programming – and very gradual emergence of custom. The cost of cabling, district by district, does not immediately generate a proportional number of subscribers, first, connecting up this or that block of flats must hang on a co-ownership decision. Then there is the particular decision of each household as to whether or not to become a subscriber. To get round the difficulty, operators have a number of initiatives available: they can reduce cabling costs with solutions that are less onerous than that of the initial fibre optics; they can accelerate linkage with blocks of flats through developing a strategy with the bigger property managers; or they can alter the customary image of what is on offer by making it no longer an individual purchase but one of a number of urban services, along with water, refuse collection and heating provision. There have been discussions with the local social housing administration in an attempt to include subscription in overall charges.

But the furtherance of these initiatives comes up against legal obstacles which have to do with property rights and with how the prerogatives of the public authority are defined. Cable networks do not constitute public services from a legal point of view. This principle has been laid down by Parliament and confirmed by the *Conseil d'État* or else in judgements given by different adminis-trative courts, in Nancy and in Versailles. Cable is counted as a private commercial activity, hence its operators are not entitled to benefit from public authority prerogatives any more than they are entitled to receive public grants. It is not difficult to see how these two elements determine the freeing of the cable market. Major cable operators have devised a strategy of negotiating on every parameter so as to change the terrain and devise legal and pricing conditions in French law which will allow a market to develop. Taking the financial aspect, the 1992 report of the *Cour des comptes* on financial practice in the Île de France shows that very many *communes* have had a financial share in the development of the network in spite of its being a private activity. As regards public-authority prerogatives, an Act passed in 1990 gave tenants a right to cable in the same way as they have a right to an aerial. Hence tenants can oblige a proprietor to connect up the property they occupy. Nevertheless, this right comes up against possible refusal on the part of the co-ownership for the block in question to be connected up. A 1992 bill tends to establish constraints on proprietors who allow cable to be linked up. Hence jurisprudence as it has evolved has continued to keep cable outside local public services, in a private frame of reference, while allowing operators considerable public authority prerogatives. Thus it is that the growth of markets and operators does indeed lead on to a new type of law, and as the latest attribute of market organization, a pricing policy reflecting consumption; this is what now makes a strategy such as 'pay-as-you-view' possible. Accordingly, over ten years combined initiative has set up legal and pricing conditions enabling a new product to come into the home. With the merging of images, texts and databases this is no small achievement!

A further example is that of the *marché d'entreprise et de travaux publics* (*METP*), which is a good illustration of how the quest for expansion leads firms to seek markets and put forward new legal dispositions so as to procure them. Public lighting in France has, since the 1980s, been a fairly substantial growth market for two reasons. EDF, in comparison with the past, covers a smaller proportion of the total number of services now, which allows private operators to enter the field. The electorate via its local representatives registers a high demand for public lighting, now seen as linked to the quality of urban life, for reasons of security, as an expression of vitality, and to provide for sports and recreational activities in leisure hours.

If they want to call upon private firms, *communes* have two standard types of contract at their disposal – one involving construction and one operation if the installations are to be privately administered. The disadvantage of the formula for private firms is that each contract is separate, renewable after a period and is open to bidding following the procedure of procurement contracts. These practised legal formulas, which vest overall control in the *commune*, entail a cost in that they require a degree of involvement on the *commune*'s part. Financial know-how is necessary to undertake the work; tenders must be invited, bids followed up and choice of an operator settled. On the other side, clearly the firm's policy is to stabilize its bid in correspondence with the legal formulas linked to the concession.

In this context, some private companies have proposed a new legal formula – *METP* – to local authorities, by which they take on the cost of construction and carry out the work and, further, operate the service over a period of ten to fifteen years, during which time they are reimbursed by the authority. Even though this type of contract cannot be compared with that governing a concession, since it applies only to one part of the service and the firm is remunerated by the *commune*, not the consumer, firms have succeeded in bringing about a profound change in the rules applying to the market by introducing a long-term relationship with the same authority.

Credit for the formula belongs not to parliamentary debate, to a working party of an association of mayors or to a ministerial white paper, but to firms themselves in their quest for markets. Legal experts acting on their behalf examined legal formulas that were relevant and in force. *METP* existed but was in abeyance. It was resuscitated and proposed to certain municipalities. One would like to know where early experiments were made so as to describe how this innovation developed. The formula took hold because it met the need felt by mayors from 1983 onwards, to disengage. It was applied in the case of modernizing university buildings in the Paris region. Eventually, the state was forced to recognize the significance of the formula and adopt a position.

A situation thus comes about in which the state finds itself not at the source of a legal construct but at its completion, no longer providing the initiative but a response, no longer imagining new solutions but ensuring sound accounting of solutions proposed under the existing legal framework. The state, which was once the agent of modernization, is here become the guardian of an order.

This example also reveals the reason for permutation among the actors. Private firms compel such recognition in the end because they need to expand year in, year out, as has been mentioned. This need represents a capital actor which imparts rhythm and objective to the whole sector. Their strength also comes from extremely close knowledge of needs and problems. These major groups are rooted in their territories, just as local authorities are. They know the municipalities and follow the debates of the various elective bodies. Hence they have every means to anticipate their markets. Sooner than adopt a passive role and wait for a local public contract to find its way to them, they prefer to develop a strategy that is genuinely dynamic.

Flexible municipal management

Decentralization was conceived in line with a plan for the modernization of public initiative. Withdrawal by central government should logically have been accompanied by a concomitant reinforcement of local government. In fact the outcome has been an unexpected success of urban service groups; a twofold development has occurred. It is possible to develop several lines of argument to account for this unlikely situation. Elsewhere I have sought to pay stress on an internal political rationale (Lorrain, 1993b). One may also look at changing conceptions of 'sound' management in public services and its effects. When the state was the major actor, its influence was widespread and, through its policy of modernization, it had an impact on local government. In this way, the so-called *économie concertée* of the 1950s re-emerged twenty years later in the guise of the contractual state.

Today the enterprise and the market stand out as the emerging actors for collective action. Central government has receded, in France as elsewhere, less because of the size of its budget than because of the expectations people place in it. Thus one can explore the productive side of municipal action and compare what takes place in *mairies* which have a direct productive component and in enterprises (Coriat, 1979; *Sociologie du travail*, 1993, papers by Weltz and Zarifian, and Maurice). Twenty years ago they evolved under state supervision but, because their productive role was played down, they were referred to as municipal administration. Withdrawal by central government has enabled the productive dimension to be recognized and, as a natural consequence, there is a shift from the notion of administration to that of management.

How can organization be achieved for the best in *mairies*, when the pricing of public services becomes a sensitive question? Just as for the Japanese motor industry in 1950, described by Benjamin Coriat, the problem is to produce a limited range of products at acceptable prices. It requires the ability to adapt quickly to customers, to elected officials who come up with new ideas and who repeatedly bring up individual requests in the municipal organization that are by definition specific. From this angle, the increasing recourse to contracting out can be analysed as a form of arrangement well adapted to the municipal productive system – to both productive and political constraints. Subcontracting introduces flexibility. Nor between one municipality and another is the private sector entrusted with identical services, hence there is political liberty. The *mairie* is not obligated to do everything on its own, and this is a factor of productive efficiency. Contracting out further introduces an element of stabilization *vis-à-vis* the politician because it involves a greater organization autonomy than does a municipal department. A space is created where a degree of planning is possible and which is free of purely political considerations. Even though operators remain subject to the choice of elected officials, day-by-day decisions are taken on an independent basis (Barthélemy *et al.*, 1992), which is certainly a very significant factor in enabling medium- and long-term policies to be developed.

But one question remains: who will ensure the coordination of the whole and maintain its efficiency as a system?

Notes

1. Since, to the best of my knowledge, no comprehensive evaluation exists I have relied on a number of different sources: press, interviews and surveys. Certain cases, however, are beginning to be documented: see recent studies by Ascher, Padioleau and Demesteere, and Verpraet (*Annales de la recherche urbaine*, 1992); Lorrain, Novarina and Thomas (*Techniques, territoires et sociétés*, 1993); Barthélémy *et al.* (1992); see also Guigo, Le Gàles and Marié.
2. Survey of centre *communes* in 210 urban areas with a population of over 23,000.
3. Conversation with an EDF official (local authorities section).
4. Major arteries and nerve centres though which the bulk of the traffic flows will be channelled to the detriment of smaller

centres and the extremities of the network (Dupuy, 1992, p. 10).

5. This group, known at the time as EEI, took the name Transexel a little later before merging with the Groupe de transport interurbain (GTI) to form the largest urban transport enterprise in France, Via-Transexel.

6. Interviews with the chairman of Lyonnaise des eaux-Dumas, Jérôme Monod, *Le Monde*, 3 August 1985, 13 August 1987, 22 August 1991.

7. This notion, conceived on the basis of central government policy (Jobert and Muller) has no relevance to our field, where an altogether different interpretation of history is being given (Lorrain, 1992) by actors who are experimenting, feeling their way and seeking pragmatic solutions to problem-solving and, to this end, constructing mechanisms for contingent action (Crozier and Friedberg; Padioleau, 1986; Olson, 1978; Schelling, 1980; Roqueplo). For this reason the privatization process cannot be studied merely from the point of view of firms. Market must be brought in continuously. Are they in recession? What possible alternative outlets exist at international level?

8. See note 6, p. 26.

6

THE PRIVATIZATION OF PUBLIC SERVICES IN SPAIN[1]

Carmen García Fernández

Spain has lately been experiencing the most sweeping redefining of the state in its entire history under the impact of two opposing forces; the drive towards regional autonomy, and Europeanization. The former corresponds to a democratic urge and works to the advantage of local communities; the latter expresses the desire to integrate the country within a larger whole. The consequences of these two tendencies are the more extreme in that the country had for long been organized on the basis of a strong centralized state, supported by large nationalized enterprises within an economy that was highly self-contained.

The changing context

The *autonomies within the state* undeniably constitute the most original feature of the political order set up in 1978 ... The novelty of the system in force has probably enabled post-Franco Spain to avoid giving way to the separatist current which some sought to promote by resorting to violence.

Couffignal, 1993

The Spanish state is made up territorially of localities (*municipios*), provinces, and autonomous regions (*comunidades autónomas*). All these communities enjoy self-government in the management of their respective interests,[2] and the resulting plurality of independent organizations embodies the state, conceived in a way that is far-reaching and complex. Principles of mutual respect, solidarity and subsidiarity inform their relationships. A distinction has to be made between the seventeen *comunidades autónomas*, which are more or less coextensive with the former regions, and the local communities comprising fifty provinces, 8,050 *municipios* and the islands. If, in certain respects, this system may have resembled the three French tiers of region, department and *commune*, it is fast distancing itself from the model. Indeed, the degree of independence of the *autonomías* goes beyond that of existing instances of decentralization in Europe.

The Constitution, promulgated in 1978, declared communities and 'nationalities' to be autonomous, the latter being regions in which the state recognized historic rights. So much for the question of principle; in reality this transfer in favour of autonomous communities represents both a variable and an unfinished process. It is variable in the sense that the Constitution provides for a range of systems so that the *comunidades autónomas* do not have the same attributes; each one separately negotiates the transfer of powers from central government and each one has elaborated its own formal status. It is unfinished because the unfolding process involves permanent negotiation; this uncircumscribed process has given and continues to give rise to some concern.

Table 6.1 The different autonomías

Autonomy in acc. with Art. 151 of the Constitution (with transfer of health)	
Andalucía	Canarias (Canary Islands)
Cataluña (Catalonia)	Galicia
Valencia	
Autonomy in acc. with Art. 143 of the Constitution (pluri provincial communities)	*(Single-province communities)*
Aragón	Asturias
Castilla-León	Baleares
Castilla-Mancha	Cantábriso
Extremadura	Madrid
	Murcia
	La Rioja
Communities with special status (forales)	
Navarra	
País Vasco (the Basque country)	

In 1992, the government and opposition signed a pact whereby the ten 'communities' on the slow track were to approximate to the degree of autonomy reached by those named by Article 151 of the Constitution (see Table 6.1). In spite of this agreement, the demand for new powers has continued. For instance, an organic law relating to community financing defined the share of state revenue they would receive, but the need for the Socialist Party to win nationalist support following the loss of its majority in the June 1993 elections resulted in an increased pay-out to the communities, who obtained the transfer of 15 per cent of income tax revenue in a gesture of which the poorer communities were highly critical.

The strength of the *comunidades* in relation to the other regional authorities is leading to the virtual disappearance of the provinces. In law they have been given no powers; their role is limited to representation on administrative commissions to do with economic cooperation or with dispensing assistance to *municipios*. The reinforcement of the role of the autonomous communities in public administration is clear from Figure 6.1.

Between the start of the present century and the 1970s, Spanish

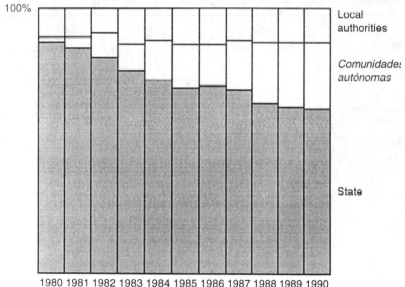

Figure 6.1 *Distribution of consolidated public expenditure in Spain*

Table 6.2   Local authority expenditure within that of overall public administration

Year	Real costs (%)*
1958	22.55
1963	19.74
1967	16.38
1975	20.05
1981	23.05
1991	22.46

*Running and real investment costs.

municipios lost a number of their prerogatives. Supply of gas and electricity, which had been considered local services following an Act of April 1924, as well as other services such as education, provision of health care,[3] even prisons, were taken over by the state. Once the process of democratization began, *municipios* started to win back functions, which explains the gain in their share of public expenditure from 1974 onwards (Table 6.2). Such functions cover social and cultural activities but also, and increasingly, economic and urban initiatives.

Among their varied activities, the law[4] defines the basic services that municipalities or their associations must supply; water, drainage, refuse collection, street-lighting and paving, cemeteries, and health standards and inspection governing food and drink. Responsibilities grow in line with population. *Municipios* with more than 5,000 inhabitants must provide and maintain public parks, libraries, markets and refuse treatment. Above 20,000, public services including policing, welfare provision, fire-fighting, sport and recreational facilities and abattoirs. Above 50,000, there is the addition of public transport and environmental issues.

So as to be able to fulfil these tasks, particularly in urban services *municipios* can form syndicates. The *comunidades autónomas* can help to this end by assisting to a degree with the financing of infrastructure so long as end management of a service is in the hands of a syndicate. The sectors in which syndicates are involved are refuse collection and treatment, water supply, transport, street and beach cleaning, maintenance of country roads, fire-fighting, abattoir management, markets and cemeteries, and tax collection. This facility is not yet fully applied to small and medium-size *municipios*. At the end of 1990, the Ministry of Public Administration (Ministerio para las Administraciones Publicas) listed 538 syndicates, grouping 3,395 *municipios*; but only 42 per cent of *municipios* of population less than 20,000 form part of a syndicate, syndicates mainly being used by larger *municipios*, among them Barcelona, Málaga, Seville, Gijón, Guadalajara, Gerona, Tarragona, Badajoz, La Coruña, Pontevedra, Pamplona and Alicante.

Following local elections in 1991, the picture in its background details became further altered by political changes which affected the position of administrative elites. The Socialist Party (PSOE) re-established itself as the dominant political force. It moved ahead in small towns and rural *municipios* but lost ground in the larger cities, among them Seville, Madrid and Valencia (the two last municipalities falling to the Partido popular (PP) and Seville to the regional Partido andalucista (PA), though retaining control in Barcelona and Zaragoza. The Basque nationalist party (PNV) retained Bilbao. The communists benefited from the Socialist setback and in a large number of cases their support enabled Socialists to hang on to their majority.

Political changes in town halls frequently leads to confrontation between politicians and local officials, there being on both sides mistrust and unreadiness, even inability, to meet the electorate's expectations. Three problems that affect local authority employees are recruitment, training and promotion. In theory and in law, recruitment should be on the basis of equal opportunity, merit, qualifications and advertising. In fact, a form of competitive entry has been devised which favours a preselected type of candidate, rather than a form of entry which promotes technical competence over and above ideological considerations; technical competence is often lacking. Then, existing employees often find that newcomers are preferred to them for posts which they could expect to be chosen for if proper training and internal promotion were applied.

Given this, the attitude of local employees to privatization is by no means uniform. If some look on it with optimism as affording them more attractive career prospects, the vast majority would prefer to stay with the advantages of being under public control, frequently because they jib at the notion of what private enterprise may demand of them. Certainly, an obligation to keep employees on may mean that policies to improve efficiency are endangered.

Table 6.3   Distribution of modes of water management

Public management			72%
Direct management	60%		
state		48%	
municipal		12%	
Canal Isabel II	12%		
Private management			26%
Joint enterprise			2%

Source: Roque Gistau Gistau, 'Los abastecimientos v sanaemientos en el Plan Hidrológico Nacional', *Revista de Obras Públicas*, no. 3321 (1993).

Private competition for urban technical networks

In the local public services sector the issue of privatization is hotly debated. Clearly there is the ideological division between left and right, but in reality the chief preoccupation is the more banal financial one. With their developing economic activity, *municipios* are facing increasing indebtedness. Political life in Spain is at a juncture where both left and right municipalities are calling on the government for more money, which always comes late.

A sector where privatization is marked is water and sewerage (Table 6.3). Traditionally water has been considered as a social possession, and this has led to very low pricing. The budget for water is balanced within the general budget, enough indication of the age of the installations plus the backwardness of the treatment plant. It is now necessary to find capital, which in turn is a recommendation for privatization.

Refuse collection and street-cleaning comprises the most widely privatized sector, probably because it is the most specific in terms of function and personnel. Public transport also lends itself to privatization, an issue which has been a matter of controversy for a long time.[5]

Private enterprises gain access to the operation of urban services through the procedure of procurement contracts, and the form of management is normally concession – in fact, leasing, since it is concession without investment. In Spain one term stands for both concepts. It is worth noting the traditional presence of French firms in the public services market, alongside a few Spanish companies, as well as the recent arrival of British companies (Thames Water and

Northumbrian Water) and even American ones (Waste Management and BFI).

The largest private urban services group in Spain is Fomento de Construcciones y Contratas SA (FCC). It came into being in March 1992 with the merger between big companies in the sector, Construcciones y Contratas (Cycsa) and Fomento de Obras y Construcciones (Focsa). Its share capital and administration are in the hands of the Koplowitz sisters, whose fortune is one of the biggest in Spain, with a consolidated turnover of 382 billion pesetas in 1992, one-third of its relating to building and public works. The group has long been associated with the environment, which accounts for a quarter of its activity. Its subsidiary, SERAGUA, recently won the contract for supplying water to Vigo (1991) and Lérida (1993). In domestic refuse collection and street-cleaning, FCC occupies the position of leader, with a turnover of 78 billion pesetas. It serves 230 *municipios* and a population of 16.5 million. It has established itself in Britain (Focsa Service), in France (with a share in Française d'assainissement et de service SA) and in Venezuela. It is also represented in urban transport across Corporación de Transportes SA, where it is associated with the French number one (VIA GTI), but for the moment development is sluggish, with only a few services being managed in medium-sized towns; Almería, Avila, Tarragona, Tarrasa and Talavera de la Reina.

SGAB (Sociedad General de Aguas de Barcelona) is the other major private group in the sector. It was founded in Liège in 1867, bought in 1881 by Lyonnaise des caux, which sold it thirty years later, while retaining an interest in it, to a group of Catalan bankers and entrepreneurs. Since 1981 SGAB and Lyonnaise des eaux have consolidated their alliance. Early in 1992, Lyonnaise des eaux-Dumez and Caixa de Ahorros y Pensiones de Barcelona, the main shareholder in SGAB, divided out some of their interests in public services, including water, waste and motorways. SGAB supplies Barcelona and surrounding suburbs – some 3 million inhabitants– with water. Its subsidiary, the Agbar corporation, has been the group's vehicle for expansion, supplying water to nearly 7 million people. It covers the country by way of different subsidiaries, which operate water as joint companies – in Alicante, Murcia and Tarragona – or through leasing – in Zamora, Palencia, Santiago de Compostella, Ciudad Real, among other towns. Cespa, another subsidiary, provides refuse services for 2.8 million people.

The Compagnie générale des eaux is represented in Spain

through several subsidiaries, supplying water to a million or so in towns such as Almería, Avila or Puerto de la Cruz. It further holds a concession for the construction and operation of a treatment plant in Zaragoza, via its subsidiary OTV, in which it has invested 25 billion pesetas. Its subsidiary Ciudad Limpia is trying to establish itself in the waste sector.

The other Spanish companies have been fighting for a place in the market. The Obrascom–Northumbrian Water partnership won the water contract for Soria in 1993, the first provincial capital supplied by a British company. Dragados y Construcciones SA, number one in building, has diversified into waste and cleaning after tying up an agreement with Bouygues. Bouygues controls GESTAGUA, which has become the main shareholder in Aguas de Valencia. Abengoa has gone into partnership with Thames Water, number one in the sector in the United Kingdom. Mention must be made too of the activity of Lain and of Cadagua, a subsidiary of the BTP Ferrovial enterprise. In the domain of public transport, the twenty-six municipal transport companies count for 80 per cent of the traffic. The private firms running transport in cities such as Bilbao, Zaragoza and Alicante represent Spanish capital.

Restructuring the major network companies

The state has lost some of its powers to the *comunidades autónomas*, but it has retained control over water resources, air and rail transport, telecommunications and energy, evidence of the importance accorded to the sectors which, in defining a network, give a strategic structure to the territory.

The state has retained control of water resources because of water's scarceness. In the matter of arbitration it has chosen to call upon the river basin authorities rather than the *comunidades autónomas*. In theory, they are responsible for the river basins which are coextensive with their territory, but in law such responsibility is given only to the regional communities which follow through the process of self-government according to Article 151 of the Constitution. In the energy field, the state controls the gas network and is enhancing its presence in the electricity supply network. In the energy and telecommunications sectors it is getting ready to confront the European market and, with this in mind, urging measures for integration and privatization of state enterprises so as to cut losses and improve results in the short term and be in a position to withstand more open competition.[6] Sell-offs are prompted not so much on doctrinal as on managerial grounds, a policy that sometimes benefits private firms in Spain, as in the case of the 40 per cent privatization of CAMPSA (Compañía Arrendatiria del Monopolio de Petróleos, SA).

The oil sector

The largest privatization has resulted from Repsol being quoted on the stock-exchange. This subholding company in the INI group was set up in July 1987 to gather together all the state-owned companies in the oil sector, thus creating Repsol-Butano, Repsol-Exploración and Repsol-Petróleo. The parent organization – Instituto Nacional de Hidrocarburos – has seen its stake fall from 100 per cent to 74 per cent in 1989 and to 40.5 per cent in 1993, and privatization is set to reduce it further to the 30 per cent mark.[7] An analysis of privatization in the case of CAMPSA, the commercial arm of the oil industry with its monopoly of petrol stations, is also of interest. The government's aim was to encourage vertical integration within the oil industry by allowing refining companies access to distribution.

The initial measure was to set up two service station networks in 1985: the one distributing the national product as a monopoly, i.e. unchanged; the other, as a parallel network, constituting 1,084 service stations, and, in conformity with European rulings, supplying EC-imported oil products. The two marketing networks, though with different suppliers, must conform to the same pricing regime; price-setting is free but subject to a maximum set by the administration.

In 1991, the Ministry for Industry decided to split CAMPSA. Repsol was authorized to sell off its shares in CAMPSA to the private refining companies, thus reducing the public stake to 64.4 per cent. The split came into operation in March 1992. The company, valued at 174 billion pesetas, was divided between PETRONOR (23 billion pesetas), Repsol (92 billion pesetas), CEPSA (43 billion pesetas) and PETROMED (16 billion pesetas).

Gas

The gas industry is nationalized on the basis of a ruling dated 27 January 1956; if its justification was to follow in the steps of French and British nationalized industries, reorganization of distribution did not ensue and the structure remained regionally based, an example being Cataluña de Gas. Only in the late 1980s did the government start to develop a policy for the use of natural gas.[8] The Constitution lays down that the utility is the concern of the state, the *comunidades autónomas*, or of *municipios* if they choose to administer it themselves. In 1987, the distribution of gas was declared a public utility; by an Act of June 1987 it took on a national character. Central government plans the system of pipelines, their international interconnection, strategic stocks, priority zones, progressive stages of development and the coordination of relations between public and private sectors. The Ministry for Industry and Energy (Ministerio de Industria y Energía) grants concessions and authorizes the construction of plant, a prerogative that is sought by the *comunidades autónomas*.

Management of production, transport and distribution – except in Catalonia and the Basque country – is in the hands of the state-owned enterprise ENAGAS, which has exclusive rights to procuring gas, stocking and transport, also to supplying power stations. Distribution is effected by public or private firms that are concessionaries in the utility. Municipalities have preferential rights over private firms to administer the supply of gas within their area. Government policy has been to beef up ENAGAS so as to display a strong and homogeneous sector to European competition. Its aim is to promote integration within the different phases of activity, and this entails firms being merged to the point almost of creating a monopoly.

Regarding distribution, Cataluña de Gas, Gas-Madrid and Repsol-Butano concluded an agreement to merge in December 1991, setting up Gas Natural,[9] which provides for 95 per cent of domestic and commercial consumption and which should in time take over the independent distributors remaining in the Asturias, Galicia and the Basque country. The government has managed to avoid weakening the sector through an abundance of regional networks. The restructuring operation within the sector led in 1994 to the merging of ENAGAS and Gas Natural. Although the state has lost 100 per cent control of ENAGAS, the objective again is to meet liberalization with a strong company and be in a position to conquer external markets such as Portugal or Morocco.

Electricity

Since 1954, the distribution of electrical energy has been a public utility. In 1984 the operation of the high-voltage network became a public utility under state tenure. Electrified transport is run by a joint enterprise (51 per cent state-owned, 49 per cent private) named Redesa.

The sector is one of those most affected by the process of Europeanization. For eight years the government has been applying pressure of one sort or another to strengthen the private firms with a share in it and extend the public-sector role in distribution. Until the start of 1991 the sector consisted of a large, publicly owned producer, Endesa – 76 per cent subsidiary of INI and trying to find a foothold in distribution – and seven private companies handling distribution. Within two years the sector was totally reorganized. A first step took place in 1991 with the merging of the two largest private companies, Hidroeléctrica Española and Iberduero, which gave birth to a new company, Iberdrola, that represented 5 billion dollars of market capitalization. Restructuring continued in December 1993 with an agreement between Endesa and Iberdrola, resulting in a very substantial exchange of assets which gave Endesa access to distribution. The company acquired control of HIDRUNA, plus 4 per cent of FECSA, in which it now has a 49 per cent stake, as well as 11.5 per cent of Iberdrola's stake in Aguas de Barcelona. Endesa's subsidiary, ERZ, acquired the hydroelectric power stations Iberdrola owned in Aragón as well as its market in the region; its subsidiary, ENECO, took 25 per cent of Saltos de Guadiana.

The Ministry for Industry proceeded to an agreement between the two major electrical groups before the bill organizing the electrical sector was drafted. On the basis of this agreement, the state-owned group, Endesa, became an enterprise for both production and distribution, capable of competing in the open market, as the European Union requires. In order to gain access into distribution, Endesa has been forced to renounce its privileges and the maximum valuation of its assets, but it has the peace of mind of not having to face EU tribunals as Iberdrola claimed would be the case.

The electrical sector in Spain thus remains organized round two major companies, Endesa and Iberdrola, controlling between them 80 per cent of the total, the remaining 20 per cent being shared between Union Eléctrica Fenosa and Hidrocantábrico.

Telecommunications

The telecommunications sector will be liberalized in Europe in 1998, but Spain has been granted a moratorium until 2003. Against a background of increasing links between European firms, and with American ones too, the Spanish company Telefónica signed an agreement with Unisource in December 1993. Unisource represents the combined telecommunications companies of the Netherlands, Sweden and Switzerland. The addition of Spain makes it the number three for international calls, bellow AT&T and the consortium formed by Deutsche Telekom and France Telecom, on a level with the union between BT and the American MCI (*Actualidad Económica*, 20 December 1993).

Furthermore, Telefónica participated in the privatization of the telecommunications sector in Argentina in 1990. Turnover for 1993-94 reached $1.8 billion and investment $925 million (this figure could reach $5.7 billion before 1997).

Conclusion

In Spain we can again see that the conception of local public utilities has evolved in a society undergoing constant change. Services such as education and occasionally health, which were once the responsibility of *municipios*, have now been transferred from the state to the *comunidades autónomas*; others – gas, for instance – the state jealously guards or else, as in the case of electricity, seeks to develop. Certain utilities which by law belong to *municipios* – water and refuse collection – have been transferred to syndicates of *municipios* at the incentive of the regions. Both state and *municipios*, moreover, have been affected by the international wave of privatization.

The development of several forms of privatization in Spain is real enough even if the government chooses to be discreet on the subject. Certain sections of the press, right-wing politicians and certain groups are alone in openly declaring themselves in favour of contracting out or the joint management of services. Gradually the state has been selling off its stake in the more prosperous nationalized industries – in the key energy sector for instance. In others, privatization will take place only when company performance has been improved the better to attract private investment. The first option is to sell off sound assets and reduce the deficit. The formula preferred by *municipios*, when they call on the private sector, is that of concession.

The question occurs as to why joint enterprises have not shown more development. Very probably there is pressure on the part of private firms in making out their requirements and their preference for independent management; but another element is the small size of *municipios* and their consequent inability to offer a stake on equal terms with the larger competitors for the utilities market, which maintain their privileged position when concessions are drawn up.

The scenario of public utilities in Spain is a developing one. The actors are taking up positions, though as yet the rules of the game are not entirely clear.

Notes

1. Adapted by Dominique Lorrain.
2. Article 137 of the Constitution of 1978.
3. Central government took charge of personnel in 1962.
4. Act of July 1985, Article 26, *reguladora de las bases del Régimen Local*.
5. One calls to mind remarks made by the deputy mayor of Madrid, Mercedes de la Merced, suggesting that privatization of public transport in the capital was a possibility.
6. F. Ferro, vice-chairman of INI (Instituto Nacional de Industria) speech at the Universidad Internacional Menédez Pelayo, La Coruña, 13 July 1989.
7. Even with 30.5 per cent, the Spanish state is the largest shareholder, followed by PEMEX with 5 per cent and the Banco Bilbao Vizcaya (BBV) with 4 per cent.
8. With gas representing 5.6 per cent of the consumption of primary energy in 1990, government measures are aimed at raising this to 12 per cent by 2000.

9. Gas Natural is owned by Repsol (45 per cent), La Caixa (25 per cent) and INH – Instituto Nacional de Hidrocarburos (3 per cent).

7

TRANSNATIONALIZATION IN LATIN AMERICA

Henri Coing

The reverberations of the privatization of urban services are worldwide and the process of internationalization cannot, by definition, be studied in one country alone, hence the interest afforded by a survey of privatization in the Third World. The focus is necessarily a narrow one on a subject which needs to be situated in context and explicitly related to the crisis in the economy, in urban government and in public policies that is occurring in the countries concerned (Coing, 1988, 1989, 1990, 1991, 1992). Thus the approach is frankly one-sided, if only for the following reason: everywhere in Latin America there is evidence of massive change in the ways in which society assumes responsibility for urban services, and the reorganization of the roles of the social actors concerned raises problems.

Privatization certainly does not provide the key to understanding this change. It is not by a long way the major factor in the picture nor the one giving shape and meaning to what has occurred. Decentralization, for instance, and a substantial transfer of responsibility from central government to local authorities are certainly more significant. The transformation in systems of financing and the distribution of costs between consumers and taxpayers represents another crucial dimension. So an approach to the problem from the angle of privatizations is a dangerously distorted one, though not absurd: the process of privatization is ongoing and developing, and polarizes debate; besides, its effects touch on our present concern since it is a contributing factor in Latin America's becoming further drawn into the process of the internationalizing of the urban services 'industry'.

In Latin America, the scenario displays the following features:

- concentration is taking place, with the emergence of powerful private groups in the field of 'urban engineering';
- vertical integration, with the divide between construction and operation disappearing; and
- diversification, since the actors now proffer a complete portfolio of activities.

Instances abound to show that concentration, vertical integration, diversification and internationalization are pertinent issues for Latin America. Major Western firms are developing strategies for establishing themselves at one and the same time in Europe and in developing countries. Lyonnaise des eaux hold water services concessions in Buenos Aires, China (Shenyang and Tanhzou), Malaysia as well as in the Czech Republic. Conversely, the technological attainment and know-how achieved by public entities and private firms enable some developing countries to compete with their opposite numbers in industrialized countries. SOFRETU, for instance, found itself competing with its offspring, the Santiago Metro Company, in the tender for the privatization of the Buenos Aires metro. The mayor of Curitiba, by exporting bus shelters to New York, managed to sell his model for refuse management to the United States. SAUR is competing with a Tunisian firm for water management in Guinea. Factors of concentration at a national level allow countries to play an active role beyond their frontiers. A private urban transport group in Brazil operating in a number of towns owns 8,000 buses, and this should be seen in connection with the strategy adopted by a German bus construction firm for the whole region.

Does this observable tendency for urban services to become increasingly bound to the world market, and to an emerging scenario of actors who are new in terms of scale of operation, degree of integration and omnipresence, represent anything more than a series of isolated cases, or is it deep-seated? To the best of my knowledge no comprehensive study exists to throw light on the question. I shall concentrate here chiefly on Latin America; an exhaustive description is out of the question, but I can perhaps pick out a number of tendencies and relate them to what is going on in Europe.

A transformation championed from outside

What is occurring in Latin America is the more bound up with trends occurring in Europe in that over recent years doctrines, idealogies and even systems have taken on a global dimension. It is impossible to find a World Bank report on the subject which does not contain an account of the 'French model' for administration, management and leasing, nor cite it as an exemplar for developing countries.

Every day the World Bank grows more insistent on the need to cut back on government interventionism and develop the private sector's role, in particular in financing operating services. In the 1980s, the aim appeared to be erect in place of the 'myth' of the primacy of the public arena a counter-myth whereby the private arena was extolled. It was explained to governments in developing countries that all their ills derived from the state's assuming direct responsibility for public services and that the problems would be solved miraculously by privatization (Roth, 1987). Documents issued in the 1990s are more qualified, but they dwell no less on the need rapidly to develop the private sector's role in urban services management. All reports contain a remark much like the following: 'The central issue confronted here is whether or not a larger role for the private sector can diminish the problem by improving efficiency and coverage in the matter of service' (Bartone et al., 1991, on municipal cleaning services). For its part, the International Finance Corporation published a book by W.C. Baum in 1992, recommended by the World Bank as an element in the campaign to promote environmental issues in developing countries. Thus such countries are directly implicated in the process of creating a world market for urban services, in which they play a not insignificant part.

The obligation to issue international tenders for surveys, public works and operational contracts is a contributory factor in this opening up of markets and process of internationalization. Anything which in a Third World client of the World Bank savours of a 'Buy American' Act and protectionism in regard to a publicly owned urban services market is anathema and its suppression is a necessary condition for the award of a loan. An example is provided by the conflict in Brazil surrounding the urban public transport programmes financed by BIRD. BIRD called for the bus markets to be opened up while Brazil stood by the oligopoly represented by two national coachbuilders; and the conflict resulted in BIRD's suspending payments.

But doubtless the most important factor is to be found in advance of the decisions to open up and has to do with the nature of the regulations enforced in this domain: 'Infrastructures will be more economically efficient and more conducive to development if they are financed by users, insofar as possible, on the basis of economic prices and on users' readiness to pay', which implies mechanisms 'adjusted to the market' and services defined according to demand. And the text here quoted concludes that efforts are combining to 'intensify the urgency there is to seek out means to incorporate the instruments of the market – competition and price-fixing – and engage the interests of the private sector in supplying these services' (World Bank, 1993). This has to be seen in the setting both of the crisis of indebtedness and public finances and of policies for structural realignment: strong pressure for reducing public deficits and subsidiaries, the objective of applying market prices and recovering costs, the further objective of public enterprises being freed from political pressures and becoming independent. In short, a move in favour of the market.

Similarly, in the context of sector borrowing, one is aware of an increasing insistence on 'institutional reinforcement' with the aim of making legal, statutory, institutional and organizational devices conform to this new positioning. In the water sector, for example, this meant the elaboration of a programme at national level in the context of the international decade of the water industry, implying institutional restructuring and reforming of the entire sector. To take the example of Colombia, the InterAmerican Bank brought about the dissolution of INSOPAL, the nationalized enterprise until then responsible for the management of water in small and medium-sized towns, whose combined purpose was to act in place of local authorities, which were considered to be too small and inadequately equipped to take on the service, to ensure the raising of the finance required for investment, and to apply a redistribution of resources at national level. It has been replaced by municipal firms whose aim is to attain self-sufficiency.

Everywhere, with the vigorous backing of multilateral banks, action is developing to increase the recovery of costs: true cost-pricing policies or at least policies that set out to achieve equilibrium; the installation of appliances for such recovery, i.e. water meters. This is noticeable in Argentina, which hitherto followed the practice in the United Kingdom of levying a fixed payment based on property valuation (the generalization of meters is a prime objective in the recent concession); it is noticeable in other countries too where meter installation applied only to a minority of consumers, and in Mexico, where the resort to private enterprise has prioritized the following aim: 'The first stage will include the constitution of an inventory of water users, instalments of meters and of new methods of invoicing' (*Financial Times*, 18 March 1993). Along with the system of recovery, invoicing is being reorganised, and there are a number of plans to stamp out the practice of being illegally connected: for instance, in Argentine (Guigo, 1992) or Columbia (Cuervo, 1992), where a start has been made by publishing in the press the names of those found acting fraudulently. In short, everywhere, beyond – or rather within – the confines of privatization programmes, a policy of market-oriented urban services is coming into being, based on market prices, even when these are not known.

Outside initiative on this scale for market conditions and privatization to be set up would certainly not have been effective but for the existence of a strong current of opinion in favour in each of the countries concerned and, in particular, the decisive crisis affecting the previous model of services management, which had clearly exhausted its possibilities. The same outside initiative also played a significant role in propagating models and solutions as well as in the opening up and internationalization of markets.

Argentina in the steps of Margaret Thatcher's Britain

Only a few countries have embarked on massive privatization programmes in the field that concerns us. By a curious irony of history, Menem's Argentina, heir to that of Juan Perón, who had fought to be rid of British interests, which were present everywhere and especially in public services concessions, has taken up the torch of massive privatization of these same services following a model that is close to Margaret Thatcher's. After privatizing telephones (France Telecom being allocated the network in the north of the country), the production and distribution of electricity in Buenos Aires (the EDF-SAUR consortium receiving half the capital), gas, railways and 10,000 km of toll motorways, the Menem government has recently privatized water distribution and the Buenos Aires metro; plans are in hand for privatizing hydroelectricity production and postal services, and the sale of public entities in the provinces, including water distribution, electricity, roads and ports, is envisaged.

This programme of privatization has allowed massive entry on the part of foreign enterprises. The Soldati group (SCP), which has taken on water distribution, in fact has a 23 per cent stake in a consortium including Lyonnaise des eaux (28.1 per cent), Sociedad general de Aguas de Barcelona (14 per cent), Meller SA (12 per cent), the Banco de Galicia (9 per cent), Générale des eaux (8.9 per cent) and Anglian Water (5 per cent). Foreign companies also play a decisive role in telephones, electricity and gas, as well as in refuse, railways and so on. There are two observations to be made at once. First, the foreign groups involved have all already acquired an international dimension and a presence in many different countries (SLEE, Waste Management, etc.). In the main these are North American, British and French groups, but Spanish ones are there in force and Italian firms are determinedly seeking to break into the markets. Second, these companies have widely differing forms and a number of them are state enterprises (France Telecom, EDF and Iberia among them). Thus the term 'privatization' may well serve to describe the purchase of one state enterprise by another state enterprise representing a third country. 'Public' and 'private' have certainly become highly adaptable terms!

Argentinian firms are also involved. The weekly review *Noticias* proclaimed 'the birth of a national oligarchy; water, electricity, gas, trains, metro roads and oil are in their hands', and continued:

> From now on, the water you use will be supplied by Soldati, the electricity by Pérez Companc or Grüneisen, gas by one or the other of these two; if you go by train, you will have the choice of Roggio or Techint; your telephone bills will go to Pérez Companc, Grüneisen or Techint. If you take the metro, you will have no choice since the system belongs to Roggio.

These are not small firms but groups of substance: Pérez Companc has a turnover of $2 billion dollars, Soldati of $1.3 billion; Techint employs 18,000 people, Macri 15,000.

How have these groups emerged? They comprise the leaders in the field of building and public works, Techint followed by Sade (Pérez Companc) and Roggio. On the other hand, Fortabat, which is dominant in the cement industry, has not managed to find a place

Table 7.1 Principal beneficiary groups of recent Argentinian privatizations

Utility	Pérez Companc	Soldati SCP	Rocca Techint	Roggio	Macri Sideco A.	Grüneisen Astra
Electricity						
production	X	X				
distribution	X		X			X
Gas						
production	X	X				
transport	X	X	X			
distribution	X	X			X	X
Water		X				
Toll roads	X		X	X	X	
Telephone	X	X	X			
Railways						
inter-urban	X	X	X			
urban					X	
metro		X				

for itself in this wave of privatizations. Astra's sources are chiefly in the oil industry, as are Soldati's. But Bridas (Bulgheroni), which is important in gas production has not managed to penetrate either. Macri is first and foremost a large, highly diversified group, but the same is true of several others: Soldati (agribusiness), Pérez Companc (transport), Techint (steel) and so on. None of them is new to the urban services sector. Techint, Roggio and Macri were in refuse; Soldati (SCP), known now as number one in water, once had a name as number one in electricity when it controlled Italo-Argentina de Electricidad, itself taken over only in 1980 by SEGBA, the state enterprise at the same time.

Is there evidence of vertical integration? It requires a much closer analysis of the different groups to be able to give a precise answer to the question. But there are some immediate pointers. First, there is the clear and deliberate coordination between construction and public works activities and the production, transporting and distribution of fluids, or with railways and toll motorways. Techint, Pérez Companc and Roggio, where there is already integration between engineering and construction, provide an illustration of this. There was the same motive at work with Lyonnaise des eaux in France in reconstituting its construction and public works sector shortly after relinquishing it. In announcing the acquisition of the Buenos Aires contract, Jérôme Monod made the point that this type of contract represented 'the absolute justification' of the merger with Dumez: 'We are integrating conception, engineering, construction and commercial capacity' (interviewed in *Le Figaro*, 11 December 1992). And the statement is understandable in view of the fact that the contract called for a network investment of more than $4 billion, the construction of a treatment plant, the renovation over five years of 1,200 km of the network, connecting up a further 2.3 million inhabitants also over five years, with the prospect of this becoming 5 million within the term of the concession. Equally, it is understandable why the number two and number three in construction and public works in Argentina also applied for the tender. There are also instances of the classic alliance between construction and public works, on the one hand, and waste management (Roggio, undertaking refuse collection, with Clima, Cliba, Sur, Ayres and Coslim, or else Techint, with refuse disposal and site improvement, linked to SYUSA).

Other developments in vertical integration include Soldati, for instance, investing in a gas deposit, a gas pipeline, a gas-fired power station and a gas distribution network, and Pérez Companc, too, in the production, transportation and distribution of gas. Soldati's name crops up again in telephones (Telefónica) and, in a larger capacity, in communications in conjunction with Cointel, Produfé, Telefé, Cabtel and Cable Chile.

Thus a body of big, multi-service, private groups has emerged, the firms mentioned above representing the most powerful economic groups in the country. Though they are often minority shareholders in a consortium dominated by a multinational, they seem able to develop their own strategy. Perhaps they will become significant actors on the urban and even international stage.

Various legal forms of privatization

Let us begin with a summary account of two contrasting areas, water and refuse.

Water is the domain *par excellence* of public enterprise, where until recently the private sector played only a minor role. Roth (1987) found evidence only of two small firms operating in Santiago on the fringe of public enterprise. Yet events move fast, as is shown by the concession of the Buenos Aires service and the announcement of other similar privatizations affecting provincial enterprises in Argentina. Caracas has issued an international tender for the management of its network. Mexico City has recently awarded a ten-year concession for water and cleaning services covering a population of 9 million to four consortia (grouping British and French as well as Mexican firms). Water services in Lima have been privatized. In Colombia, following the municipalization of water distribution in small and medium-size towns which had previously been administered centrally, a number of cases of privatization or partial contracting out are under way, and even major cities such as Baranquilla and Bucaramanga are following the trend. So in this respect and in this field, developments in Latin America are no different from those in Africa and Asia.

Refuse is certainly the sphere in which the trend is strongest. One cannot put a figure on all the municipalities affected, which include Bogotá, Santiago (21 out of 23 *municipios*), Buenos Aires and Córdoba, Caracas and most of the larger towns in Venezuela, and so forth. Statistics for Brazil will suffice. According to IBGE (Instituto Brasileiro de Geogonfia e Estatistica), in 1989 only 2.5 per cent of the country's 4,125 municipalities had contracted a service out to private enterprise. And the figure itself is misleading, first because the overall number of municipalities has grown rapidly, from 25 in 1977 to 64 in 1983 and to 116 in 1989, second, because the development particularly affects the major urban areas and largest *municipios*: out of the inner cities in nine metropolitan areas, seven had contracted refuse services out in 1989 (as against three in 1983); third, because this pattern is limited to specific regions, those that are the most wealthy and the most economically dynamic: of the 116 municipalities involved, 52 are in the state of São Paulo, 64 in the south-east and 24 in the south, i.e. 76 per cent of the national total in these two regions.

Together, the private enterprises concerned as yet display little concentration. Ninety-five of the companies identified are active only in one town, ten of them in two, eleven in more than two; the two largest companies each function in ten towns. However, these figures are based on the name of the firm, the only information available, and may well conceal the existence of groups with a number of subsidiaries, each with a different name. Also, since the practice of contracting out has only recently become generalized, firms are to be found with only a reduced scale of operation in the refuse sector, which belong none the less to groups that operate on a large scale: PAVITER, operational in Salvador, is a subsidiary of

OAS, one of the biggest construction and public works groups in Brazil and one which for a long time has been active outside Brazil. It has recently bought up the number one in the sector, VAGA-SOPAVE, with interests in ten cities and three states.

As everywhere else, the term 'privatization' serves to designate very different types of situation, points in a spectrum that ranges from the simple subcontracting of secondary assignments to the state's making over the entire responsibility for a given area. Thus one comes across the whole range of relationship between government and the private sector. Refuse collection is the characteristic sphere of private enterprise contracting, contracts being awarded following tendering at national or international level. What was formerly a public monopoly is not for the most part spatially organized for competition. In the larger municipalities, the territory is assigned into zones and each zone to a different firm; there are four in Caracas, two in the Federal District of Buenos Aires and six in São Paulo. Fairly often, the municipality retains a zone under its direct authority, thus having a point of comparison for performance and costs. Zoning among several operators is also practised in Argentina, as mentioned, for nearly all services including telephone, electricity and gas. In Brazil it is virtually general in regard to urban transport.

Nor is deregulation only subject to zoning. As has the United Kingdom, Argentina has made systematic practice of segmenting services, each one being subject to a different contract and a different firm. With gas and electricity, production, transport and distribution are contracted for separately; the same is the case with refuse, collection being distinct from transfer and dumping in Buenos Aires, São Paulo, Caracas, Santiago and elsewhere, or from treatment (involving disposal, composting, waste-to-energy systems and incineration in Brazil), or frequently also from street-cleaning. As regards water, Argentina has conceded the totality of the service to a single consortium, but in Venezuela the programme planned implies a separation between production and transport, treatment and distribution, with each of these functions being assigned to a different operator. In El Salvador plans for contracting out take into account the phases of production, treatment and supply, and the private enterprise will be remunerated according to the quantity of cubic metres of water treated and sold for public distribution. The patter here is similar to that developed in the United States and Europe, and is based on the principle that different segments of a service represent very different features in regard to the relative importance of capital and labour, technological complexity, external factors, economies of scale, as well as social and institutional variables.

Such segmentation of services is radically opposed to the tradition of public monopolies in Latin America, where the monopoly applied not only to territory but involved the integration within one organization of every stage and division in the process of conception, financing, carrying into effect and operation of a service. It implied management by a single actor. The consequence of segmentation is to introduce a variety of actors into one and the same service, distinct by their form (public or private), by their scale of operation (local or national) and also by their nature, whether they are administrative, entrepreneurial or even non-governmental organizations or consumer associations. The inference is that there is no tradition or experience or mechanism for contractualization, nor any system for coordination between actors and that everything has to be reinvented.

The form of *concession* remains rare except in the transport sphere, though very different in content. Elsewhere, the concept has disappeared. This type of relationship with private enterprise played a predominant role in Latin America at the end of the nineteenth century and during the first half of the twentieth. Most of the networks of water, electricity, telephones and tramways were developed on this model. The British-owned City of Santos Improvements Co., to take but one example, was founded in 1889 to exploit the services of electrical energy, tramways and gas production and distribution under a concession granted by the municipality; in 1893 it took over the water service in addition and retained the concession until 1953. Over the same period, the São Paulo Tramway Light and Power Co., Canadian in origin, provided services for the São Paulo municipality. For the most part, the technology was imported, the capital foreign and the operation too. In Buenos Aires, the Anglo-Argentina, the dominant force in transport, was owned by the SOFINA group, which was made up of British but also Belgian, French and German capital. It is easy to understand how within the entire area concession became identified with the dominant position of European or North American enterprises; the nationalization of public services represented not merely their appropriation by the state but the fact of the nation coming into its own. A generation or so later, an Argentinian writer observed:

The experience was a profitable one and it can be said that, however costly, it was an error that had to be perpetrated, since never again was the government challenged on its right to take charge of these services or to run them.

So one might have considered the concession formula to be conclusively abandoned, yet it had surfaced again, notably for water management in Buenos Aires and even for waste management in Caracas. Private enterprises can be found taking charge not only of the running of urban services but of investment too, and to a certain degree of the risk involved; certainly it is one of the chief political surprises in this sphere.

Leasing, on the other hand, has no tradition in Latin America. Today it has made an appearance, but, as elsewhere, the actual forms of contract are so diversified as to mean there is no watertight division between provision of services, operation and maintenance, delegated management, leasing and concession; a settlement on the basis of the situation is made, concerning the value of existing installations, debt servicing, new investment – involving a renewal or extension of capacity, financial or fiscal amenities granted to the operator, guarantees or subsidies, etc. It is frequently very difficult to muster the body of information required to establish a contract in law. For water especially, one comes up against the same problems here as those described by Dominique Lorrain in the case of France (Lorrain, 1989a), and for transport services (the Buenos Aires metro or recent forms of special track transport in France), where concession goes hand in hand with subsidization (not to mention varied mass-transport projects which have appeared all over the place, furnished with intricate schemes for financing that are as bizarre as they are unreliable), the difficulties are similar. Besides, one often comes across evolving forms of contract, which gradually take on a different substance, whether or not this was provided for at the outset (witness the case of water in Guinea and in Guinea-Bissau and, as it appears, in Caracas and Mexico City), modifying the degree of financial involvement and risk for the firm. Further, in urban transport in Brazil, one finds a growing number of public–private combinations, varying from one municipality to another, which makes it impossible to characterize a contract without looking closely at each case (Henry and Pacheco, 1993).

Formulas of the Build, Own, Operate and Transfer (BOOT) or Build, Own, Operate (BOO) type are uncommon. Cointreau-Levine in his study on waste management (1992), cites only rare instances, in Hong Kong, Indonesia and Argentina, where in fact a composting cooperative is concerned. For water, the few known cases concern Malaysia and Indonesia, not Latin America, at least for the moment. Venezuela is trying to develop the formula in the field of electricity. Everywhere there is evidence that provision of services, sometimes known as peripheral privatization, is multiplying – delegated management, a multitude of forms of subcontracting; in the water sector, for instance, there is meter reading, invoicing, recovery, upkeep and maintenance of networks and meters, public works, but also supervision of public works, and so forth. All this is relatively new, since public enterprises have until recently held on jealously to their monopoly over the whole range of operations the service requires and dropped considerably behind the private sector in partitioning policies. But in the present situation there are two possible courses: to make up lost ground in the matter of partitioning, so bringing about a greater ability to achieve control and strategic development, or to go for stage-by-stage, fragmented contracting out, a creeping process guided by the urgency of problems needing attention and little by little depleting public enterprise of its substance. Recourse to partitioning indeed presupposes a greater potential of strategy and control, not a reduced one, as some appear to think. Hence the most significant privatizations are not always those one imagines them to be.

A cyclical phenomenon, a transition or a new model?

In Latin America, unlike in France, privatization is frequently resorted to in conditions of acute crisis, as an emergency. It might be a 'technical' collapse, as for instance with the refuse service in Caracas, where the scale of the crisis affecting the municipal enterprise responsible led to the creation of a nationalized enterprise, which, when within a few years it itself became crisis-ridden, made over refuse collection to the private sector (Coing and Montano, 1988). Or again, a vicious circle of decapitalization has led to the bankruptcy and disappearance of countless public urban transport enterprises all over the subcontinent. The Latin American model of urban services provision was dominated by the image of the public enterprise, whose mission was to create the infrastructure needed for economic development (within the strategy of becoming less dependent on imports), mobilize financial resources at home and abroad so as to undertake massive investment, and implement both territorially and socially the cross-subsidizing required. Thus it was a fundamentally public and centralized model, one whose financing was largely budgeted for. This model has been overtaken by crisis and seems to have exhausted its potential. Even Brazil, where 'rationalization and modernization' in this sector were highly successful throughout the 1960s and 1970s, saw the backbone of the system for financing urban services, the Banco Nacional de Habitação, collapse and go under at the start of the 1980s with the consequent paralysis of sector-based investment programmes it had fed; such a financial débâcle led to the model's being impugned. From this viewpoint, the crisis in urban services in Latin America is comparable not so much to parallel services in Europe as with the crisis and misgivings over our systems of social security, unemployment insurance and pensions.

One may wonder whether these misgivings, the extent and gravity of which clearly vary considerably from one country to another, will lead simply to the substitution of public enterprise by private enterprise in a concentrated, multi-service, transnationalized form. However, this is a purely notional consideration; the changes occurring are more complex than might appear, which is why a few crucial features need to be dwelt on.

What private sector?

The private sector was already there in the previous model. Urban services in Latin America never developed as isolated, self-sufficient units. The nineteenth-century system of concessions turned them into economic units that were closely integrated with world markets, providing capital, delivery and operation. But later on the existence of large state monopolies depended on relationships that were no less close with suppliers, just as they did in Europe. The close and complex links in France, for example, between the SNCF, RATP, EDF or France Telecom and the manufacturers of equipment are well known. In Latin America few countries evolved a strategy for development across the spectrum of relevant branches, so treating urban services as a springboard for constituting a national industrial sector (Brazil was one of the exceptions here). Consequently, supplier partners were often transnational firms, now directly concerned by the crisis the model has undergone. The effect of this is that their role has to be redefined, as has the role of engineering and of each link in the chain. Thus a new model coupled to the world market is being set up. Will it be of North American, German or French design? Yet these are themselves being redefined under the impact of global competition, in particular from markets that are open to the Third World. Conflicting forces evidently have a role to play; is the systematic opposition of the World Bank to any form of vertical integration likely to influence the global trend? Clearly there is total interdependence between what is happening in France and in Third World countries.

Conversely, within the previous model itself, there had evolved a whole area of private activity ordained to mitigate the inadequacies of the public service, where tiny niches of private service developed by way of substitution, either where markets were solvent (in postal services and telecommunications, and in energy production) or where there was a high population (the well-known so-called 'unofficial sector': trucks delivering water to areas deprived of it, Jeeps supplying a collective transport service in districts out of reach, refuse collectors and salvagers). Are such forms of private initiative likely to move towards being made official as a range of provision on offer according to level of service, so reinforcing the place of small-scale enterprises, or will they disappear, or again will they, as in the past, continually re-emerge in clandestine form to fill the gaps left by official service provision?

What stability?

The chief drawback of a purely ideological debate on privatization is the lack of any historical sense. In disregard of time as it is, it tends to forget that a decision to modify a method of management is not an event to be seen in isolation but a link in a long historical chain, within a process of successive changes over a long period which alone gives it significance. In the previous paragraph we laid stress on the need to relate privatizations occurring in Latin America to the acute crisis of a model that resembled neither that devised by Haussmann in the last century nor the welfare state which it yet took pleasure in emulating. But in fact, for most of the time, management modes have experienced not so much change as a series of transformations amounting to instability. The transport sector, for instance, has gone through a rapid succession of phases ringing the changes on the balance between public and private, monopoly and competition, regulation and deregulation, formal and informal (see above). All these are witness to structural instability in the sense that solutions successively adopted are rapidly undermined by unresolved contradictions, and by the lack of coherent and stable sociopolitical compromise on questions of financing, redistribution and quality of service.

So the question that arises today in respect of privatizations that have occurred is to know whether they are the result of a new and stable form of compromise or whether they are indicative of loss of control, a solution taken *in extremis* and without weighing up all the determining factors; in other words, are they anything other than an episode in a cycle of instability? In the wake of the abolition of the public enterprise, INSFOPAL, some Columbian cities, Santa Marta and Cúcuta among them, experienced a toing and froing between private and public water management. The same has been true for waste management; Salvador de Bahía, for instance, over a period of twenty years has shifted three times between public management and contracting out. In some Mexican cities, water services have been passed successively between very different actors within the public sector, each anxious to be rid of the hot potato.

What can one say now about the stability of the new formulas adopted? Are the mechanisms that led to instability no longer present? Is the change that has taken place simply a stage in a cyclical pattern, is it a transitional phase towards a new model whose outline is not yet clearly perceived, or rather can one point to the foundations of a new and durable model?

The number of solutions already tried out and the diversity of contracts provide an answer. Latin America, as elsewhere, is a laboratory for experimentation, characteristic of a period of transition (which does not rule out the possibility that a single model may emerge eventually); however, the toing and froing one sees puts one in mind not so much of cyclical movement as of a process of apprenticeship through trial and error, with a view to a new allocation of tasks, competence and costs. There is a shift in the traditional opposition between central and local, public and private, just as there is in the institutional arrangements between administrations and consumer-occupiers, or between organizing authority and service providers, whether public or private. It is the very notion of urban public service which is being repudiated and reconstructed, privatization being no more than a figure, a symptom, indeed a stage in an unfolding process. Besides, such redefinitions are tentative and by no means certain to thrive; there has been so much turning back or setting off in a contrary direction, ample evidence that the huge process of restructuring now under way is proceeding by trial and error.

Experience shows that to oversee the contracting out of management requires of a public authority a capability that is different and far harder to draw on than that required by direct management, since it implies a radical change in forms of organization and control. In turn, such capabilities have a role within direct management, thus investing it with a degree of credibility and the proficiency to present itself as an alternative to contracting out. This process of reciprocal transformation and apprenticeship is discernible in several countries and deserves close analysis. Pacheco has observed it in the case of urban transport in Brazil and has shown that all over the country new forms of relationship between local powers and transport firms are coming into being, new types of contract and of remuneration for these firms, and devices to reduce differences in profitability between operators, etc. In the same context new functions are being invented for public enterprises, new methods of regulated competition (Pacheco, 1992). If a metamorphosis has taken place it affects public authorities and private enterprises simultaneously, as well as the forms that regulate their relationships.

It should be added that, for the private sector, instability means risk. Accordingly, it will only commit itself in return for inordinately high compensation or a substantial monopolistic security, and in any event on the basis of highly short-term calculations of profitability. There is ample historical illustration of the shattering effects of such situations; for instance, the processes of accelerated decapitalization observed at the end of a concessionary contract.

A sector-based or transversal vision?

The theme of privatization has long been accompanied by an explicitly sector-based view of urban services, namely that all should conform to the same assumption of being rationalized and made profitable, but each being subjected to a business form of rationalization with the object of producing one service and one alone. A typical example is afforded by the fierce opposition shown by the World Bank to any cross-subsidizing between services, even when they are administered by a single public authority, as is frequently the case in Colombia or in Germany. Links that exist between urban services should conform to the market, and the link between infrastructure services and overall urban management is of secondary importance. Yet over recent years it seems that a more integrated vision is developing in the World Bank itself, one which emphasizes the decisive role cities play in economic development and the strategic importance of urban infrastructure to such development; their quantitative deficiencies, their inadequacy in the face of demand, are obstacles to development. This argues for a reform of ineffectual regulations, a reinforcement of local powers and their finances and the modernization of public enterprises and their administration. But that implies, to the same extent, taking an overall view of these infrastructures - 'an interrelated set of infrastructure services, the complex of infrastructure services in the context of overall strategy' (World Bank, 1993, p.3). Such a step leads directly to an emphasis of the importance of regulations which ensure that decisions are meaningful in space and time, hence the crucial role of government in the planning and mobilization of the financial resources necessary. The logical conclusion is that 'the institutional arrangements appropriate for infrastructures will be far more diverse than either the traditional public monopoly or the free market model' (ibid.). In practice, we are still a long way from this cross-sector vision of urban services (Coing and Henry, 1990) but it is certain that this question will bear heavily on the development of modes of management in the future.

The term 'strategy', applied to urban services, signifies that the cross-sector and the sector-based, the long-term and the short-term, are no longer seen in opposition to one another but in combination. Certainly in the nineteenth century these were the questions that the policy of concessions came up against, in particular in the area of water, as much in Europe as the United States, and the recurring conflicts to do with the rate of investment, anticipation of needs and pricing regime led to a decline in management contracted out. It was no different in Latin America, since for example the Buenos Aires water concession, granted for a duration of forty-five years in 1888, had to be rescinded three years later (in return for 25.5

million gold pesos in compensation!). At the time the concession represented a transition towards direct management, because of its inability to take account of the long-term and cross-sector dimensions. The history of public transport concessions in Latin America has not produced a satisfactory answer to the question; that is all that can be said.

Urban management, social management

The solvency of the population will play a crucial role in future developments. In Mexico City the zone entrusted to the consortium led by Lyonnaise des eaux represents 2.3 million inhabitants and to date has only 330,000 registered customers. Even allowing for a large number of corporate customers, the question of the generalization of the network is crucial, with the likelihood of its having to face the insolvency of a portion of the population. In Buenos Aires the venture embarked on is to reverse the tendency for the level of cover to show a constant fall; indeed, the targets set aim to raise cover from 55 per cent at present to 100 per cent in thirty years' time, gaining twenty points in the first five years. To suggest simply that poor public management was responsible for such a state of affairs and that sound private management will see a turn-round is manifestly absurd. The fundamental problem is a political one even in its purely management aspects. Unquestionably, sizeable margins for manoeuvre can be recovered to the extent that solvent consumers can be made to pay, consumers who frequently and unfairly escape the costs they incur because of inefficient pricing policies, failure to follow up non-payment, illegal connecting or the entrenched system represented by the concentration of public investment in 'legal' areas of urbanization. But this cannot all be simply reduced to a problem of 'management'; it has to do with politics, and contracting out, even the concession of services, is no guarantee at all that things will be different. The manner in which the privatized transport services in Brazil are responding to the crisis by falling back on profitable segments in the market, cutting back on services for sections of the population who are insolvent and withholding investment is evidence of this (a vicious circle for the firms concerned, a vicious circle for the users, Pacheco calls it).

Likewise, much of the manifest problem of service exclusion originates upstream of services, in the control of urbanization and the development of so-called spontaneous settlement, which the enterprise handling services comes across subsequently as an obstacle it cannot cope with single-handed. Yet, within the frame of contracting services out, there is no reason at all why a dualist approach should not be pressed, profitable areas being left to private enterprises and 'problem' ones being subject to social compensation policies or being provided by other means with low-cost, low-level services in order to make up the leeway. Privatization may try to evade the problems but they will soon return; social and political pressures, or quite simply rioting, will soon bring back earlier practices. Whatever mode of management is favoured, none will stop those who live in the slum quarters of Lima from staging a demonstration in front of the presidential palace to demand water. And the history of urban transport in Latin America precisely illustrates the way in which the scope afforded by concession-granting enables the formula to be adapted for this type of situation, by developing a form of interplay between government, private enterprise and consumer which is radically different from what economic theory appears to suggest.

Discourse on services management remains silent on the subject of urban conflict and works on the assumption of its always being possible to establish a basis of trust between supplier and consumer. But inhabitants have too long a history of unkept promises and specious arguments for the lack of public action and the unequal distribution of investment to be justified. Their root experience is that of being cheated. Behind the question of trust, necessary in any business relationship, there is, ineluctably, the question of legitimacy, which is of essence political.[1]

Hence, the task of totally redefining the objectives, the means and the roles of every actor in the services sector is one that cannot be avoided; the facile alternatives of public and private, commercial or non-commercial, management centralized or decentralized, offer no solution. Otherwise, current management changes will be merely episodic, a prelude to new upheavals. One may also turn the question round and speculate whether privatization is not itself an effect of the breakdown of earlier compromises, which, having already come to grief, make any thought of retreat impossible.

Note

1. The catalogue of political struggle for physical or financial access to urban services is virtually endless, whether for water (Peru, Brazil, Mexico), transport or whatever. So much so that one has to look on such struggle as one of the more effective means of regulating the previous model. How would it be with a model based on contracting out? At a time when sophisticated instruments for regulation are being devised, one would do well to remember this one and its habit of appearing, uninvited.

8

LOCAL SERVICES IN POLAND IN THE WAKE OF PUBLIC PROVISION

Pawel Swianiewicz

The democratization of the political system and the transition from a command to a market economy constitute the two most important elements in the reforms undertaken in Eastern Europe at the start of the 1990s.

Some authors (e.g. Clark and Wildavsky, 1990) claim that these two items are interrelated – that democracy cannot perform effectively in a non-market environment. Under the communist regime, the economy was dominated by large, inefficient, state-owned companies. The public sector's share of the economy was not as large in Poland as in other countries of the region (see Table 8.1) since a large part of agriculture as well as some retail trade and some craft industry still remained in private hands. In 1985 more than 75 per cent of agricultural land belonged to private farms, and about 5.4 per cent of employees in non-agricultural sectors worked in private firms.[1] But the economy was generally dominated by the public sector.

When the present reforms in Eastern Europe are analysed, marketization and privatization are sometimes treated as synonyms. The Polish case suggests this is an over-simplification. Until the beginning of 1990 even existing private firms operated in a highly monopolized, non-market and non-competitive environment. In particular, such private firms operated in the framework of an economy whose growth was limited by the shortages of materials, workers, etc., not by consumer demand (Kornai, 1980). This fact has had important psychological implications for the behaviour of

Table 8.1   The share of the public sector under various communist regimes: international comparison

Country	Year	Share of public sector
Bulgaria	1970	99.7
Czechoslovakia	1988	99.3
East Germany	1988	96.4
Hungary	1988	92.9
POLAND	1988	81.2
Romania	1980	95.5
Yugoslavia	1987	86.5

Source: Kornai (1992).

'old' private firms in a time of economic transition. Shock therapy was not much less shocking for them than for the public-sector companies.

Demonopolization and privatization of the major part of the economy are among the most important strategies for reform in East European countries. Balcerowicz (1992), main author of the Polish economic reform, and deputy prime minister in 1989–91, assumed that the goal of reforms should be a Polish economy characterized by a dominant private sector, competition (not monopoly), openness to international trade, a strong and convertible currency, and a state which does not limit entrepreneurship by bureaucratic regulations but secures stable conditions for economic activity; at the same time one strong enough to resist lobbying by different pressure groups.

Changes in the local government system, and in the organization of urban services in particular, are closely interrelated with these more general changes in the national economy (Iwanek, 1992; Nejman, 1992a). Reform of local government is usually seen as less important than changes in industry or in large state-owned companies, but taking into account the fact that services provided on a local level affect most of everyday life, municipal reform may be more crucial than is commonly realized. It is also worth stressing that Balcerowicz mentions local government reform as being among the most important institutional changes leading to the creation of the new economic system in the country.

Privatization of the Polish economy in the 1990s

Iwanek (1992) summarizes different methods used in the Polish strategy to privatize state-owned enterprises as falling into three basic categories:

- transformation into state-owned corporations followed by sale of their stock to the general public;
- liquidation in order to be sold off wholly or in part; and
- leasing in whole or in part to partnerships with the option to purchase after some time (partnership of employees usually preferred).

Another important element of the reform is so-called mass privatization, an idea based on offering a share in ownership of a group of six hundred privatized enterprises to every adult citizen, the enterprises being managed by specially created investment funds. This programme became a hotly debated political issue; final approval was given by Parliament in April 1993 by a very narrow majority. Janusz Lewandowski, Minister for Property Transfers, called privatization in Poland 'the sale of enterprises that no one owns, and whose value no one knows, to buyers who have no money'. This remark illustrates three basic problems:

- *Unclear property rights.* It would be enough to mention complications relating to claims by former (pre-war) owners who now want to get back their property, or who at least claim that they should be compensated for the loss. But the situation is further complicated by the re-creation of communal property and the process of division of public property between the state and the municipalities. A lack of decision here concerning the legal status of claims of former owners is one of the major obstacles to the speeding up of privatization.
- *The unknown values of factories, and also of land and buildings.* In such circumstances authorities responsible for selling property may be subject to the accusation of selling off national property and of corruption, or, alternatively, of blocking privatization by demanding too high a price.
- *A capital market too restricted for the private sector to invest in and buy state-owned companies.* Foreign investments may sometimes be a good solution but foreign capital is not always interested in investing in Polish companies with outdated

technology and uncertain markets for their products; also, there are numerous examples of threats of potential foreign domination of the Polish economy. The weakness of Polish capital may be illustrated by the fact that out of more than fifty medium and large-sized enterprises sold during the last three years, Polish private investors bought only six companies (Boczyński, 1993). On the other hand, foreign investments in privatization include more than $1 billion by Fiat, $300 million by Lucchini (also Italian) in the steel industry and $120 million by the American company IPC.

Another significant barrier to privatization is the decreasing support of public opinion. The inefficiency of the communist economies in Eastern Europe produced an enormous number of arguments for private ownership in the economy and it is not surprising that privatization easily attracted popular support at the beginning of reform. But increasing difficulties relating to the economic transition (principally high unemployment) and disillusionment regarding a quick end to the crisis threw light on the shortcomings of a pure market system and strengthened pressure to slow down the pace of change and to maintain existing state-owned enterprises. At the beginning of 1990 support for the reform was almost universal. But according to the CBOS public opinion research agency, by 1991 privatization was supported by only 65 per cent of Polish citizens whereas 30 per cent were rather against it; by 1992 the number of supporters had decreased still further to 55 per cent and the number of opponents had increased to 42 per cent.[2]

Despite all these difficulties, the past three years have brought a dramatic change in the ownership structure of the Polish economy. Part of this change has been due to the privatization of state-owned companies, but a large part is due to the creation and development of new private firms. The proportion of the private sector in the national product increased almost threefold between 1985 and 1992 and, according to a survey in *The Economist* (13–19 March 1993), is the highest among reforming East European economies. More than twenty share-holding companies are quoted on the stock exchange established in Warsaw two years ago as the first such institution in the region. The role of the private sector in the Polish economy in 1992 is illustrated in Table 8.2.

Table 8.2   Share of the private sector in different branches
of the Polish economy (1992)

	Share in production	Share in employment
Agriculture	79.9%	n/a
Industry	31.0%	41.4%
Building	77.7%	71.8%
Transport	39.3%	23.1%
Retail trade	n/a	90.5%

Sources: agriculture: *Mały rocznik statystyczny*, GUS, 1992; other data: *Polityka – prywatyzacja*, March 1993. Figures for agriculture are from 1991.

Urban services before 1990

Under the communist regime local services were delivered by state enterprises. They were called 'communal' (*przedsiebiorstwa komunalne*), but communal (municipal) property separate from that of the state did not exist and local authorities' discretion to decide about the structure of these firms or to change the fees for services was almost nil. The aim of local government was to provide services in accordance with strict rules as defined by central regulations. At the end of the 1980s there were about eight hundred such enterprises, employing over 160,000 people. More than 70 per cent of them (usually in medium-sized and small towns) were organized as multi-branch firms providing a wide range of services from public transport to the maintenance of communal housing, street-cleaning, gas supply. In the larger cities different services were usually provided by separate firms. Municipal enterprises often served areas bigger than one city. Such a situation was most frequent in the case of local transportation (40 per cent of them served more than one municipality), and water supply firms (27 per cent of them) (Aziewicz, 1993). An extreme case was that of a company providing water and sewage for forty municipalities. Under the highly centralized system it was not necessary to specify the financial responsibility nor the role in decision-making of individual local governments in regard to the area served. But this ill-defined relationship led to problems, such as bargaining between neighbouring municipalities, when local government reform started in 1990.

The old system was very ineffective and costly, heavily subsidized and wasteful in energy and materials. Kornai (1992) describes the 'causal chain' of the system: the undivided power of the Marxist–Leninist party and the dominant influence of idealogy through preponderant state and quasi-state ownership, bureaucracy, and other distinctive features of a command economy, including informal bargains and soft budget constraint, leading to inefficiency and chronic shortages. More specific factors concerning urban services include the bureaucratic formula of profit calculation based on costs of services (that is, the more costly the service provision, the higher the firm's profit), extremely limited powers on the part of local government in regard to costs and quality of service delivery, and failure to pursue non-payment of charges (in practice, it was frequently easier to demand more subsidies than to improve debt collection).

What the system delivered was of a poor quality. The nature of urban services makes it difficult to provide quantitative arguments to support this thesis, but it is possible to give examples. During rush-hours trams and buses were usually overcrowded. In larger cities (including Warsaw) it was dangerous to drink unboiled tap-water. In 1980, 55 per cent and in 1990 44 per cent of towns had no sewage treatment plant at all. Moreover, only 25 per cent in 1980 (36 per cent in 1990) had anything more than primitive, mechanical sewage treatment. In fact, many local services were not provided by most rural municipalities and even several smaller towns. They did not provide water, nor collect waste, nor was there any local public transport. Energy was supplied by a company that was independent of local government and covered several municipalities. In most places there were frequent power failures because of the lack of money needed to maintain existing infrastructure and undertake essential investment.

Privatization as a form of change after 1990

Changes in urban services became possible when political and economic reform started in 1989–90. Besides general changes in the economic system, local government reform was also of great importance. In March 1990, a new Local Government Act was voted in by the Polish Parliament, followed by free local elections a few months later. The reform changed the status of local government from that of agent of central government to independent actor on the political scene. This is not to imply that reform was introduced smoothly and without conflict, but, despite much opposition on the part of local leaders, it is clear that the power of municipal government has been substantially increased. In particular, the new Act created municipal property, set up a municipal budget separate from the state budget and allowed much more discretion to manage and organize municipal affairs.

Article 7 of the Local Government Act says that 'municipal tasks include satisfaction of the collective needs of the community'. In particular, the Act lays down the following areas in regard to urban services: local roads, streets, bridges and traffic organization; public utilities such as water supply, collection and treatment of sewage, refuse tips, and supply of electricity and heating; local public transport; welfare, including health care; municipal housing; education, including primary and nursery schools; culture, including public libraries; municipal parks and wooded areas; public order; and fire prevention. However, the Local Government Act does not state which functions are mandatory. As mentioned before, many small municipalities do not perform most of these functions in practice.

After local government reform, which created 'municipal property', most of the enterprises responsible for the provision of services came under municipal ownership. Municipalities have considerable discretion to decide the organizational form of service delivery and, in the case of some functions, freedom to determine fees or charges.

Taking into account the demand for change as well as contacts made with municipalities in Western Europe, it is not surprising that partial privatization has frequently been seen as a remedy for the inefficiency of existing enterprises. In addition, there are the large and still increasing subsidies necessary to keep at least a minimal level of service provision. General promises of privatization were given in the local election campaign of May 1990, and a survey conducted one year later among 246 mayors of Polish municipalities confirmed broad support for the privatization of local services.[3] In general, local leaders classified local services into three groups:

- to be privatized almost entirely: restaurants, the retail trade, small industrial enterprises, small agricultural firms;

- to be partially privatized: housing, public utilities (sewage treatment, waste disposal, etc.), children's day care services, health service, culture, urban transport
- to remain mostly under public ownership: schools, services for the elderly, fire brigades.

But shortly after the election it became clear that broad plans for privatization were very difficult to implement. Organizational and legal problems, difficulties in finding a potential private provider, fear of rapid and uncertain changes, and frequent opposition on the part of workers employed in existing public firms quickly tempered idealistic programmes.

None of the four post-communist governments took a clear position concerning the provision of local services (unlike, for example, the Conservative government in the United Kingdom in the 1980s) but they seemed to be in favour of privatization reforms. Restructuring of communal enterprises (which have normally provided local services) became an obligation upon local authorities in Poland, and a decision on the future legal form of such enterprises was due by 1994. Local governments also have a fiscal incentive to change the 'old' structure of enterprises, change of legal status providing an opportunity to avoid a high tax on wages and salaries (*podatek od ponadnormatywnych wynagrodzeń*) and until 1992 also to avoid business tax (*podatek dochodowy od osób prawnych*) on enterprises. But on the other hand, some regulations slow down the process of privatization. For example, local governments are allowed to sell municipal flats to the tenants at a price lower than the market value.

The emergence of new firms in urban services is limited to certain branches, being almost non-existent in the case of most public utilities which are 'natural monopolies'. However, in refuse collection the Long Frank Company has won part of the market in Warsaw and its suburbs, and some private firms are running local transport services (especially services operating between the suburbs and centre of large cities). The methods favoured are contracting out or, more frequently, franchising.

Services linked to areas of natural monopoly, such as public utilities in water, gas supply and sewage treatment, present a separate case. The privatization of such services meets resistance, sometimes unorthodox, on the part of old monopolies which try to restrict their profits when the city attempts to separate and contract out some less complicated parts of the service. A report by the Polish Committee to Prevent Monopolistic Practices (Komitet Zapobiegania Praktykom Monopolistycznym) highlights a city which decided to contract out street-lighting maintenance.[4] Previously it had been the responsibility of an electrical company supplying the whole city. Despite the fact that the contract was signed and maintenance was being provided by the private firm, the monopoly still included a fee for the upkeep of street-lighting in its electricity charges.

Changes in existing municipal firms provide the subject of a report prepared in May–August 1992 by the Institute of Market Economy Analysis and Cooperation Fund (Aziewicz, 1993).[5] In 1992 multi-branch firms predominated in towns of population under 20,000, which single-branch firms operated more frequently in those whose population is more than 50,000 (Table 8.3).

Table 8.3 Distribution of single-branch and multi-branch municipal firms according to the size of municipality

Type of firm	Percentage of firms in towns with population:		
	under 20,000	20,000–50,000	over 50,000
Single-branch	4	9	19
Multi-branch	37	17	13
Total	41	26	32

Source: Aziewicz (1993).

Regarding the number of employees in single-branch firms, the largest branches are local public transportation (44 per cent of employees), municipal housing (21 per cent), water supply and sewerage (15 per cent), heating (12 per cent). As mentioned above, the restructuring of municipal enterprises is not incumbent upon Polish municipalities. Action taken in this area can be classified as follows:

• No changes so far introduced.
• Existing enterprise divided into two or more smaller firms, since it has frequently been objected that multi-branch firms or firms serving a large area are difficult to control. Division is seen as a method of increasing a firm's effectiveness through easier management, of bringing a clearer relationship between costs and effects, and of reducing bureaucracy. Sometimes the

process of division affected single-branch companies too; for example, in communal housing a unit seeing to major repairs has been separated from a unit focused on day-to-day maintenance. The relative popularity of this approach (at least in theoretical discussions taking place in Poland) suggests considerable influence of British and American experiences in organizing local services. It has also been frequently suggested that the division into smaller, better-focused units may be treated as a first step towards privatization.

- Enterprise transformed into an in-house department (*zakład budżetowy*); such a form of transformation is relatively simple and gives local government the possibility of stricter control over local services, itself an economic reason for this choice. But usually the deciding factor has been political: wage demands on the part of employees. The 'in-house department' option contains the tax advantages already mentioned (exemption from wage tax and, until the end of 1992, from business tax), consequently funds are usually available for more increases. The main argument against this option is that it lacks a mechanism for regenerating capital stock in the long term.

- Municipal enterprise liquidated and privatization process started (*prywatyzacja przez likwidację*). *The most frequent means of privatization is to create a company in which a large proportion of shares is owned by the previous employees; selling the whole firm to a single private investor is another, less frequent option.*

- Local authorities setting up companies owned by the municipality (*jednoosobowa spółka gminy*). Authors of legal regulations relating to this option assumed it would be a tentative form of privatization. However, studies undertaken (Aziewicz, 1993) suggest that municipalities usually find such companies more convenient and practical than the traditional system of provision.

Figures given in Table 8.4 show that, for all the expression of opinion in favour of privatization, progress towards this end has been slow. The process has begun in 14 per cent of municipal firms – most often, those responsible for street repairs (33 per cent) and municipal parts (33 per cent); less frequently, in public transport (5 per cent). It is interesting to observe what has happened with firms which have been divided into smaller units. More than 20 per cent

Table 8.4 Changes in different branches of municipal enterprises (July 1992)

Type of enterprise	No change	division of existing firm	Percentage of firms transformed into		
			in-house department	privatization through liquidation	companies owned by municipality
Local transport	22	3	67	5	2
Water supply, sewage	37	6	37	21	0
Municipal housing	32	6	47	13	2
Street repairs and maintenance	33	0	17	33	17
City parks	56	0	11	33	0
Heating	47	5	21	14	14
Street cleaning and waste collection	31	0	38	25	6
Single-branch firms (total number)	34	5	39	17	4
Multi-branch firms (total number)	28	13	43	13	4
Total	30	11	41	14	4

of them (15 per cent of divided single-branch and 30 per cent of divided multi-branch firms) have undergone privatization, which supports the thesis that the aim of privatization underlay the creation of small units.

Certainly each situation is different, just as each municipality is different. In rural areas there are usually no enterprises providing local services, so there is nothing to privatize. In larger cities, the problem is more complex and any change requires longer and more careful preparation. Medium-sized towns probably lend themselves more easily to reform, although this depends on the political options of local authorities, on the entrepreneurial spirit of local political leaders as well as on local circumstances. A good example is provided by Zduńska Wola (population 45,000, located in central Poland), which decided to privatize four out of five municipal enterprises (the exception was the one responsible for street cleaning and waste disposal). The method usually adopted was leasing to companies established by employees, a strategy much used by Polish municipalities.

Demand for change, the need for substantial investment and the very limited financial resources of both local governments and other potential local investors have created a favourable environment for large foreign companies. On the other hand, strict government regulations concerning fees for services and a not always positive attitude in public opinion (suspicion of 'foreign domination') make the situation less attractive for potential outside investors. In fact, the only well-known example of such international cooperation is the Gdańsk water supply. The Gdańsk municipality accepted an offer made by a big French firm (Saur, in the Bouygues group) and created a company in which the French partner has 51 per cent and the municipality 49 per cent of the shares. However, the agreement stipulated that the price of water would be decided by local government. As might be supposed, such change was criticized by the opposition in the council, who attacked the decision as illegal and also accused mayor and municipality of being bribed, and even called for an inquiry by the public prosecutor. Over the first few months wages did not change; some organizational changes in management were introduced but it is too early for a more comprehensive evaluation of the new company.

Housing

In 1990 about 18 per cent of the Polish population lived in municipal housing. This number has decreased systematically during the past thirty years (in 1968 the figure was 22 per cent, in 1984 20 per cent) because of the very limited number of new apartments built by local authorities. During the 1980s municipal flats constituted only about 2 per cent of newly built housing stock. Municipal housing is certainly more important in urban than in rural areas. In the former, municipal apartments provide housing for 30 per cent of the population but in the latter for only 3 per cent.

In discussing local housing policies we must keep in mind the severe housing crisis, which is perhaps the most important social problem in Poland. The number of new apartments has been decreasing for many years. A large number of young families do not have their own flat. In Warsaw (as in other big cities) the market price per square metre exceeds $600 while average monthly salaries are only about $250. At the same time, because of high inflation and high interest rates, mortgages are not readily available. This situation, which is a greater problem in larger towns, calls for action on the part of municipalities. On the one hand, it is obvious that an improvement in housing conditions should be among urban priorities; on the other hand, it is a great temptation to increase local budget revenue through selling apartments.

In such circumstances one may suppose that housing policies are at the top of local political agendas and that every decision in this field is highly visible. There is scope for privatization in municipal housing either in maintenance of existing stock or in selling apartments to the tenants.

As regards the first category, maintenance of existing stock, figures presented in the previous section suggest that most mayors would prefer some forms of privatization, but only 13 per cent of municipalities have started this process. The reform of communal enterprises in public housing is especially difficult and complicated. Moreover, local politicians have to consider employees in these enterprises, who are frequently against such rapid changes. Whatever its form, the main goal of privatization is the reduction of costs spent on maintenance (spending on public housing eats up a large proportion of the budget in some big towns) and a better quality of service.

As regards the sale of municipal housing, we need to distinguish between two kinds of flats: those built by the state after 1945, and those built before 1945 by private owners and nationalized after World War II. In the latter category most former owners want reprivatization, but, owing to the delay in arriving at a decision, a large proportion of this stock is 'frozen'; it is impossible to sell these flats to the tenants, and local authorities are unwilling to spend money on major repairs.

Government regulations determine rents and fees paid for water or central heating in municipal flats. Rents and some fees are below cost, so municipalities are forced to subsidize municipal housing. On the other hand, rents have been raised considerably during the past few years and there are increasing problems with collecting rents from poorer tenants. In such circumstances readiness to sell a large part of the stock is not surprising. But, unlike in the case of recent privatization of housing in the United Kingdom, legal regulations are slowing down this process. Significantly, following several conflicts between state administration and local governments, a court has decided that municipalities are not allowed to sell apartments to tenants at a discount; that is, at less than the market value of the flat.

Conflict between municipalities and the state administration, which supervises local government activity, began when the decision to sell some flats was declared invalid because 'there was not law allowing the price of public property to be reduced'. Municipal authorities argued that there was no law forbidding such a solution and that public interest was not threatened because it was difficult to talk about loss with public housing in deficit and highly subsidized by the municipal budget (Nasierowska, 1992). But the court was of the same opinion as the state administration and its decision invalidated privatization programmes in many cities. As a consequence the number of sales is relatively low, an extreme example being provided by Warsaw, where the new local authorities sold only about three hundred apartments. Be that as it may, local politicians and specialists are not agreed on the question. Those who support quick privatization are sometimes accused of squandering public assets, even of corruption. It is also objected that selling municipal flats may result in a situation in which the only public tenants would be those living on welfare, hence that housing stock owned by municipalities would be in very bad shape. Proponents of privatization maintain that the present situation may lead to the physical deterioration of an even larger part of the stock because of lack of money for necessary repairs. Opponents are described by them as conservatives who do not understand the market economy and block the reform (Majewski, 1992).

The full range of different policies may be found in decisions concerning municipal flats which are at present unoccupied. Options differ from distributing (freely or almost freely) apartments among families with very poor housing conditions to selling them by auction to those who can pay the most. Differences and conflicts between options are sometimes seen inside the same municipality. A good example is provided by the case of Świnoujście (Nejman, 1992b), a small port on the Baltic. The vigorous entrepreneurial and pro-privatization policy of the municipality is contested by local labour unions and some influential citizens, who call for greater attention to be given to redistributive policies. The mayor's reply is that his activity is focused on development because otherwise the cake to be divided would shrink and from a long-term perspective even more serious cuts in redistributive programmes would be inevitable. The conflict became very sharp in the autumn of 1992, when the municipality decided to auction apartments left in the city by the departing Soviet troops. Opponents argued that these apartments should be freely allocated to those in poor housing.

Local transport

The problem of an extremely ineffective monopolized local transport system concerns all urban municipalities and numerous rural communes surrounding the bigger cities. Local transport is one of the services which, according to a majority of Polish mayors, should be 'left to market forces', but Table 8.4 indicates that privatization has been implemented in only 5 per cent of existing firms. Changes to public transport, especially in big cities, are very difficult and much slower than some optimists supposed. One of the factors is that radical restructuring is frequently opposed by employees in monopolies, who at the same time insist on a wage increase, witness the urban transport strikes in 1991.

A strategy much used by big cities has been to demand a share in subsidies from small surrounding municipalities. The city buses have usually served the surrounding areas but under the previous system transport companies were financed by the central municipality. This new financial demand caused local authorities in small towns or rural areas to scrutinize the effectiveness of the old monopolies, and some municipalities decided to organize their own local transportation service. Transport in municipalities surrounding large cities is relatively simple: the system is not dense, the main passenger flows are known, and profitability is highly probable. These are the reasons why privatization of local transport, usually in the form of contracting out, frequently began in this type of municipality. The solution has been adopted in many municipalities surrounding Warsaw, but also around other big cities. In Zgierz (a small town close to Łódź, the second biggest city in Poland), the local government claims that it pays only $13,000 monthly to a private contractor instead of the $30,000 paid previously to the transport monopoly in Łódź; moreover, the private firm employs a hundred local citizens and pays taxes to the local budget (Łodwig, 1992). A similar solution has been adopted by three municipalities to the east of Warsaw which have cooperated to organize their own public transport as a response to excessive demands on the part of the Warsaw monopoly. In 1991 each of these municipalities spent $70,000 (in the form of credit for a private firm) instead of $260,000 demanded by the Warsaw company (Swianiewicz, 1991a).

Evaluation of the first year of the new firms' operation is rather positive, and the long and dramatic strikes of public transport in some Polish cities have been an additional argument for reform.

But the picture is by no means always perfect. Some of the initial assumptions have appeared too optimistic. In the example cited above, first, it has not been possible to keep fares very cheap, and now the private firm's tickets are slightly more expensive than those in Warsaw. But councillors think that this is compensated for by better and longer private bus routes. Micro-buses take citizens almost to the centre of Warsaw while the Warsaw buses went only to the outskirts, where a transfer was necessary. Second, there are no reduced fares for children, pensioners, etc. Third, there are problems with the weekend and evening services, which are not profitable. A form of subsidy as well as frequency of service has been the subject of negotiation with the private contractor. Sometimes competitive tendering has been tried as a form of pressure on monopolistic enterprise so as to reduce costs (Swianiewicz, 1991b).

Certainly the situation in big cities is much more complicated.

Rapid, unprepared changes might well lead to chaos. In Warsaw plans to reform public transportation have been prepared by a British firm, Drawlane Consultants Europe Ltd, which is proposing privatization, be implemented very slowly and carefully over the next few years. The immediate reaction by the labour unions was a strike by bus drivers in May 1993, protesting against plans leading to some reductions in jobs.

Is privatization the future of local services in Poland?

Changes in local services are not at the top of the current political agenda. Discussions are usually limited to specialists and local politicians, whereas public opinion is concerned with the more general problems of economic and political transition. Even this limited debate is very seldom based on any hard analysis of the real effects of implemented changes. The report prepared by the Institute of Market Economics (Aziewicz, 1993) is probably the first attempt to analyse the process of change in local services in a detailed way, but it represents only a first impression, not deep, indispensable analysis. Discussions (and also decisions) are based instead on an ideological assumption – for example, that private ownership is by definition better than public – or on a borrowed analysis of Western experiences.

The best known are the British and American experiences of privatization. Experts connected with the Liberal-Democratic Congress (the part led by one of the post-communist prime ministers, Bielecki) often quote papers and books published by Savas.[6] Privatization is frequently related to the breakup of large, ineffective municipal enterprises into smaller, independent parts. The long-term aim of many theorists, and also some local politicians, is that the Polish model of privatization of urban services should be similar to that implemented in the United Kingdom in the Thatcher era.

In general, it is possible to identify the main forces leading to privatization as:

- Theoretical or sometimes ideological debate. These were more influential at the beginning of economic and political transition, having lost their impetus in view of the growing disappointment at the results of reform.
- Budgetary pressure. Local governments are looking for a way to

reduce the pressure on public spending relating to the maintenance of existing stock. Privatization is frequently seen as one possible solution.

- Demand. The very low standard of some services – water, for example – coexists with a lack of resources to finance necessary investment. Cooperation with the private sector, especially with a foreign company, may be seen as a strategy for coping with this problem.

- Ambitions of managerial staff. It is difficult to quantify this factor but some case-studies suggest that former directors of municipal enterprises who expected to retain an important position in a privatized firm have sometimes been proponents of change.

As against these, there are forces slowing down the process of privatization. One of the most important is the mistrust of public employees and unions. Furthermore, local politicians and administrative staff are not skilled enough to organize a transfer of ownership and are not trained to manage the complex relationship between consumer, local government and private provider of services. There is also a political aspect to the problem: some local governments are afraid of losing control over services after privatization.

There exists a gap between campaign declarations by local politicians in support of privatization and real, implemented reforms. Since most of the changes take the form of 'in-house services', the role of local government as direct provider of services has grown. Many municipalities insist that this form of closer control is no more than a tentative solution and that further forms of change from actually 'delivering' to 'organizing' delivery of services (through a system of contracts, incentives and control) are still being considered. It is too early, however, to decide how reliable these declarations are. Almost certainly, in many municipalities, commitment to privatization will remain verbal. It is difficult to say that privatization represents the future for local services in the majority of municipalities, but there is no doubt that the future will be much more diversified than the past. Instead of one – centrally implemented – model, we shall witness many different solutions in different places.

Two possibilities may be envisaged: a 'liberal' option with more attention to privatization, and enabling private-sector development; and a 'social democratic' one, with more focus on public-sector activity. However, observations suggest that the same governments which are the most active in privatization are also the most active in expanding and innovating municipal sector activity (Kowalczyk and Swianiewicz, 1991). Rather than these two 'classical' options we may distinguish two other types of local authority: 'active' and 'passive'. The former one would be active in both privatization and its own economic activity while the latter usually passive in 'enabling' as well as in 'providing'. Similar conclusions may be drawn from analysis of ownership changes in municipal enterprises (Aziewicz, 1993). In general, municipalities may be divided into two groups: those which have not introduced any changes in organization of urban services and those which have started different reforms (including those which have privatized enterprises but also those which have transformed them into in-house departments, companies owned by the municipality, etc.). A further study would be needed to explain why some local governments adopt a 'passive' and others an 'active' solution, but, tentatively, it is possible to formulate the hypothesis that political, cultural and economic factors are of some importance. The smallest proportion (20–25 per cent) of 'unreformed' enterprises may be found in Galicia (south-eastern Poland) and, especially, Wielkopolska (mid-western Poland) – two regions with relatively strong traditions of self-government. The largest proportion (more than 60 per cent) we find in regions close to the eastern border (the so-called 'Eastern Wall'), the region which is the least developed and with an almost total lack of tradition in self-government. Similar regional differentiation has been found in voting behaviour and the innovative behaviour of public enterprises, but as regards urban services this should be treated as a 'recognized hypothesis' only.

Notes

1. Source: author's own calculation based on materials of GUS (Central Statistical Office).
2. Source: *Gazeta Wyborcza*, 11 December 1992.
3. The survey was organized as part of the International Local Democracy and Innovation Project, partially financed by the Norwegian Ministry of Foreign Affairs and the Norwegian Research Council for Applied Social Sciences (NORAS). The data cited was published in the Polish report of the project (Jał

owiecki and Swianiewicz, 1991).
4. Quoted from *Gazeta Wyborcza*, 29 January 1993.
5. Most of the statistical data used in the rest of this chapter is based on a study conducted by a group directed by Aziewicz.
6. His *Privatization as a Key to Better Government* (Chatham, 1986) has recently been published in Polish.

9

THE PRIVATIZATION OF URBAN SERVICES IN HUNGARY

Tamás Fleischer

Infrastructures: the background to privatization

Eastern Europe has always been characterized by radical changes of direction. Following World War II and the setting up of the Soviet satellite system, a number of developments, nationalization among them, occurred far more rapidly than in the West; and they were carried into effect unopposed since in the main they were linked to the dispossession of property-owners by way of a form of expropriation that had no legal basis whatsoever. Leaving the legal aspect to one side, by 1950 the so-called Eastern bloc countries, including Hungary, had all the appearance of state monopolies. It was this economic predominance of the state, given support by ideology and national policies, which enabled wages to be held down at a generally low level, thus obliging women to work, at first principally in the cities, and bringing about the two-wage family model. Simultaneously, the urban population rapidly became dependent on communal services.

In line with the idealogy of the time, low incomes were made up for by free municipal services – education and health, for instance – or by very low prices for transport and other services, rents included. The ideal of 'the state as provider', coming to the aid not merely of those in need (who are non-existent under socialism) but of all according to their needs through the instrument of prices, was a constant theme during the forty years socialism lasted, even though in Hungary the stability of prices and charges was not guaranteed over the last ten years, whereas elsewhere wages kept at some distance behind inflation. Eastern European countries thus moved into a phase of transition characterized by distortion of market prices and price structures.

In Eastern Europe economic theory centred on production to the neglect of public services. The ideal of 'the state as provider' did not imply a 'state providing services', and the development of public services was a low priority. The concept of 'the state as provider' was admirably suited to another ideology: the survival of a 'wartime economy' which required everything to be organized for production. Accordingly, a service was provided not for the individual as such but for the workforce as a whole, so that services could be guaranteed only where there were workers. The stock example here is provided by workers' hostels, built like a barracks to house the labour force from other regions, which was paid for and maintained by the employers. These may in some way be considered as 'urban' services but, in view of their exclusive nature and their highly specific purpose, hardly as 'public' services. The course of development over recent years highlights the problem. As production in several of the industries responsible for maintaining these hostels dropped, and with it the demand for unskilled labour, the premises became increasingly dilapidated, and were bought up and turned into a chain of cheap and unprofitable hotels.

If this example were applied to networks, it could be said that even if the official ideology and economic statistics tended to ignore services because of the priority given to industry, a number of infrastructural defects in relation to production were eventually put right. Certain networks whose absence impaired the overall efficiency of the system were created or, where they already existed, made good and extended.

Hence, the marginalization of public services prevented them developing in the way they might well have done, while some services that were directly linked to production, and that had the benefit of support within groups whose influence and bargaining position were strong, were improved and able to meet the needs in their sector. Given that such pressure groups also represented state property, they can hardy be described as 'private' services; yet their essence was clearly distinct from the principle of 'public services', which would have implied the inclusion of features detrimental to their functioning.

Political economy also determined the way in which town planning developed. With accelerating industrialization, the recruitment of rural labour took on a degree of importance, with migration into distant areas, construction of workers' hostels, as mentioned above, and a consequent growth in city population. At the same time, towns as opposed to villages tended to represent the 'controlling' function and 'industry', whereby they came to benefit from a preferential status in the system of redistribution. The redirection of revenue in favour of urban investment first favoured the capital, Budapest (as well as new mining communities and industrial towns built in the 1950s), before in the 1960s spreading to industry in general and to the regional capitals and, to a lesser extent, remaining towns at the start of the 1970s. In the context of services as previously described, the growth of some particular urban services was fairly exceptional. The higher standard of living in towns encouraged rural depopulation, while the concomitant growth in cities wiped out the advantages gained.

The technical level of urban services is directly attributable to these circumstances. In most cases infrastructure is a hundred years old, and what was once perfectly efficient has now become obsolete. Urban policies applied over the past forty years that were mindful of investment but neglected existing stock have largely brought about this result. Public services have not enjoyed increased investment unless this happened to coincide with specific industrial projects. But the basic network for supplying water and electricity and gas was a relatively satisfactory one.

At the close of the nineteenth century Hungary was among the countries that led in the development and application of electrical energy. Arc lamps were invented in the Ganz foundry in 1878; the first electricity power station was put into service in 1884 in Temesvár (now Timisoara in Romania) and in Matészalka in 1888. The supply of electricity in Budapest was begun in 1893 almost at the same time as in other European cities. By the end of 1944 40 per cent of the country was being supplied. Electricity production was nationalized in 1948, and the sector was reorganized a number of times before MVM, the Hungarian electricity companies, were established in 1963; that year also saw the last village linked up to the network.

Before World War II, the public supply of gas depended on coal-fed plant built at the end of the last century. Gas became publicly owned well before electricity. During the second half of the nineteenth century, several gasworks were constructed to supply street lighting; at Pest in 1856, Szeged and Debrecen in 1864, Sopron in 1866 and Gyór in 1869; by the end of the century ten cities, including the capital, were so provided. Coal gas was used for cooking, heating and hot water. The Obuda gasworks, built in 1912–13, and that at Pécs, built in the 1930s, were technically advanced for their period.

Following nationalization in 1948, development was to an extent held back by reconstruction, but it accelerated in the 1960s as the reserves of natural gas (Zala) began to come into production; industry was the big customer, taking around 60 per cent. This growth went hand in hand with major structural changes in energy. Coal gas (produced locally) gave way to natural gas. The changeover began in Debrecen and Miskolc, where it had been completed by 1970.

Public urban transport development in Hungary also compares favourably with that in the West. Sewerage systems are of a good standard in urban areas, water supply slightly less so. The difference is very marked in rural areas. Central heating is fairly common in residential areas; obviously there is the matter of its not becoming too costly with the removal of energy subsidies. Telecommunications, even in urban areas, has been relatively underdeveloped. The housing stock, state and other, is clearly in poor shape.

There are considerable – often regional – differences in technical services which are not network-delivered, even as regards the way they are run. Examples include chimney-sweeping, funeral undertaking, swimming baths, green spaces, refuse collection and so on. At the same time, this type of activity seems to lend itself more readily to being privatized than the public services mentioned above.

The third phase of privatization is now complete.[1] The first phase took place before the political changes at the end of the 1980s. It was marked by its 'spontaneous' character and the interest shown by the West in the Hungarian economy. 'Spontaneous' here implies that initiatives were taken at company level and legally ratified afterwards. Legislation in regard to company and business changes was voted by Parliament in 1987 and 1988 to formalize ongoing practice, which began with a kind of restructuring of state enterprises into a group of companies nominally in the hands of partners and independently run. The transition enabled foreign capital to become available for investment in some of the new entities so as to enhance their market profile.

The second phase of privatization, between autumn 1990 and autumn 1992, was termed 'controlled'. The main instrument of privatization, AVÜ (Public Property Authority), was set up just before the 1990 elections in order to control, regulate and promote, under parliamentary supervision, the process of change towards privatization. The newly elected Parliament subsequently modified AVÜ's role so as to make it an important instrument in fighting spontaneous privatization. During this phase, irrespective of various public utterances, the whole process was analysed in terms of the increase in revenue obtained and, more particularly, of the degree of success attributable to the input of foreign capital. In fact, the revenue was not excessive. Privatization slowed down in the autumn of 1992 with increasing variance between supply and demand aspects. There was less foreign interest shown in Hungary, in part because of its position *vis-à-vis* its neighbours, in part because the bout of euphoria over Eastern Europe had worn off. The view of some market analysts was that the Hungarian economy had lost its attraction and its dominance, so investors switched their short-term attention to Poland, then, more hopefully, to the Czech economy. This period was further marked by privatization having to face internal pressure and increasing sniping.

The third phase is generally dated from August 1992 when a parliamentary bill on privatization became law. By its terms, AVRt (Company for the Administration of Hungarian State Assets) was set up to oversee and actively participate in the partial privatization of assets that had always belonged to the state. The Hungarian electricity companies (MVM Rt), Hungarian oil and gas company (MOL Rt) and the gas distribution companies were among the 160 firms selected. The Act aims to provide a framework for the long-term administration of strategic activities in which the government will retain shares. At the same time, AVÜ's role was modified to bring it into line with the new Act, so making it possible for privatization of selected companies to be carried out in the short term. AVRt was given three principal missions with regard to ownership of government shares in companies, improving company performance and company privatization.

This phase in privatization was marked by:

- political changes in the administration of national assets (there were detractors who accused the government of seeking to be rid of them entirely;

- a new strategy in privatization (scrutiny of state assets with a view to privatization and development of market conditions so as to launch new share issues);
- growing anomalies in the privatizing process. Declared priorities at the time were to change the structure of ownership by rapidly increasing the number of Hungarian shareowners and thereby to give a productive, entrepreneurial impetus to the economy. In the event, a form of privatization under state control seemed to emerge in opposition to spontaneous privatization. While the regulatory framework was put into place (with the law governing concessions and that mentioned above), the process slowed down, occupying itself successively with bigger cases – privatizing the food and agriculture industry, then Malev (Hungarian Airways) and later Matáv (Hungarian Telecommunications) – rather as if a bottleneck had appeared.

It is still too early to talk of a fourth phase, but there are several signs of difficulties ahead. The balancing act between AVÜ, AVRt and the ministries has given rise to controversy. Some suggest that AVRt is now redundant and should be replaced by one large holding company under state leadership. Government ministries have begun to oppose ownership transfer where some public utilities, in which they feel the state should continue to have a majority stake, are concerned. At the end of 1993, following an alteration in the relevant government decree, ownership of regional plant for providing water and sewerage was transferred from AVRt to the Ministry of Transport, Communication and Water Management.

A rapid glance back over the laborious process of recent privatization allows one to see that it has been accused of being too little and too controlled, too fast and too slow; but the real question was to know who actually did the controlling and handled the changes. The same period has seen a clear tendency emerging for the state to extend its control of the privatization process as well as of its own assets.

The privatization of urban services

Given that there are no immediately available statistics or data on the privatization of urban services in Hungary, what follows can be no more than a sketchy account of what is taking place. This section, while instancing individual cases, gives an overall account of various Hungarian localities. In conclusion, I shall try to draw the consequences of the experience thus far.

The 1990 Act on administrative autonomy was one of the first Acts to be passed by the new democratic Parliament, preceding the first free elections in autumn 1990. In general, it enabled a direct transfer of assets to be made from the former municipal councils to local independent administrations. But since for the most part these had only been assigned to the councils, the Act determined how they should be integrated as local assets. This is why privatization, in the restricted sense, required certain steps to be taken beforehand. The privatization of public utilities conformed to the following sequence:

- audit of each utility;
- transfer of ownership of the public firms (in the hands of the former councils) to the local administrators;
- transfer of these same administration-owned companies into joint-stock companies, with the entirety of shares owned by the said administrations; and
- market issue of some – and, in some cases, all – shares.

At the outset the situation in the capital differed from that in the nineteen rural departments (*comitats*). The special position of Budapest put it outside the general application of the Act, and a particular set of regulations was voted following the municipal election. In Budapest,[2] fourteen public utility[3] companies, employing 40,000 people, were placed under municipal authority. Audits were carried out during 1991, and the transfer of assets continued until the end of 1992.

Elsewhere the situation is less straightforward because utilities in general do not serve specific localities, thus making the transfer of ownership more complex. Levels of service varied greatly between regions. At first, every locality wanted ownership for itself, which meant splitting companies in a way that threatened their reasonable functioning. A portion of a network may be owned by a small village without the wherewithal (personnel or plant) to ensure its maintenance and efficiency. The experience was an apprenticeship in democracy and authority, and local communities had to learn this lesson before they saw the virtues of cooperation.

Public utility audits

The aim of a utility – to provide an efficient service – frequently has to take into account the social and economic context in which the company is assessed. The most serious problems encountered were the following: lack of any legislative or regulatory framework, of any overall environmental concept, and of a clear grasp of functions and tasks; lack of any coordination between functions and sources; constant and irrational changes in accounting and economic regulation; and chronic lack of certainty about the future.

Such an economic context has certainly shaped the way public utilities function. Firms had to operate in an economy of scarcity, hence they set up the necessary 'pre-service' requisites – building, vehicle maintenance, upkeep of green spaces, etc. – so as to be able to pursue their activities. The result was that, while endeavouring to optimize their basic services, they found themselves unable to develop 'consumer services'. The market held no interest for them since their method of functioning fell outside its mechanisms.

By way of example, each spring the management of the swimming pools in Budapest threatens the municipality with keeping some of its pools closed on the grounds that the resources at its disposal are inadequate for all of them to be kept open. Current practice is for the company to manage only the establishments, which are not profitable, while services used by the public – restaurants and cafés, sale of goods and so on – are franchised and do show profits. Most of these franchise-holders make their profit by virtue of the swimming pool functioning but from an activity that is secondary to that of the pool itself and the service it provides.

Strictly speaking, the financing of baths and accessory services should be linked. Such restructuring would be an ideal preliminary step towards privatization. However, it would entail assessment of each service rather than that of the different firms involved. But it is also true that the past few years have seen big improvements in consumer services, with the Budapest baths management directing its investment, possibly beyond its means, towards setting up a hydrotherapy establishment.

Each company's audit has provided evidence that the following priorities must be ensured before ownership ties are transferred:

- reasonable certainty of continuity and smooth functioning of the principal activity;

- awareness of the environment on the part of the decision-making and regulatory bodies;
- importance of social factors: some public utility firms are subsidiaries of major employers;
- heed given to long-term factors, implying that the transfer of assets should be carried out with appropriate circumspection.

Some companies encountered particular problems when the service enjoyed a (natural) monopoly position: water, for instance, sewerage or electricity and to a certain extent gas, heating, and telephones; or when the only customer was the local administrative body in a monopoly position, for example street-cleaning, refuse disposal or upkeep of green spaces. In the latter instance it is indispensable to look closely at the benefits that could be had if the legal form of the company belonging to the municipality were modified and examine whether the charges provided for are proportional to the cost of transformation.

The transfer of state enterprise assets and the formation of companies belonging to local administrations

In Budapest the transfer of assets was spread out over a fairly long period and completed, more or less successfully, in the course of 1992. In the previous two years the local government obstructed attempts to convert two or three companies after their managers had put forward different schemes for speeding up the process.

A report that drew on the evidence available was presented to the assembly of the Budapest municipal government defining the basic functions of each company as well as additional activities, in accordance with the principle that assets should not be dissipated but directed towards the company's chief purpose.

The Budapest municipality then appointed new commissions to supervise the firms, inspected their balance-sheets and established the procedure once the transfer of assets was complete.

Dissension had mainly to do with the interpretation of what assets were necessary for a company's basic activity. Proper market conditions did not exist; moreover, with the shortages, companies were obliged to accept responsibility for 'inputs' or services needed to pursue their activity. The situation is a characteristic one in

Eastern Europe. Consequently, nearly all the companies concerned set up a maintenance service for machines and vehicles, a construction and building maintenance unit, and on occasion a workshop to produce piping or parts for assembly, etc. Such specialized units found themselves generally underemployed, hence sought to place orders elsewhere, thus spawning a healthy secondary activity. It only needed the secondary to move into profit, unlike the main service, for the firm to seek to develop it. And when it came to transferring assets, the company was only too ready to claim that it stood to lose the activity which enabled it to finance its main task.

As mentioned above, various types of opposition arose across the country during the transitional phase affecting utilities. Three levels of ownership led to problems during the process of change. First, in relation to the infrastructure: underground piping, for instance, could officially be divided between localities. Then, functioning: when it comes to company functioning within this or that region, who is to define the rightful share in it that each locality can lay claim to, with no previous work having been done on the marginal cost involved? Division becomes a complex affair that may well prejudice normal functioning. Company assets constitute the third level and the question of secondary activities mentioned above (a problem encountered in Budapest as well). In the regions, workshops of this sort may belong to hundreds of localities; thus, breaking up the principal sector is not a definitive solution.

The instance of water supply and sewage treatment at a local level is a case in point. Formerly, there were twenty-eight companies in the business; they began breaking up into smaller regional and urban units until they numbered 160, still with no change in their status. A firm covering a particular area used to serve the main town and probably hundreds of small localities. Asset division and the inability of administrations, representing towns or villages, to recognize their common interests and achieve cooperation led increasingly to their trying to 'go it alone'. At the same time, the infrastructural network generally mirrored the former organization in the manner of its functioning, so did not lend itself to being divided up. Naturally enough, all this led to endless wrangling as well as to court cases. Heavily populated areas, large towns and their suburbs, may have profited by the change, but for the remainder the cost of water and sewerage went up considerably, further widening the gulf in living conditions between town and country.

The transformation of companies owned by local administrations into joint-stock companies

Concrete schemes for the conversion of the larger networks – water, gas, urban heating, sewerage – is well under way, water being at the most advanced stage. If the present scheme continues to apply, 80 per cent of the service company, with 3,000 employees and assets worth 16 billion forints ($160 million) can be regarded as representing the main activity; this nucleus will become a joint-stock company, exclusively owned by the municipality of Budapest, while the accessory shops (steel piping, vehicle spare parts and maintenance, etc.) will be sold off separately.

Elsewhere there are cases that present problems as to who are authorized shareholders. Legislation stipulates that the government must retain 50 per cent of shares plus one as a guarantee of state property, while in regard to local autonomy legislation provides for identical conditions in certain cases, such as water provision. There are five major companies supplying water throughout the country and, with the regulations governing price and their public utility obligations, they have virtually no chance of attracting capital other than from the government and independent local authorities. Furthermore, current regulations disallow any form of dividend distribution. It would need only a brief amendment to overcome the problem but the case serves to show how new difficulties constantly crop up and delay a programme that was seemingly well conceived.

Privatizing utilities poses a number of general problems to do with removing government control over prices, the natural monopoly position of certain utilities and the dearth of capital to enable recovery to take off. A foreign investor could bring in the capital but only in return for free price-fixing and a continuing monopoly position. With telecommunications and in part with gas, price regulation can be rapidly diluted but the change is a good deal slower with water, electricity, housing or public transport; and it has to be said that sometimes elected officials are reluctant to take the necessary steps.

A survey undertaken in Hungary in 1991 has looked at local

government intentions in the matter of privatization. Elected representatives were questioned a year following their election in more than 200 municipalities (from a total of 3,070). Their views were calibrated on a scale of 0 to 100, 0 signifying total absence of any privatization project, 100 full implementation. Intentions in regard to privatizing fourteen sectors are given in Table 9.1. The list clearly shows services coming half-way down the list, with public utilities and transport – the stock urban services – in the middle. The sample taken from people living in the same localities provides figures which in general are 10 per cent lower than those for elected officials.[4]

The market issue of shares

If by privatization of urban services one means no more than private capital committed, Hungary affords no ground for assessment. An earlier survey in Budapest showed one single offer of capital as having been put forward by the city gasworks, an offer which, in order to be substantiated, required negotiation over several points, one of them probably being that the municipality retain a 51 per cent stake.

Most public utilities would like to raise prices. The company

Table 9.1 Intentions to privatize various sectors on the part of Hungarian municipalities

Sector	Percentage intending to privatize
Retail trade	82.5
Cinemas	74.3
Small industrial firms	74.3
State farms	46.1
Banks	42.2
Large industrial firms	42.2
Public utilities	37.4
Urban public transport	31.7
Regional public transport	31.7
Health care	28.5
Postal services	26.7
Schools	22.1
Railways	15.1
Prisons	3.4

managing the Budapest water supply has made known its desire to raise prices for water and sewerage, and a survey it has conducted calls for prices to be doubled.

With housing the situation is different. Housing is not a typical 'urban service', but the problems of low-rent municipal or state housing are frequently encountered in urban areas. The main problem has to do with the upkeep of buildings; a quarter of the 800,000 flats in Budapest are in buildings that date from before World War I. Expert opinion suggests that a rehabilitation programme in the centre of Budapest would cost around 500 billion forints ($5 billion) and affect 200,000 flats. Between the mid-1980s and the end of 1993, municipalities across the country sold off 200,000 state-owned flats to their tenants at between 15 and 30 per cent below market price, with a fixed interest rate of 3 per cent – advantageous conditions, it would seem, but purchasers were made to bear the backlog in lack of upkeep. The result has been that tenants in better residential districts have been able to purchase property of some value at reasonable prices, whereas flats in poor condition continue to be the responsibility of municipalities.

From an economic viewpoint, municipalities are better able to draw good revenue from ground-floor space when it is let to businesses. Such revenue, which provides 10–20 per cent of the local budget, can be earmarked for building maintenance, hence municipalities would sooner provide lettings for shops than hand over ownership. Once legislation on housing had been voted, Parliament saw an opportunity here for privatization by obliging municipalities to sell off commercial premises, a move not unconnected with the fact that the newly elected municipal officials were members of the parliamentary opposition or else independents.

Energy monopolies

In conclusion, we shall look at two major services in the energy sector; gas and electricity.

MOL, the Hungarian oil and gas company, was formed on 1 October 1991 on the foundations of OKGT, the national oil and gas consortium. The new company aims to lead the field in Hungary. Fifteen former subsidiaries out of a total of twenty-three (on the manufacturing and service side) have been shut down and a two-divisional (upstream/downstream) operating structure set up. The result is a streamlined limited-liability company with a workforce – cut by nearly half – of 23,000.

In the 1980s six companies supplying gas were members of OKGT. Five of them distribute gas throughout the country, excluding Budapest, the city gas company traditionally being the property of the municipality – now, independent government – of Budapest. The five companies mentioned belong to the Association of Gas Supply Companies, of which the Budapest company is still not a member.

The privatization process of these regional distribution companies was interrupted in May 1992 because of the lack of interest shown in the international market offer, whose closure was postponed indefinitely. In February 1994, AVRt intervened again in the process in anticipation of legislation on gas and some changes in energy-sector regulations. The new provisions follow the old in keeping a one-quarter stake plus one in each distribution company under state ownership.

MVMT had the nationwide responsibility for providing electrical energy and a virtual monopoly of production. This range of activity from source to consumer meant a workforce of about 40,000, making it one of the largest companies in Hungary.

On 1 January 19992, MVMT underwent conversion into a group of public companies, part being made up of the Hungarian electricity companies (MVM Rt). They were given the task both of managing company assets and of ensuring the operation and strategy of electricity production. By the terms of the Act of Conversion, the member companies became limited-liability companies with 50 per cent of capital belonging to the group and the remaining 50 per cent, corresponding to the distribution companies' stake, in the hands of the Authority for Public Property (AVÜ), minus shares that went to municipalities in exchange for the use of their land. By the terms of the 1992 Act on privatization, MVM Rt was required to transfer its stake to AVRt, which would provide long-term management. Then AVRt and AVÜ together set about privatizing the capital. This gave rise to fierce debate which lasted until November 1993, when the government modified the list of firms that were to remain under national ownership; whereupon AVRt took over the entire stake the state had held in the electrical industry which enabled the privatization launch to start on a uniform footing.

Local government also has a look-in as regards ownership of the energy sector. A tiny part – 2–3 per cent depending on area size – of the electricity supply companies' stake is allocated to municipalities. Further, urban heating companies are now no longer controlled by central government but by local administrations.

Conclusion

The purpose of this chapter has been to examine the context of urban services in Hungary and especially the problems that came in the wake of political change. Privatization tends to be seen as an end in itself and its objectives are not generally clarified. The best illustration of this is the fact that success measured in terms of revenue has been forsaken in order to proclaim that the priorities and true purpose of privatization awaited definition: organizational changes, an economic structure that accords with the market, greater transparency, or the rapid dismantling of nationalized firms and consequent budgetary relief, or else guaranteed capital inflow.

A number of questions need answering in regard to general economic policy. Privatization began in the sector with no preliminary statement, no agreement as to the method to be used in administering a public utility nor as to the attitude to be taken up by local government in this respect.

Public utilities reflect the economic policy of the past forty years. In the absence of market conditions, they tended to take less notice of consumers since their survival and development depended chiefly on the size of the budget slice they received. In the recent past they have had to adapt to rapid and somewhat eccentric changes in the system of regulations, whereby they have been forced to abandon the circumspection proper to planning preparation and which in other circumstances they would sooner have chosen.

Consequently, whereas central and local government have been rather slow in determining the prospects and long-term context of privatization, the firms directly involved have been equally reluctant to give the matter consideration and devise long-term strategies; they have allowed themselves to be bogged down by the question of distribution policy.

This question, then, has tended to dictate a bit-by-bit application of privatization, with the persistence of negotiation over unresolved issues that pre-date it, and no one seems to know whether a slower or more cautious approach for public utilities represents an advantage or a disadvantage in the overall process.

In Budapest, privatization is being implemented less rapidly than was expected but in a systematic way. A first phase has seen all the public utilities audited. Transfer of assets at the end of 1992 has marked a second phase, with these firms passing into the control of local government. In 1993, firms were converted into joint-stock companies under sole ownership. This step will be followed by full or partial privatization of each company.

Notes

1. Privatization here implies change in the ownership of state assets. A further significant trend at the start of the 1980s was the growing number of small and medium-sized firms in trade, industry and agriculture as well as in certain services.
2. For the twenty-two districts of Budapest there are twenty-two independent administrative bodies, each led by a mayor. The capital itself forms the twenty-third, its mayor the mayor of Budapest. Prerogatives drawn up in 1990 are now being put into effect and certain anomalies are appearing.
3. The following sectors are represented: transport, water supply, sewerage, maintenance of public property, cleaning, heating, gas supply, chimney-sweeping, funeral undertaking, swimming baths, upkeep of green spaces, property maintenance, cinemas and leisure activities. Power stations, telecommunications and railways are not within the competence of the authorities of the capital, though theoretically they should be.
4. In my opinion privatization has come to be more acceptable since 1991.

CONCLUSION: PRIVATIZATION, URBAN GOVERNMENT AND THE CITIZEN

Gerry Stoker

This book has examined the privatization of urban services in different countries and therefore has focused on one of the major trends in public policy. Privatization in its various forms has for a long time been part of the make-up of the service provision in urban areas but it has in the past decade or so gained the status of being an overarching paradigm or even a panacea. Privatization has achieved a prominent place on the agenda of policy-makers in different countries for a variety of reasons. For some its benefits to urban government and its citizens are clear and substantial. Others see privatization as posing a threat to governmental capacity and the role of the urban citizen. This concluding chapter compares the diverse forces behind privatization trends in different countries and examines contrasting assessments of privatization in practice.

Complexity in the development of privatization

The rise of privatization would appear to be a response to the fiscal pressures faced by those responsible for urban services. A key rationale behind privatization is that it enables governments to achieve more within existing resources. Asset sales can 'create' resources to be used for other public purposes. Competition and market-testing offer the prospect of savings in service provision. Drawing in resources from voluntary and private-sector providers would also seem to help close the gap between spending plans and taxation. It may be that the fiscal distress claimed by some governments is exaggerated. Certainly there is nothing automatic in the connection between financial constraints and the adoption of privatization. Rather it reflects perceptions and awareness among policy-makers. As Henig *et al.*(1988, p.445) put it, 'Economic forces do not affect policy directly; rather, they influence policy through their effect upon the perceptions, calculations, and balance of power among political actors.' The concerns about fiscal pressures provides a key part of the backcloth to privatization. Such concerns are noted in each of the country-specific case-studies in this book.

The rise of privatization also reflects the advent of a range of private-sector companies and markets keen to exploit the opportunities that an expansion of privatization can provide. Private companies with a stake in privatized provisions have a substantial interest in expanding the market and their position within it. The case of France would appear to be a particularly strong illustration of this phenomenon. The profit-seeking aspirations of private companies and investors provide an important background factor in the development of privatization. This broad influence is observed in all the countries examined in this book.

A further factor explaining the rise of privatization may be processes of cross-national policy learning or transfer. Policy entrepreneurs may 'self consciously mine the experiences of their or other nations for political and economic lessons that they can introduce elsewhere' (Henig *et al.*, 1988, p. 458). Eastern European countries have received more than their fair share of visits from 'think-tanks' and experts recommending privatization solutions. In the case of Latin America it is the World Bank and other international organizations that have taken on this promotional role. Sometimes a genuine attempt at learning may be made. On other occasions a looser process of transfer may occur in which 'successful' policies are copied as a fashion or ideological statement. The symbolic value of privatization is perhaps at its strongest in the cases of Poland and Hungary. Germany provides an interesting example of the spill-over of privatization measures initially targeted at the newly incorporated eastern *Länder* but increasingly seen as having some potential application in the rest of the country.

Fiscal stress, private-sector interests and cross-national learning or transfer help to explain the convergence towards privatization in the development of urban services provision. Yet as the chapters in the book show, different countries are heading down different paths in the unfolding of their privatization programmes. Following Henig *et al.* (1988), three factors can be seen as helping to explain divergence: pre-existing institutional arrangements; political culture and objectives; and the power balance between affected interests.

The evolution towards increased privatization in France in contrast with the more rapid and radical processes observable in the United Kingdom reflect substantial differences in pre-existing institutional arrangements between the two countries. In France companies involved in water distribution and production, sewerage and waste treatment, refuse collection and other urban services were in many cases formed over a century ago. They have an established role. The companies' economies of scale and the technical efficiency they offer cannot be matched by municipalities or communes that are small in size and lack adequate human resources. The fragmentation of French urban government and the established position of companies in service provision provide key factors in explaining the evolutionary path taken by France.

In contrast, the United Kingdom's privatization has come through a great political push and effort since 1979. The pace and speed of change has been revolutionary. The history of the development of urban services in the United Kingdom has some marked contrasts with the experience of France. The former country experienced large-scale industrialization earlier than France and it was the local authorities or municipalities in the rapidly expanding urban centres that in many cases took the lead in providing key urban services such as highways, gas, sewage treatment, water supply and public transport. The post-war settlement saw responsibility for much provision passed on to nationalized quasi-governmental agencies. Yet local authorities retained a strong role in direct service provision, were reorganized into large-scale units and, at the beginning of the 1980s, employed roughly 3 million full- and part-time employees. Nationalized industries and utilities along with local authorities dominated provision, and the break-up of this monopoly has required the display of considerable tenacity and determination by the Conservatives, who have been in national government since 1979. With the institutional framework loaded against the development of privatization, the Conservatives opted for a directive and interventionist strategy in order to achieve their objectives.

The influences of political culture and the values and objectives of governing coalitions also help explain the divergent paths taken by countries with respect to the privatization of urban services. The United Kingdom stands out as an example of a country with a strongly politically driven and ideological programme. Privatization was seen as part of a crusade to roll back the state and create the conditions for a new political settlement with increased responsibility in private, voluntary and family hands. The welfare state that dominated post-war years was seen as a drain on national efficiency and individual initiative. Privatization was about liberating British society from the heavy hand of the state. This is not to deny the influence of pragmatic considerations in the British case but it is to emphasize that the programme of privatization was part of a broader ideological and political project. In Germany, in contrast, privatization was seen largely as a technical, pragmatic tool. Politicians did not see the issue as one of rolling back the state. Only when privatization measures for the recently incorporated Eastern bloc developed did a more ideological debate emerge. In France the political debate over privatization has largely been low-key. The Polish case offers an interesting twist. Some difference can be observed between those local councils with 'liberal' or 'social democratic' preferences, with the former displaying greater interest in privatization. Yet evidence also exists that those most active in privatization are also those most active in expanding and innovating in municipal activity. In short, the crucial political divide might be between those who are 'innovators' and those who are 'parochials' out of the mainstream developments.

The final factor explaining divergence is the balance of power between various actors. In the United Kingdom the establishment of a sustained majority in Parliament and the lack of constitutional or political protection around local government created a situation where the Conservatives' privatization programme could be pushed through despite the strength of organized opposition in trade unions and labour movement. A greater degree of compromise, consensus and negotiation would appear to have accompanied the programmes in most other European countries. The picture in each country is complex and the balance of power may shift according to which aspect of privatization is being promoted. Understanding the distribution of power between relevant interests or groups provides a valuable contribution to explaining the divergent shape taken by privatization in different countries.

The impact of privatization: promise or threat?

Policies or programmes such as privatization call out for a judgement of their impact. Which interests are gaining? Which are losing? These simple questions often require very complex answers, however, and the accumulation of evidence which is difficult to obtain and interpret (Walsh, 1994). With respect to contracting out, for example, the issue of financial savings poses formidable problems. A high proportion of the relevant data comes from those who are seeking either to promote or to attach this form of privatization. Questions of commercial confidentiality or secrecy may colour or limit the date. Before-and-after comparisons are often difficult because a move to contracting out is often accompanied by other organization shifts or changes in the standard of service provided. There is also the problem of time. Many of the changes discussed in this book are relatively recent phenomena. Privatization, as Henig *et al.* (1988, p. 442) put it, 'is still unfinished business'. In such circumstances any assessment of the impact of privatization has to be tentative and to a degree speculative.

Two concerns underlie the evaluation offered here. Does the urban citizen gain through privatization? Is urban government made more effective? Other interests, such as that of private companies looking for new markets under privatization or the managers and workforce of state-run service providers, are left to one side. For the advocates of privatization it is the positive impact on urban government and urban citizens which is seen as the great virtue of privatization. It seems reasonable to assess the programme against these goals. The case for privatization is examined first before I turn to the arguments of its critics.

In praise of privatization

The citizen as tax-payer gains through privatization, according to its advocates. There is the once-and-for-all gain from the sale of assets with the long-term bonus of shifting responsibility for funding future investment plans to the private sector. Competition between privatized providers will encourage lower prices for services. If no such competition is present or competition is only weakly developed then a regulator can provide the necessary check on any 'monopoly' behaviour. The wider introduction of competitive tendering, contracts, internal markets and charges within urban service provision also encourages efficiency in terms of more service produced per unit cost. Sometimes savings in the region of 50 or 25 per cent are claimed, but a recent estimate of the average savings made by competitive tendering in British local authorities suggested a figure of 6 per cent of the total value of contracts let (Walsh, 1994).

Good news for the taxpayer is accompanied by good news for the citizen as service user, according to the advocates of privatization. The search for profitability stimulates private-sector producers to discover and provide what the customer wants (Waldegrave, 1993). Introducing market mechanisms such as competition, choice and opt-out in the public sector creates an environment which likewise encourages organizations to be responsive to consumer demands. Competition between public-sector schools for pupils, for example, leads to improved standards throughout the system. To survive, schools must be attractive in a system where public money follows pupils. More generally, privatization in its various forms encourages a more outward-looking approach to service providers. Thinking abut how to satisfy the customer becomes central to the operation of all organizations.

The advocates of privatization also claim that their programme can enhance the quality of urban government (see Mather, 1989). One benefit is that politicians and senior policy-makers, by developing an arm's-length involvement with service providers, have more opportunity and capacity to concentrate on strategic decision-making. The details and daily practice of service provision and implementation are left to others, allowing those in control of urban government to think about long-term and major issues. When it comes to service provision their role is to specify the standard of service to be provided matched by available finance. Thereafter their role is to monitor and then if necessary respecify what should be provided. Freed from commitments to 'in-house' producers, senior policy-makers are able to perform these functions more objectively and effectively. Privatization encourages an 'output' or 'results' orientation among senior policy-makers which improves the focus and quality of their decision-making.

Doubts and difficulties over privatization

The citizen as tax-payer, the critics argue, is likely to gain from privatization only in the short run or in limited circumstances. The gains from asset sales are by definition a once-and-for-all windfall. Investment in water, gas and other utilities will still be necessary in the future. If the citizen as taxpayer does not have to pay, then the citizen as service user will face higher charges to meet long-term investment needs. The efficiency gains from competitive tendering are greatest with respect to relatively simple, repetitive tasks such as refuse collection. Other functions which demand a greater amount of professional and expert involvement and are less subject to low-cost monitoring techniques may offer much less or no savings when market-tested (Walsh, 1994).

A wider concern is that privatization can create perverse incentives leading to poor management, waste and corruption. The performance culture can lead to the narrow focus on measurable targets to the detriment or exclusion of the main public purposes of the organization. It would be ironic if the ideological rush to privatization led Eastern European countries to repeat the mistake of the state-planned system in which quotas and plans drove the production process. A too simplistic approach to performance targets can lead to an emphasis on inappropriate outputs and a neglect of the wider purpose of the organization. The greater autonomy available to service providers under privatization can lead to waste, as managers of former state-run services reward themselves with perks and benefits. The increased salaries paid to top managers in the privatized utilities in Britain– especially in the case of water companies – has been the subject of critical comment.

Beyond these 'creaming' activities there is a fear that privatization will open the way to more explicitly corrupt practice. Probity in public affairs is threatened by privatization, according to some critics. The more commercial ethos associated with privatization and the opportunities provided by increased contract-awarding activity would seem to provide some foundation for these concerns. The issue can be over-played, and critics ignore the corruption associated with state-run systems of the past. In Britain, at least it is a matter of public debate and concern.

The critics of privatization do not see the range of its reforms as necessarily providing good news for the citizen as service user. Above all, the objection is that in reality, despite the rhetoric about customer service and choice, the service user is generally given a rather passive and limited role. Customers are offered various services by privatized utilities and charged according to their 'choice'. The range of options available emerges from a mix of influences from utility managers, regulators and politicians rather than users. With respect to competitive tendering, the ultimate users of service are rarely involved in the specification and writing of the contracts; their needs or wants are defined by others. Internal markets like those in the British National Health Service are driven not by the direct choice of users but by professionals and managers who act for them. This is not to deny that the responsiveness of services is sometimes improved under privatization. It is to argue that what emerges depends on processes outside the control of the individual customer.

A wider issue raised by critics is that if privatization is pushed too far it neglects the difference between the public as customer and citizen. The citizen has rights that differ from those of the customer. They are not merely the right to vote but also include the right to know, the right to explanation, the right to be heard, the right to be listened to and the right to be involved. Public services and the actions of government rest ultimately for their legitimacy on the granting of consent and support from the public. Opportunities to exercise this wider citizenship should not be squeezed out by the rush to privatization (see Stewart and Stoker, 1995).

Critics also raise doubts about the impact of privatization on urban government. The separation of policy-makers from those responsible for service provision and implementation creates a number of difficulties. First, the opportunity for learning is reduced as direct, hands-on involvement gives way to a more hands-off relationship. Information reaching policy-makers is likely to be tailored by service providers and limited to particular performance targets, reducing the quality of feedback. More developed mechanisms for learning about service failings and inadequacies will have to be considered if they do not already exist. In the French system, Lorrain (1991) suggests, there is an alternation between two solutions: global regulation and detailed control. The former rests on the assumption that producers are concerned to win customer approval and will take steps to do so. If no complaints emerge the system is working. In the case of detailed control personnel are appointed to monitor and oversee the privatized operators. Both approaches have difficulties associated with them. 'In the first case there is an absence of knowledge, and in the second, the knowledge is available but at a high price' (Lorrain, 1991, p.108).

A related concern is that the rationale for privatization repeats the old fallacy that policy and administration can be easily separated. Yet implementation issues have a habit of gaining high political salience and status. Politicians, although they may be tempted to pass off responsibility to privatized providers, may find themselves dragged in to arbitrate or make judgements over difficult cases. Rather than freeing political time for strategic concerns, a privatized system might overload politicians with complaints, scandals and special cases which require their attention.

A final point made by critics is that privatized systems may lack the capacity for integrated governance. Privatized utilities and other organizations operating to contract bring specialization and focus to their task, but there is a danger that differentiation will decline into fragmentation. Will urban governments have the capacity to coordinate and network with other relevant interests to meet the complex social and economic challenges of their areas? In the British case the growth of privatization raises severe doubts about the capacity of elected local authorities to undertake this function unless they are given new responsibilities and a greater legitimacy (Stoker and Young, 1993).

A final comment

Just as the development of privatization reflects the diverse dynamics and history of different countries, so the benefits and advantages of privatization are likely to vary from country to country. For countries such as France, with relatively 'mature' privatized systems, or in the case of Germany, where forces in favour of continuity remain strong, the dilemmas posed by privatization may be more manageable. In the case of Britain and Eastern European countries, where the pace, or at least the commitment to change, is radical, there is a greater urgency and difficulty in the quest to balance the advantages and disadvantages of privatization. The debate about the contribution of privatization to urban services will continue. This book has, I hope, provided some cross-national information and insights, and some analytic aid to the debate.

SELECT BIBLIOGRAPHY

Adam Smith Institute, *But Who Will Regulate the Regulators?*, London, Adam Smith Institute, 1993.

Annales de la recerce urbaine, special issue: *La Planification et ses doubles*, no. 51, 1992.

Aoki, M. Gustafson, B. and Williamson, O.E., *The Firms as a Nexus of Treaties*, London, Sage, 1990.

Appleby, J., Little, V., Ranade, W., Robinson, R. and Smith, P., *Implementating the Reforms: A Second National Survey of District General Managers*, Birmingham, National Association of Health Authorities and Trusts, 1992.

Audit, Commission, *Realising the Benefits of Competition: The Client Role*, London, HMSO, 1993.

Aziewicz, T. (ed.), *Przekształcenia w sektorze usług komunalnych*, Fundusz Wsółpracy i Instytut Badań nad Gospodarką Rynkową, Warsaw, 1993.

Balcerowicz, L., *800 dni: szok kontrolowany*, BGW, 1992.

Barthélémy, C. *et al.*, 'L'autonomie: une troisième voie pour la gestion municipale', Paris, Rapport Plan urbain, 1992.

Bartone, C. *et al.*, 'Private sector participation in municipal solid waste service: experiences in Latin America', *Waste Management and Research*, No. 9, 1991.

Batley, R., 'Comparisons and lessons' in R. Batley and G. Stoker (eds), *Local Government in Europe*, London, Macmillan, 1991.

Baudant, A., *Pont-à-Mousson (1918–1939): stratégies industrielles d'une dynastie lorraine*, Paris, Publications de la Sorbonne, 1980.

Baum, W.C., *Investing the Environment: Business Opportunities in the Developing Countries*, Washington D.C., International Finance Corporation, 1992.

Baumol, W.J., and Panzar, J.C. and Willy, R.D., *Contestable Markets and the Theory of Industry Structure*, New York, Harcourt Brace Jovanovich, 1982.

Beaud, M. and Dostaler, G., *La Pensée économique depuis Keynes*, Paris, Le Seuil, 1993.

Bericht der Arbeitgruppe der Bundesregierung 'Private' Finanzierung öffentlicher Infrastruktur, Bonn, 1991.

Bishop, M and Kay, J., *Does Privatisation Work?*, London, London Business School, 1988.

Boczyński, P., 'Worek bez kota', *Polityka – prywatyzacja*, March 1993.

Bonaïti, J.P., 'La réforme des industries électriques en Europe centrale', *Flux*, no. 10, Paris, CNRS, 1992.

Byrne, T., *Local Government in Britain*, Harmondsworth, Penguin, 1986 (4th edition).

Campagnac, E. (ed.), *Les Grands Groupes de construction*, Paris, L'Harmattan, 1992.

Clark, J. and Wildavsky, A., 'Why communism collapses: the moral and material failures of communism are intertwined', *Journal of Public Policy*, 10, 4: 361–90, 1990.

Coing, H., 'Privatisation des services urbains: transition ou nouveau modèle?', communication à la réunion du Groupe Latino Américain de Recherche Urbaine, Mexico, 1991.

Coing, H., 'Les services urbains révisités in *Servicios Urbanos en America Latina*, Santiago, Ed. REDES, 1992.

Coing, H., *La Privatisation des Services Urbains au Vénézuéla 1989–1993*, Noisy-le-Grand, Latts/CNRS, 1994.

Coing, H. and Henry, E., 'Pour une analyse transversale des services urbains dans le tiers monde', Actes des journées internationales de Lille, *Villes, moteurs de développement économique dans le tiers monde*, 1990.

Coing, H. and Montano, I., 'Hacia una privatización del servicio de agua potable?' in Actes du colloque Ciudagua, *Encuentro América Latina–Europa sobre el acceso de la población a los servicios de agua y saneamiento en las ciudades de América Latina*, Noisy-le-Grand, Cités Unies, 1988.

Coing, H., de Lara, Ph. and Montano, I., 'Privatisation et régulation des services urbains, une étude comparative (Argentine, Brésil, Sénégal)', Paris, LATTS (mimeo), 1989.

Cointreau-Levine, S., *Private Sector Participation in Municipal Solid Waste Services in Developing Countries*, Bridgewater, CT, 1992.

Commissariat Général du Plan, *Rapport du groupe Réseaux 2010*, Paris, 1994.

Coriat, B., *Penser à l'envers*, Paris, Christian Bourgois, 1991.

Couffignal, G., *Le Régime politique de l'Espagne*, Paris, Montchrestien, coll. Clefs politiques, 1993.

Coyaud, D.P., 'Private and public alternatives for providing water supply and sewerage services', World Bank INU, Report no. 31, 1988.

Crew, M.A. and Kleindorfer, P.R., *The Economics of Public Utility Regulation*, London, Macmillan, 1986.

Crozier, M. and Friedberg, E., *L'Acteur et le système*, Paris, Seuil, 1977.

Cuervo, L.M., *De la vela al apagon. 100 años de servicio eléctrico en Colombia*, Bogatá, CINEP, 1992.

Curien, N. and Gensollen, M., *Économie des télécommunications, ouverture et réglementation*, Paris, ENSPTT-Economica, 1992.

Demsetz, H., 'Why regulate utilities?', *Journal of Law and Economics*, 11: 55-65.

Dente, B., 'Italian local services: the difficult road towards privatisation' in R. Batley and G. Stoker., *Local Government in Europe: Trends and Developments*, New York, St Martin's Press; London, Macmillan, 1991.

Department of the Environment *Competing for Quality*, London, Department of the Environment, 1991.

Dobek, M. 'Privatisation as a political priority: the British experience', *Political Studies*, 41, 1: 24–41.

Dromet, D., *L'Industrie de l'Eau dans le Monde*, Presses de L'Ecole Nationale des Ponts et Chaussées, 1987.

Dumez, H. and Jeunemaître, A., *La Concurrence en Europe*, Paris, Le Seuil, 1991.

Dupuy, G., *L'Informatisation des villes*, Paris, PUF, 'Que sais-je?', 1992.

Eatwell, J., Milgate, N. and Newman, P. (eds), *The Invisible Hand*, London, Macmillan, 1989.

Économie et humanisme, special issue: *Les Services urbains en France*, no. 312, 1990.

Esser, J., 'Allemagne: privatisation symbolique dans une économie sociale de marché', in V. Wright (ed.), *Les Privatisations en Europe*, Arles, Actes Sud, 1993.

Etner, F., *Histoire du calcul économique en France*, Paris, Economica, 1987.

Garrison, R.W. and Kirzner, I.M., 'Friedrich August von Hayek' in Eatwell, J., Milgate, N. and Newman, P., (eds) *The Invisible Hand*, London, Macmillan: 119-30, 1989.

Goldberg, J. and Janssen, J., 'Les stratégies d'entreprises et la structure du bâtiment en Allemagne', in Campagnac, E. (ed.), *Les Grands Groupes de la construction*, Paris, L'Harmattan: 135-53, 1992.

Goldsmith, M. (ed.), *Essays on the Future of Local Government*, Salford, University of Salford, 1986.

Guigo, D., 'La crisis eléctrica en el Gran Buenos Aires: SEGBA y los colgados', in G. Dupuy (ed.), *Las redes de servicios urbanos de Buenos Aires*, Paris, Paradigme, 1992.

Ham, C., *Locality Purchasing*, Birmingham, Health Services Management Centre, 1992.

Ham, C. and Spurgeon, P., *Effective Purchasing*, Birmingham, Health Services Management Centre, 1992.

Harden, I., *The Contracting State*, Buckingham, Open University Press, 1992.

Heinz, W. (ed.), *Partenariats Public-Privé dans l'Aménagement Urbain*, Paris, L'Harmattan, 1994.

Häussermann, H., 'Les infrastructures urbaines en Allemagne avant 1945', *Flux*, no. 10, Paris, CNRS: 25–31, 1992.

Henig, J., Hamnett, C. and Feigenbaum, H., 'The politics of privatisation; a comparative perspective', *Governance*, 1, 4: 442–58, 1988.

Henkel, M., *Government, Evaluation and Change*, London, Jessica Kingsley, 1991.

Henry, E., 'Los embudos de las empresas del autotransporte urbano colectivo en desarrollo', in *Servicios Urbanos en America Latina*, Redes, 1993.

Henry, E. Pacheco, R.S., 'Grosse entreprise privée *versus* politique locale réglementaire du transport urbain', communication à la VIe conférence sur les Transports urbains, Tunis, CODATU, 1993.

Institute of Public Finance, *Direct Labour Organisations*, London, Department of the Environment, 1992.

Iwanek, M., 'Poland's property rights problem in transition', in Katz, B. and Rittenberg, L. (eds), *The Economic Transformation of Eastern Europe*, Westport, CT, Praeger, 1992.

Jałowiecki, B. and Swianiewicz, P., *Między nadzieją i rozczarowanieum: samorząd lokalny rok po wyborach*, University of Warsaw, 1991.

Jobert, B. and Muller, P., *L'Etat en Action (Politiques Publiques et Corporatisms)*, Paris, PUF, 1987.

Kemp, P., 'Housing' in D. Marsh and R. Rhodes (eds), *Implementing Thatcherite Policies*, Buckingham, Open University Press, 1992.

Kharkhordin, O., 'The corporate ethic, the ethic of *samostoyatelnost* and the spirit of capitalism', *Revue d'études comparatives Est-Ouest*, forthcoming.

King, D., *The New Right: Politics, Markets and Citizenship*, London, Macmillan, 1987.

Kornai, J., *Economics of Shortages*, Amsterdam, North-Holland, 1980.

Kornai, J., *The Socialist System: The Political Economy of Communism*, Princeton, NJ, Princeton University Press, 1992.

Kowalczyk, A. and Swianiewicz, P., 'Polytika władz lokalnych wobec przedsiębiorczoşci', in B.Jałowiecki (ed.), *Społeczeństwo i gospodarka w Polsce lokalnej*, University of Warsaw.

Laffont, J.J. and Tirole,J., *A Theory of Incentives in Procurement and Regulation*, Cambridge, MA, MIT Press, 1993.

Li You Mei and Pavé, F., 'Singularité du développement économique de la Chine actuelle' *Sociologie du travail*, Paris, Dunod, 1995.

Local Authorities Association, *CCT Information Service Survey Report no. 6*, London, Local Government Management Board, 1992.

Łodwig, S., 'Wychodzi taniej', *Wspólnota*, no. 50, 1992.

Loesch, A., *Privatisierung öffentlicher Unternehmen: Ein Überblick über die Argumente*, Baden-Baden, Nomos Verlagsgesellschaft, 1983.

Lorrain, D., 'The French model of urban services', *West Europe Politics*, **15**, 11–12, April 1992.

Lorrain, D., 'Le grand fossé? Le débat public privé et les services urbains', *Politiques et Management public*,vol.3–5, 83–102, 1987.

Lorrain, D., 'La gestion des services d'eau dans la France urbaine', in *Génie urbain, acteurs territoires, technologies*, Paris, Plan urbain, 1989a.

Lorrain, D., 'La montée en puissance des villes', *Economie et Humanisme*, special issue: *Maires aujourd'hui*, no. 305: 6–21, 1989b.

Lorrain, D., 'Public goods and private operators in France', in R. Batley and G. Stoker (eds), *Local Government in Europe: Trends and Developments*, New York, St Martin's Press; London, Macmillan: 89–109, 1991.

Lorrain, D., 'Les services urbains, le marché et le politique' in Cl. Martinand (ed.) *Le Financement privé des équipements publics*, Paris, Economica: 13–43, 1993a.

Lorrain, D., 'Après la decentralisation (l'action publique flexible)', *Sociologie du travail*, 3: 285–307, 1993b.

Loughlin, M., Gelfand, M. and Young, K., *Half a Century of Municipal Decline, 1935–1985*, London, Allen & Unwin, 1985.

Marsh, D., 'Privatisation under Mrs Thatcher: a review of the literature', *Public Administration*, 69, 4: 459–81, 1991.

Mather, G., 'Thatcherism and local government: an evaluation', in Stewart, J. and Stoker, G. (eds) *The Future of Local Government*, London, Macmillan, 1989.

Majewski, Z., 'Sprzedawać czy chomikować?', *Wspólnota*, no. 49, 1992.

Mintzberg, H., *The Rise and Fall of Strategic Planning*, Englewood Cliffs, NJ, Prentice-Hall, 1993.

Nasierowska, G., 'Pełna wartość mieszkania', *Wspólnota*, no. 44, 1992.

Nejman, M., *OECD Survey*, Poland, 1992.

Nejman, M., 'Linia demokracyjna', *Wspólnota*, no. 44, 1992.

OECD survey: Poland, June 1992.

Olson, M., *The Logic of Collective Action*, Cambridge, Mass., Harvard University Press, 1966.

Osborne, D. and Gaebler, T., *Reinventing Government*, London, Addison-Wesley, 1992.

Pacheco, R.S., *Transportes e Servicos Urbanos pos-80: Desafios a Gestaoe a Pesquisa*, Sao Paolo, NERU, 1992.

Padioleau, J.G., *Ordre Social (Principes d'Analyse Sociologique)*, Paris, L'Harmattan, 1986.

Pickvance, Ch., 'Le gouvernement local anglais en souffrance', *Annales de la recherche urbaine*, no. 28, 88–93, 1985.

Rhodes, R.A.W., *Beyond Westminster and Whitehall*, London, Sydney and Wellington, Unwin Hyman, 1988.

Ridley, N., *The Local Right: Enabling Not Providing*, London, Centre for Policy Studies, 1988.

Rioux, J.P., *La France de la Quatrième République*, Paris, Le Seuil, coll, 'Points', 1980.

Robson, W., *Local Government in Crisis*, London, Allen and Unwin, 1966.

Roqueplo, P., *Pluies Acides: Menaces pour l'Europe*, Paris, Economica, 1988.

Roth, G., *The Private Provision of Public Services in Developing Countries*, Oxford, Oxford University Press, EDI Series in Economic Development, 1987.

Saloman, L., 'Rethinking public management', *Public Policy*, 29: 255–60, 1981.

Saltman, R.B. and von Otter, C., *Planned Markets and Public Competition: Strategic Reforms in Northern European Health Systems*, Buckingham, Open University Press, 1992.

Savas, E.S., 'Privatisation in post-socialist countries', *Public Administration Review*, 52, 6, 1992.

Scheele, U., *Privatisierung von Infrastruktur: Möglichkeiten und Alternativen*, Cologne, Bund-Verlag, 1993.

Schelling, T.C., *Micromotives and Macrobehaviour*, New York and London, W.W. Norton, 1978.

Seldon, A., *The Riddle of the Voucher: An Inquiry into the Obstacles to Introducing Choice and Competition in State Schools*, London, Institute of Economic Affairs, 1986.

Seoane, M. and Martinez, O., 'El nacimento de una aggiornada oligarquia nacional', *Noticias*, 3 January 1993.

Sharkey, W.W., *The Theory of Natural Monopoly*, Cambridge, Cambridge, Cambridge University Press, 1982.

Sharpe, L.J., 'Reforming the grass roots: an alternative analysis' in D. Butler and A. Halsey (eds), *Policy and Politics*, London, Macmillan, 1978.

Simon, J.P., *L'Esprit des règles: réseaux et réglementation aux États-Unis*, Paris, L'Harmattan, coll. 'Logiques juridiques', 1991.

Sociologie du travail, special issue: *Systèmes productifs: les modèles en question*, no. 1, 1993.

Sparks, D., 'Public versus private bus transport in the Third World: the cyclical nature of providing a public service', in Mathe, H. (ed.), *Managing Service Across Borders*, 8, Eurolog.

Steinheuer, W., 'Privatisierung kommunaler leistungen: theorische Grundlagen und praktische Erfahrungen nordrhein-westfälischer Städte und Gemeinden', *Schriftenreihe des Bundes der Steuerzahler Nordrhein-Westfalen*, no. 17, 1991.

Stewart, J., 'The changing organisation and management of local authorities', in J. Stewart and G. Stoker (eds), *The Future of Local Government*, London, Macmillan, 1989.

Stewart, J., *Accountability to the Public*, London, European Policy Forum, 1993.

Stewart, J., and Stoker, G. (eds), *The Future of Local Government*, London, Macmillan, 1989.

Stewart, J. and Stoker, G., 'Fifteen years of local government restructuring 1979-1994, in J. Stewart and G. Stoker (eds), *Local Government in the 1990s*, London, Macmillan, 1995.

Stoffaës, C. (ed.), *Entre monopole et concurrence: la régulation de l'énergie en perspective historique*, Paris, Éditions PAU, 1994.

Stoker, G. and Young, S., *Cities in the 1990s*, London, Longman, 1993.

Swianiewicz, P., 'Local government in Poland in transition: the case of Wesola Town', in G. Péteri (ed.), *Event and Changes: The First Steps of Local Transition in East-Central Europe*, Budapest, 1991a.

Swianiewicz, P., 'Polityka gospodarcza władz lokalnych', in B. Jałowiecki and P. Swianiewicz (eds), *Między nadzieją i roczarowaniem: samorząd lokalny rok po wyborach*, University of Warsaw, 1991b.

Techniques, territoires et sociétés, special issue: *Acteurs publics, acteurs privés dans l'aménagement*, no. 26, 1994.

Veljanovski, C., 'The political economy of regulation', in P. Dunleavy, A. Gamble and G. Peele (eds), *Developments in British Politics 3*, London, Macmillan, 1990.

Vickers, J. and Yarrow G., *Privatization: An Economic Analysis*, Cambridge, MA, MIT Press, 1988.

Vincent-Jones, P., 'Contracts and business transactions: a socio-legal analysis', *Journal of Law and Society*, 16, 2: 166–86, 1989.

Waldegrave, W., *The Reality of Reform and Accountability in Today's Public Service*, London, Public Finance Foundation, 1993.

Walsh, D., and Davis H., *Competition and Service*, Birmingham, INLOGOV, 1993.

Walsh, K., *Competitive Tendering for Local Authority Services: Initial Experiences*, London, HMSO, 1991.

Walsh, K., 'Competition and public service delivery', in J. Stewart and G. Stoker (eds), *Local Government in the 1990s*, London, Macmillan, 1994.

Walzer, M., *Spheres of Justice: A Defence of Pluralism and Equality*, New York, Basic Books, 1983.

Williamson, O.E., *The Economics Institutions of Capitalism*, New York, Macmillan, The Free Press, 1985.

World Bank, *Infrastructure Sector Policy*, Washington DC, 1993.

Wright, V. (ed.), *Les Privatisations en Europe*, Arles, Actes Sud, 1993.

Young, S., 'The nature of privatisation in Britain, 1979–1985', *Western European Politics*, 9: 235–52, 1986.

INDEX